Gambling and Speculation

Gambling and Speculation

A Theory, a History, and a Future of Some Human Decisions

Reuven Brenner

with Gabrielle A. Brenner

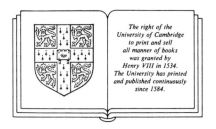

The right of the
University of Cambridge
to print and sell
all manner of books
was granted by
Henry VIII in 1534.
The University has printed
and published continuously
since 1584.

Cambridge University Press

Cambridge

New York   Port Chester   Melbourne   Sydney

Published by the Press Syndicate of the University of Cambridge
The Pitt Building, Trumpington Street, Cambridge CB2 1RP
40 West 20th Street, New York, NY 10011, USA
10 Stamford Road, Oakleigh, Melbourne 3166, Australia

© Cambridge University Press 1990

First published 1990

Printed in the United States of America

Library of Congress Cataloging-in-Publication Data
Brenner, Reuven.
  Gambling and speculation. / Reuven Brenner with
Gabrielle A. Brenner.
    p. cm.
  Includes bibliographical references.
  ISBN 0 521 38180 0
    1. Gambling. 2. Gambling – United States – History.
I. Brenner, Gabrielle A. II. Title.
HV6710.B74 1990   89–17378
363.4'2'09 – dc20   CIP

British Library Cataloguing in Publication Data
Brenner, Reuven
  Gambling and speculation: a theory, a history, and a future of
some human decisions
    1. Gambling
I. Title II. Brenner, Gabrielle A.
  795

  ISBN 0 521 38180 0

Contents

v

Preface and acknowledgments

If readers expect this book to be about the follies of gamblers and of speculators, they will be disappointed. As it turns out, the follies are mainly of those who have condemned them.

The evidence we have found has led us to the conclusion that the negative image of gamblers, of speculators, and of gambling is due to prejudice, to the distorted image heavily promoted by some powerful groups who, however, have not had much evidence to support their views.

We did not intend to give this message when we started to write the book. Our interest was to try to answer the questions: Why do people gamble? Who are the gamblers? Are they really spending their money recklessly, committing crimes, destroying family lives? What is the difference between gambling and speculation? What is the impact of speculation? Why do people gamble and speculate sometimes more and sometimes less? Can one propose a general view of human nature that sheds light on the gambling instinct and confront it systematically with facts?

The answer to the last question is yes. We examine the history of gambling, the origins of antigambling and antispeculation legislation, and events that led to changes in such legislation against the fixed backdrop of human nature. This examination leads us to the conclusion that behind the condemnation has lurked, at times, a resistance to the idea that chance, rather than divine will or talent, can have a significant effect on the allocation and reallocation of property. In other words, the condemnation was linked with the idea that people can get rich because of sheer luck and the fact that people's hopes could be ritualized around the idea of chance, embodied in some market institutions, rather than that of providence, embodied in some religious institutions.

At other times, the condemnation disguised some groups' selfish interests. These groups were afraid of losing their fortunes when people suddenly preferred to devote their time and money to gambling instead of to traditional pastimes. In societies committed to the idea of competition, such groups, who thus feared falling behind, could not be expected to state bluntly that this threat shaped their opposition to gambling. Thus, words were used as a curtain to cover these groups' selfish motivations. Unfortunately, later generations frequently seemed to take words at their face value, leading both to the invention of some theories and to prejudice.

Gambling was linked with additional broader issues; for instance: How and why did societies move from a somehow established status quo? How can such societies hold their members together?

When the status quo was no longer maintained, some people's greater willingness to gamble and to speculate was viewed by others as a symbol of chaos. The confusing debates about gambling mirrored this view. Gambling was also linked with fears of envious reactions. Part of the middle class perceived accurately that since in a competitive system not all can succeed, the envy and the frustration of those falling behind may find one outlet in games of chance. The increased willingness to gamble was interpreted as implying that the poorer people felt excluded from the system that provided the established ones with a comfortable living. Thus, the establishment sensed that the wealth they owned and the institutions that insured them were threatened, and realized that envy and the sense of illegitimacy – sentiments that were linked with people's increased propensity to gamble – led some people to actions that threatened the status quo. But even these were just a fraction of the broader issues that were tightly linked with gambling.

Prohibitions on gambling led to the involvement of organized crime in the United States and elsewhere. This impact, in turn, led both to further legislation designed to control the crime rate and to even further confusion about whether or not it was gambling itself or its prohibition that promoted involvement in criminal acts.

Legal scholars frequently confused gambling with speculation, and the antigambling laws were at times interpreted as implying the prohibition of various contracts in both futures and insurance markets. One consequence of all this confusion was that during this century, in both the United States and England, the whole law on betting and gaming was ambiguous in its working, leading Justice Swift to declare in 1936 that the English betting laws were "in a tremendous mess, and something ought to be done about it, but nothing is done. Nothing will be done. It is a hopeless mess and everybody is afraid to touch it."

We also deal with the legal issues in this book, and make suggestions about what should be done. But before arriving at these pragmatic implications of the investigation, the reader must first get acquainted with some theories as well as some facts and discussions about gambling and about speculation from antiquity to our times. As the story unfolds, it becomes more comprehensible why the law was and still is in such confusion, and why people might be afraid to touch it. The change would require discussion of the principles of equality, capitalism, and the role of religious influence, and would also lead to reexamination of a wide range of existing legislation, a reexamination that many groups may have the incentive to oppose.

The discussion around this wide array of topics is presented as follows. Chapter 1 summarizes the history of gambling and especially that of lotteries, paying special attention to the origins of some games and showing that devices used today in games of chance were originally used for making decisions during religious rituals. Chapter 2 examines the current lottery scene: Who are buyers and why do they gamble? The evidence suggests that a sharp distinction should be made between games played for passing the time and for entertainment, and others where there is a chance of winning large prizes and becoming rich. The evidence also suggests that compulsive gamblers represent, and apparently represented, a tiny proportion of the players. One cannot, therefore, explain the special indignation toward gambling and its prohibition in many countries and across time by the existence of this tiny proportion of the gambling population.

So how can one explain the frequently severe condemnation of gambling and the antigambling legislation that persisted, at times, for centuries? Chapters 3 and 4 give some answers to this question, framed in a broad perspective. Such a perspective is necessary, for there have been times when gambling and other pastimes were linked together and attacked in England, in the United States, and elsewhere by commercial groups, political parties, and the church. Chapter 4 shows that at times condemnation of gambling was also linked with the church's negative attitudes toward risk taking in general and toward speculation and some business ventures in particular. This chapter also makes it clear why there has been a confusion among

gambling, speculation, and insurance, and to what erroneous legislation this confusion – still alive today – has led. The discussions in
Chapters 3 and 4 also reveal that by deepening and expanding the
analysis, one inevitably has to link the examination of gambling
with a fundamental inquiry into human nature and the structure of
societies.

After we answer the questions why people gamble and who are the
gamblers, and then why gambling was condemned, Chapter 5 examines the options that governments have today for regulating this
activity. The conclusions are reached after we examine the impact of
the various policies adopted in the past.

Chapter 6 puts all the pieces together and adds some reflections on
the elusive notions of chance, happiness, the "social good," and the
relationship among them.

The book examines the facts, the events, and these elusive notions by combining what some historians perceive as two opposed
methods. It uses narrative when describing a sequence of events, but
it also relies on structure when pointing out some regularities. These
methods have been perceived as opposites, some historians suggesting that narrative is used in order to impose some order on a
sequence of random events, whereas a structural presentation is used
by those who see historical events in a different light. The reason that
these two ways of looking at events can be combined here is that we
view human behavior as being shaped by both chance and the
structural notion of social ranks, and see the two as inseparable.
Thus, instead of becoming opposites, the two methods of describing
historical events are shown to complement each other.

We are indebted to Alan Blinder, Frank Buckley, David Burton,
Charles Clotfelter, Leonard Dudley, William Eadington, Milton Friedman, David Henderson, John Hey, John Hughes, Roy Kaplan, Rod
Kiewit, Ejan Mackaay, William McNeill, Claude Montmarquette,
Mark Perlman, Pierre Perron, Anatol Rapoport, and T. W. Schultz
for many helpful comments. We were also helped by André Tremblay's dedicated research assistance.

We are grateful for the excellent secretarial and other support
provided at the C.R.D.E. (Centre de Recherche et Développement en
Economique) by Jocelyne Demers, Sharon Brewer, and Francine
Martel. Special thanks are also due to the staff of the library at the

Ecole des Hautes Etudes Commerciales (H.E.C.), who located rare documents, especially Mr. Vasile Tega, Mr. Réal Lemieux, and Ms. Nicole Dupont.

The research was supported by grants from H.E.C., from the Center of Entrepreneurial Studies at the Wharton School, and the F.C.A.R. (Fonds pour la Formation de Chercheurs et l'Aide à la Recherche), whom we thank.

Last, but not least, we thank our copyeditor and production editor, Jane Van Tassel, for her meticulous work.

1. The uneasy history of lotteries

Thomas Jefferson called the lottery "a wonderful thing: It lays taxation only on the willing." But Jefferson's statement is erroneous. After all, taxing alcoholic beverages and tobacco also implies that the tax is imposed only on those willing to drink or smoke. Yet this fact does not necessarily turn either alcohol or tobacco into a wonderful thing.

Jefferson's statement may be linked to Britain's tax on tea, which, when imposed on the unwilling American settlers, resulted in the tea being thrown into Boston's harbor – certainly a way to avoid paying taxes. One can only speculate on Jefferson's reaction and the future of the colonies if Britain, instead of imposing a tax on tea, had decided to sell lotteries on this continent . . .

Briefly, Jefferson's opinion notwithstanding, games of chance have frequently been attacked with a ferocity that even alcoholic beverages and tobacco – two commodities that governments have frequently found to be wonderful things to tax – have rarely been. One question is why.

To answer this question, a brief historical survey of games of chance, with special emphasis on lotteries, is necessary. This survey starts at the very beginning, looking at the origins of both words and devices today associated with games of chance.

1. Religious practice or game of chance?

The origin of the word "lot" is the Teutonic root *hleut*, which meant the pebble that was cast to decide disputes and divisions of property.[1] This is also the source of the Italian word *lotteria* and the French *loterie*, which eventually came to mean a game of chance. To this day, however, in both Dutch and English, the word "lot" has broader meanings: It refers not only to a lottery ticket but also to a man's destiny. These two current uses of the same word are not accidental: Devices used today in games of chance were originally used for making decisions during religious rituals.

Perusal of the Bible reveals that drawing lots was regularly used to discover God's will in decisions on a number of issues, ranging from the election of a king (1 Sam. 10:20–1) to that of cult functionaries (1 Chron. 24–6), to the selection of the "scapegoat" for the atonement ritual (Lev. 16:8–10), to the identification of a party guilty of some sacrilege (Josh. 7:10–26), and to the selection of a date for some future action (Esther 3:7; 9:24). One instance of such lot casting described in Exodus 28:30 shows that the high priest Aaron is ordered to wear lots – "Urim and Thummim" – when going before the Lord:

And in the breastpiece of judgement you shall put the Urim and the Thummim, and they shall be upon Aaron's heart, when he goes in before the Lord; thus Aaron shall bear the judgement of the people of Israel upon his heart before the Lord continually.

Although nobody today knows exactly what the Urim and Thummim were,[2] one interpretation given to these words is that they were two dice, one used for a positive and the other for a negative answer.[3] For example, Joshua, after succeeding Moses, is given this order:

He shall stand before Eleazar the priest, who shall inquire for him by the judgement of the Urim before the Lord; at his word they shall go out, and at his word they shall come in, both he and . . . the whole congregation (Lev. 27:20–1),[4]

whereas Saul, when looking for the one who disobeyed his order to fast until evening, says:

If this guilt is in me or in Jonathan my son: O Lord God of Israel, give Urim; but if this guilt is in thy people Israel, give Thummim. (1 Sam. 14:41)

In Joshua 7:13 lots are used by Aaron to find out who, in defiance of God's wishes, took the sacramental objects, and in Leviticus 16:10 Aaron is ordered to cast a lot between two goats to choose the sacrificial one.

Leaders and important office holders were selected by drawing lots. Saul was thus selected by Samuel to be king of Israel (1 Sam. 10), although the drawing of lots only confirmed the feeling of Samuel, who had already anointed Saul. Eleazar, Ithamar, and their sons, the heirs of Aaron the high priest, divided the priestly duties by lots among them (1 Chron. 24). The lot was also used to discern the blame for the wrath of heaven: In the midst of the storm the sailors threw Jonah, on whom the lot fell, into the sea (Jon. 1:7).[5] In the New Testament it is said that Zechariah, John's father, is assigned duties by lot "according to the custom of the priesthood" (Luke 1:9), and the disciples chose Matthias from their midst to take over the ministry that Jesus had assigned to Judas by drawing straws (Acts 1:26).

Lots were used to choose members of important groups: the inhabitants of Jerusalem after the first exile to Babylon (Neh. 11:1) and the soldiers in the first attack against the rebel tribe of Benjamin (Judg. 20:12).[6] They were also used to divide land or other forms of wealth among various claimants. In Numbers 26:52–6, for example, one finds: "The Lord said to Moses . . . the land shall be divided by lots; according to the name of the tribes of their father they shall inherit. Their inheritance shall be divided according to lot" (a custom also found in Mesopotamia). The idea that the divine will is reflected in the fall of lots is most clearly expressed in Proverbs 16:33: "The lot is cast into the lap, but the whole disposing thereof is of the Lord," although the reference to the Urim and Thummim also stresses that their use is linked with divine means of communication, and in Isaiah 34:17 it is the deity who actually casts the lot determining the inherited portion.[7]

Similar practices can be found among primitive tribes, where bones, sticks, arrows, and lots were shuffled and thrown by the tribal seer, who then disclosed the message for the future, a message revealed by the supernatural spirit who controlled the throw. Early American Indians believed that their gods were the originators of their gambling games with colored stones and that the gods determined the outcome.[8]

Lot casting was used in pre-Islamic Arabia too, in order to determine guilt, and the Qur'an refers to the biblical use of lots (*sahama*) in the case of Yunus (Jonah), who lost and was thrown into the sea (3:44/39).[9] Yet these examples, as well as the biblical uses of lots, do not contravene the wide Qur'anic injunction against gambling:

They ask thee concerning liquor and gambling [*maysir*]. Tell them: There is great harm in both and also some profit for people, but their harm is greater than their profit. (2:220)

O ye who believe, liquor and gambling [*maysir*], idols and divining arrows are but abominations and satanic devices. So turn wholly away from each of them that you may prosper. Satan desires only to create enmity and hatred between you by means of liquor and gambling [*maysir*] and to keep you back from the remembrance of Allah and from Prayer. (5:91–3)

(Maysir was a pre-Islamic game of chance with mainly charitable goals.)[10] Later commentators attributed this condemnation to the fact that gambling was so widespread in pre-Islamic Arabia that "men . . . used to gamble their women folk and property. . . . [This] used to engender hostility and hatred among them."[11] The Qur'anic injunction was believed to be so broad that it made suspect even the practice of lot casting in legal proceedings, although the Jonah case and the other prophetic traditions argued for its adoption in such cases as manumission, divorce, and the allocation of inheritance.[12]

Thus, among Muslims too the casting of lots was approved for making up one's mind in cases of judgment or for ritual and political purposes (and thus the act could be carried out only by judges or priests). At the same time, casting them for other purpose was viewed as sacrilege.[13] The practice was thus linked with the belief that fate was not capricious and that in cases where judges could not arrive at a decision the casting of lots would reveal the divine will.

Similar practices are described in Greek mythology. The gods cast lots to divide the universe among them. Zeus got the sky, Poseidon the seas, and Hades, the loser, the underworld.[14] In the *Iliad*, Zeus used a sacred balance to decide whether the Trojans or the Greeks would win the battle (book VIII) and whether Hector or Achilles would die (book XXII). Even more revealing is the way in which it was decided who would strike the first blow in the duel between Paris and Menelaos: Hector put lots in his helmet and cast them. That was the way to determine a man's fate and the wishes of the gods (book III).[15] It has been pointed out too that the root of the Greek word *dike*, meaning "justice," is another word that meant "to cast" or "to throw," a relationship also found in Hebrew.[16] On Greek coins the figure of Dike, the goddess of justice, sometimes blends with the figure of Nemesis (vengeance) and with that of Tyche, the goddess of fortune – Huizinga (1955) remarked that originally they may have represented the same idea. Cohen (1964, p. 199) also notes that Tyche "was represented with a rudder to guide the ship of life, or with a ball or wheel, or with Amalthea's horn of plenty," and often she was blindfolded like the goddess of justice to suggest her impartiality. And, as among the ancient Hebrews and in latter-day Islam, in ancient Greece lots were drawn to divide an inheritance and to select some magistrates.[17] This last custom is also found in ancient Rome, where priests were chosen by this method.[18]

It may not be surprising that not only the word "lot" but also the word "play" had its origin in the spheres of ethics, law, and religion,[19] and that the customs of many societies show a relationship among fighting, games of chance, and beliefs (religious ones in particular). The word "play," the German *pflegen*, and the Dutch *plegen* are derived from a combination of the Old English *plegan* and the Old Frisian *plega*.[20] Their meaning was "to vouch or stand guarantee for, to take a risk, to expose oneself to danger."[21] Also "with many peoples dice-playing forms part of their religious practices.... In the *Mahābhārata*, the world itself is conceived as a game of dice which Siva plays with his Queen.... The main action of the Mahābhārata hinges on the game of dice which King Yudhistira plays with the Kauravas...[and] a whole chapter [of it is devoted] to the creation of the dicing-hall-sabha."[22] In archaic language, concludes Huizinga (1955), divine will and destiny were equivalent concepts, and "fate" might have been revealed by eliciting some pronouncement from them: One drew sticks, cast stones, or picked among the pages of the Holy Book.

But now remark: All the aforementioned widespread uses of both lots and dice were related to making decisions, to making up one's mind in legal and religious matters, and had nothing to do with games of chance. The situations in which they were employed were not repetitive, and were ones where a decision needed to be made. Nor were monetary prizes involved, and the casting of the lot was not a matter of entertainment. This way of making decisions – casting lots, throwing dice – had thus initially to do with a belief in a spiritual power that was supposed to control the outcome of the cast or the throw. Therefore, no smallest element of chance may have been perceived when priests and leaders pursued such practices. The lots and dice served to make final decisions concerning unique events linked with divisions of wealth, engagement in battles, and other crucial matters. But "divinity" was perceived to be responsible for the outcome.

How were such decisions made in later ages? They were not necessarily made on firmer bases, although within the newer systems of belief they may have been perceived as being so made. In ancient Greece people flocked to the oracles to resolve their doubts and to seek guidance in private or public affairs. No decision on engagement in war, on signing a treaty, or on enactment of law was made without oracular approval. Later, for centuries monarchs and governments used astrology for forecasting; it was perceived as an exact rather than an occult science.[23] In England, from the time of Elizabeth to that of William and Mary, the status of judicial astrology was well established. In the time of Charles I, the most learned and the most noble did not hesitate to consult astrologers openly. In every town and village, astrologers – just like priests in earlier times – were busy casting birth dates, predicting happy or unhappy marriages, and choosing dates for prosperous journeys and for setting up enterprises, whether shops or the marching of an army.[24] At the same time, traces of the practice of casting lots for making decisions survived.

During the sixteenth century, borough officers in England were still sometimes chosen by lot. In 1583 the Chapter of Wells Cathedral apportioned patronage in this manner. The practice of forcing condemned men to choose by lot how many and who should die was a common feature of military discipline much employed during the Civil War. In 1653 a London congregation proposed that a new Parliament should be selected from nominees chosen by each religious congregation "by lot after solemn prayer," the implication being that decisions made in this way received some sort of divine approval. The same idea lurked behind the use of lots for condemned men: The lucky ticket was labeled "Life given by God." In 1649 the council of the army sought God by prayer and then cast lots to determine which regiments should be sent to Ireland. A decision of 1665 even allowed juries to cast lots to resolve their differences as an alternative to retrial when agreement could not be reached. Although by the eighteenth century it had become a serious offense for juries to reach their decisions in this way, John Wesley still used lots to determine the Lord's will, arguing that they could be used in exceptional cases when long prayer and debate did not help bring about a decision. He said, however, that the matter was not settled by chance, for "the whole disposal thereof is of the Lord."[25]

Can one say that the newer and more widespread methods of making up one's mind – be it by reliance on magic, witchcraft, or the position of stars – were different in their essence from the ancient one? As long as people believe in a divine power that controls the throw of the dice (thrown by leaders and priests) or in a divine power that determines the positions of stars (examined by astrologers), decisions made when people share such beliefs will not be perceived as involving chance at all.[26] The fact that *we* view outcomes based on such decisions as matters of chance is irrelevant. Future generations might perceive decisions made on the recommendation of some Wall Street gurus or some social scientists, or those based on some Freudian interpretation of dreams, as being just like the decisions based in the distant past on either the throw of the dice or the positions of stars, no matter how scientific they may seem to some of us today. After all, recall that astrology was viewed for hundreds of years as science and not occult practice.[27]

To summarize, until the beginning of the seventeenth century the use of lots was generally regarded as a direct appeal to divine providence. The clergy condemned their use in resolving trivial matters; and they were not supposed to be used if some alternative way of reaching a decision was available. All games depending upon hazard or chance were to be strictly shunned, not just because they were said to encourage habits of idleness and improvidence, but because they were disrespectful to God. (More will be said on this point in Chapter 3.) For these same reasons, some theologians condemned using lotteries for routine purposes.

2. Lotteries in history

A brief history of lotteries and some other games of chance reveals some broad characteristics that will be dissected in the next chapters. This history reveals that games were perceived as playing a number of distinct roles. For the players, they represented a way either of passing their leisure time or of having a chance, however tiny, to become rich. For governments, they served as one of the means to raise revenues during periods when financial institutions were not yet developed or when they were hard pressed by sudden expenses. In spite of such apparently straightforward roles, lotteries and other games of chance have frequently been attacked on the ground that a society becomes worse off if people are given the opportunity to play, and for long periods of time many games were outlawed. Episodes in this story will be examined in detail in the next chapters, where the reasons for these negative attitudes will be explored. Here a broad picture is drawn to provide the background.

The Greeks believed that Palamedes invented dice and played with his fellow soldiers to relieve boredom during the ten-year siege of Troy. Gambling apparently remained popular in ancient Greece.[28] Games of chance in Rome were popular too: At the Circus, the emperors threw down numbered pieces of parchment, and the "winning" numbers represented a claim on prizes, which could be either privileges or goods such as precious vases or horses.[29] According to Suetonius, biographer of the emperor Augustus, tickets and tablets were sold during the Saturnalian festivities; the prizes varied from a hundred gold pieces to a toothpick, a purple robe, or a painting (the bettors saw only the reverse sides of the paintings, which were signed either by famous painters like Apelles and Zeuxis or by unknown ones). Heavy betting took place at the chariot races,[30] and the custom of distributing gifts to guests at parties by way of a lottery (each guest receiving a free ticket) was very popular.[31] The Roman emperors did not miss the contribution that lotteries could make to the state coffers. Both Augustus and Nero used lotteries regularly to finance their building programs; lotteries were also the means by which Rome was rebuilt after Nero burned it down. At the same time, the name for a gambler in Rome was *aleator*, which had a negative connotation, and laws were passed to limit bets. Also, in order to prohibit excessive gambling, laws prescribed that money lost at play could not be recovered by the winner, whereas money already lost and paid out could be recovered by the loser.[32]

The Roman custom of distributing gifts to one's guests in the guise of a lottery was the precursor of the first medieval lotteries. Merchants in Italy, the German states, and England discovered that they could gain a higher profit if they auctioned off their relatively expensive goods as prizes in lottery drawings.[33] Lotteries existed in Flanders in the fifteenth century, their earnings being earmarked for such public works as the building of poorhouses or ports.[34] The first recorded use of lotteries to raise public revenues in that century can be found in the town of Sluis (Holland) in 1434, the goal being to strengthen the town's fortifications.[35] In Amsterdam in 1592 lotteries paid for the building of a hospital, and in Middleburg in 1615 for the city's fortifications. In 1695 and 1696 twenty-four cities in Holland organized lotteries with large prizes. In 1726, however, their sale became a state monopoly, and the revenues were used to finance a number of important monuments.[36]

The first private lottery with monetary prizes in Western Europe was apparently in Florence in 1530. It seems to have been a great success. Learning from this experience, Venice created the first government monopoly in lotteries, which yielded considerable revenue for the republic's coffers;[37] Florence, Milan, Turin, and Rome all followed suit.[38]

A lottery is mentioned in 1444 in the town of l'Ecluse, but lotteries took root in France only after being introduced by the courtiers of Catherine de' Medici. Francis I immediately saw their potential for generating revenue and proceeded to issue the first letters patent for a "loterie" in 1539 in exchange for an annual right to 2,000 livres.[39] During the same century, the proceeds of a lottery financed the building of the Parisian church of Saint-Sulpice, as well as that of the Military School of Paris.[40] In 1572 a lottery was instituted in Paris to provide dowries for impoverished but virtuous young women who lived on the estate of Louis de Gonzague.[41] "Dieu vous a élu" ("God has chosen you") was the phrase written on the winning tickets, which carried prizes of 500 francs, and "Dieu vous console" ("God comforts you") was on the losing tickets. Before the tickets were drawn, on Palm Sunday, mass was celebrated with great pomp, and Pope Sextus V granted the promoters of this lottery remission of sins. Lotteries were so successful in France that they became an important fiscal instrument, especially when the people, already burdened by taxation, refused to pay more taxes.[42]

In 1776 all public lotteries were consolidated in the Loterie Royale modeled on the very successful Lottery of the Roman States sponsored by the pope (which helped to build and maintain Rome's public monuments and also helped create the museums of the Vatican),[43] and all private lotteries were outlawed. The reason given for the last step was to prevent the French from playing in foreign lotteries, which were more attractive than their own, and thus losing foreign exchange. But one wonders if there was not another and more important reason lurking behind this act; namely, to augment the treasury's receipts at a time when the kingdom had a budget deficit of 37 million livres.[44] If this was the real goal, it was attained. This new lottery was a great success and a major support for the chronically insolvent French treasury.

It even survived the French Revolution. Whereas all lotteries were abolished by the revolutionary government in 1793 on the ground that they exploited the poor,[45] the decision was reversed a few years later. In 1799 the lotteries were reborn under the name Loterie Nationale. One reason was that, deprived of their lotteries, people played the foreign ones illegally. As a result, the French government was losing not only revenue but also currency.[46]

With the coming to power of Napoleon Bonaparte, the Loterie Nationale became the Loterie Impériale and, as befitted its new title, helped finance his imperial projects and wars.[47] The lottery survived both the fall of the emperor and the restoration of the king and was finally abolished in 1836 (although lotteries to promote the arts or for charitable purposes were still authorized, and frequently the municipal governments of Paris, Lyons, and Marseilles sold premium bonds, where part of the accumulated interest was pooled and allocated by lot). The same legislature that abolished the lotteries created people's savings banks in the hope that the poor who had previously gambled would now start saving.[48]

The English proved themselves no less inured to the charms of lotteries. Queen Elizabeth chartered a lottery that was drawn in 1569 and offered a variety of prizes in goods as well as money.[49] In addition to the first prize of £5,000, there was another prize that rendered the buyer free from arrest for seven days except for a major crime. This first lottery was not a great success, in spite of advertising.[50] The next drawings took place in 1569, 1585, and 1612, when James I authorized one to raise funds for the Virginia Company to finance settlements in the New World. This lottery was successful, and the Virginia Company used lotteries for funding in the following years. Cities and towns were at first very happy with the lottery, but some soon began to complain that "the excitement of lottery had demoralized business and industry," and in 1621 Parliament halted lotteries until "we shall be more fully informed of the inconveniences and evils [of lotteries] . . . and may ordaine due remedy to the same."[51] But private lotteries still flourished, although they were looked upon with suspicion by some members of the public who argued that "the meaner sort of people are diverted from their work."[52]

Nevertheless, monopoly privileges for promoting lotteries were granted by the king to his courtiers, and in 1627, 1631, and 1689 lotteries were used to finance the supply of London's water.[53] The year 1694 saw the return of the state lottery in an unusual guise. In order to replenish the exchequer, depleted by French war expenditures, the state sponsored a lottery whose tickets were state bonds that were to be repaid sixteen years later. The interest rate that would be paid above a minimum of 10 percent (a rather low rate for this period) was drawn in a lottery.[54] This type of lottery was very successful, and its formula was used repeatedly by the state until 1769. (And it reappeared in the 1950s in a somewhat different form, under the name premium bonds.)

Yet in 1699 an act was passed to ban lotteries. (Some other games of chance, as we shall see in Chapter 3, had been banned before.) The reason given in the preamble to the act was that they had "most unjustly and fraudulently got . . . great sums of money from the children and servants of several gentlemen, traders and merchants . . . to the utter ruin and impoverishment of many families" (Ezell 1960, p. 9). This ban did not last. From 1709 to 1826 the British government authorized annual lotteries as a means of financing the exchequer, and private lotteries were used to raffle goods, just as in medieval times.[55] Private lotteries were outlawed in 1721, but publicly sponsored ones continued to flourish: Westminster Bridge and the purchase of some famous private libraries were thus financed by the government.[56]

During these years, "insurance" began to appear. This practice essentially meant that the agents selling the tickets could also sell fractions of them, promising the winner fractions of the prize. The practice led to abuses: It gave incentives for rigging the drawing of the lottery, and such rigging did indeed occur a number of times in 1775.[57] Moreover, it was seen as pernicious, in that it enabled the poorer elements of society to gamble. When the lottery was drawn, all those who were "insured" were accused of not working and of causing near riots in the neighborhood of the drawings.[58]

These occurrences were claimed by commentators to be at the origin of a growing opposition to lotteries. To quote Sir William Petty a century earlier, lotteries became "a tax upon unfortunate self-conceited fools." Each year the passage of the Lottery Act, which allowed the sale of lotteries for that year, became the occasion of severe criticism.[59] In 1808 a committee of the House of Commons was appointed to inquire into the evil consequences of lotteries and the remedies that could be obtained from regulating them. Its final report, full of horror stories about people for whom the lottery had

proved to be their downfall, concluded by saying that "the foundation of the lottery system is so ... vicious ... that under no ...
regulations ... will it be possible ... [to] divest it of all ...
evils."[60] In the 1823 Lottery Act, provisions were made to end the
practice after a last drawing in 1826. This epitaph was written for
that occasion:

> In Memory of
> THE STATE OF LOTTERY,
> the last of a long line
> whose origin in England commenced
> in the year 1569,
> which, after a series of tedious complaints
> *Expired*
> on the
> 18th day of October 1826.
> During a period of 257 years, the family
> flourished under the powerful protection
> of the
> British Parliament;
>
> The Minister of the day continuing to
> give them his support for the improvement
> of the revenue.
>
> As they increased, it was found that their
> continuance corrupted the morals,
> and encouraged a spirit
> of Speculation and Gambling among the lower
> classes of the people ... [61]

Note that the reason given is protection of the poor.[62]

This marks the end of lotteries in England until the present time
except for their use for promotion of the arts and some other special purposes.[63] In 1836 the advertising of foreign lotteries was also
prohibited.[64]

Lotteries in the New World

Lotteries came to the New World as an import from the Old.[65] We
have seen how the Virginia Company financed the early settlers with
the help of lotteries. And, as earlier in Europe, lotteries were also
used to sell property, substituting for the nonexistent banking sys-

tem. In order to dispose of an expensive property, people sold tickets to a lottery in which the property was the prize. Thomas Jefferson explained its rationale:

An article of property, insusceptible of division at all, or not without great diminution of its worth, is sometimes of so large a value as that no purchaser can be found.... The lottery is here a salutary instrument for disposing of it, where men run small risks for a chance of obtaining a high prize.[66]

This was especially true in the case of an owner having a pressing need of money at a time when corporations and security markets were in their infancy. Before 1790 there were only three incorporated banks in America. Lotteries were a substitute for what are now customary sources of public and private finance.

Ordinary lotteries with the customary monetary prizes existed as well. These lotteries did not come without their detractors. The Quakers of Pennsylvania were the first group whose objections to lotteries resulted in the passage of laws against them. There were others who were afraid of excesses among the poorer elements of society caused by excessive gambling. Yet such concerns did not induce the colonial governments to outlaw lotteries, since they could not give up such a means of raising revenues. One must remember that the fiscal needs of the American colonies were large: They waged wars against both the Indians and the French, but the population resisted increased taxes.[67] The strapped governments turned to lotteries to provide funds, which financed the protection of the seacoast against the French (1744, Massachusetts), paid for fortifications (1746, New York City), helped to build colleges (Yale, Harvard, Princeton, the future University of Pennsylvania), and provided funding for the construction of churches (1765, Pennsylvania). The popularity of lotteries to finance public works was such that they aroused suspicion in the British administrators of the colonies and the British government; both called for their abolition. A circular sent to the colonial governors in 1768 forbade them to license further lotteries, stating:

Whereas a Practice hath ... prevailed ... in America for passing laws for raising money by instituting public lotteries; ... such practice doth tend to disengage those who become adventurers therein from that spirit of industry and attention to their proper callings and occupations on which the public welfare so greatly depends...[68]

The bans came in spite of the fact that at home in England lotteries were still allowed to flourish.

But the days of English rule were numbered, and during the War of Independence lotteries were again one of the means by which a hard-pressed Continental Congress hoped to finance its war expenses, establishing the United States Lottery. The first drawing was successful; the following, less so.

Lotteries flourished in the independent United States as they had in colonial America. The people were still wary of taxes (they had, after all, just waged a war in order not to pay them), so lotteries were used to finance public projects at both the state and the federal level. They were also used to finance county and municipal buildings, repair streets, ensure the water supplies of cities, and build roads, canals, and bridges.

At the same time, the banking system developed; by 1810 there were nearly ninety incorporated banks (up from three twenty years earlier). Still, there was no extensive specialization, and lottery financing was combined with what we now view as conventional methods of finance. Suits (1979), for example, notes that after the Revolution John Adams negotiated Dutch loans for the new country. But the credit rating of the United States was so bad that it was required to pay a bonus on the interest. Adams arranged a lottery to pay the bonus. Information given by the *Boston Mercantile Journal* is useful to give a further idea of the continued importance of lotteries. According to it, in 1832 approximately 420 lotteries were drawn in eight states (New York, Virginia, Connecticut, Rhode Island, Pennsylvania, Delaware, North Carolina, and Maryland). The tickets sold in these lotteries brought a gross revenue of $66 million, more than five times the expenses of the federal government in that year.[69]

As lottery activities expanded, their character changed. A group of middlemen, the ticket brokers and lottery contractors, developed. Contractors took over the management of lotteries and hired brokers to sell the tickets. The brokers bought large blocks of tickets at a discount and resold them. Networks of lottery contractors and ticket brokers provided the framework for modern investment banking and stock brokerage services: What they did was tap people's savings to finance big public works.

Lotteries during this time had their critics. But the critics' voices were not heeded during the eighteenth century. Their main argument was that lotteries attracted poor people's resources and energy that could have been used more productively elsewhere. This argument was reinforced by the popularity of "insurance," already seen in the British context, which enabled people who could not afford to buy a whole ticket to buy a fraction of one.[70] This system not only provided more opportunities for the poor to gamble but, as in England, also provided more opportunities for fraud.[71] Fueled by some well-publicized scandals and the realization that the middlemen were retaining the lion's share of the profits, the antilottery movement gained influence. Pennsylvania became the first state to abolish lotteries, in 1833, followed by Massachusetts in the same year. By the beginning of the Civil War all but Delaware, Kentucky, and Missouri had similar laws on their books.[72] The Civil War and its consequences for the finances of southern states brought a revival of lotteries. However, in 1868 Congress forbade any sale of lottery tickets by mail, and by 1878 all states except Louisiana had prohibited lotteries.

In Louisiana, the lottery started in 1868 helped in reconstruction. A private firm was given a monopoly to sell tickets against a fixed annual fee paid to the state. But its very success, helped by the fact that it attracted customers from all over the United States (who violated the federal law against the sale of tickets by mail), created the seeds of its own destruction. Outraged by this violation of its laws, Congress strengthened them. In 1892 the charter of the company was not renewed when an antilottery ticket elected by a finally fed-up Louisiana electorate threw out the monopolist owners, who had until then bribed officials and manipulated elections in order to ensure the continued operation of the lottery. This was the end of the legal lottery in the United States until recent times.

The colonies to the north did not escape the lure of lotteries.[73] Whereas Quebec's authorities prohibited all games of chance, they allowed a few lotteries to dispose of some property (as in the United States) or to raise money for charitable purposes or public projects. Again the reason for their appearance was to substitute for an undeveloped banking system or for a nonexistent administration and bureaucracy that could collect taxes when funds were suddenly needed.

The first legal lotteries in Quebec were severely regulated. They had to be evaluated by experts, and the organizers had to obtain authorization from the government for every game. The British conquest of 1760 did not spell the end of the lottery, which was, as we have seen, already well entrenched in England and in the colonies to the south. With the War of Independence in the United States, lotteries were used by the British governor to distribute land to Loyalist soldiers and to immigrants fleeing from the new United States.[74] As everywhere else, revenues from lotteries were also used for public works; the new prison built in Montreal in 1783 was financed by a lottery. Moreover, revenues from American lotteries were used to finance some important projects in Canada. The Welland Canal between Lakes Ontario and Erie was financed by an American lottery.[75]

Nevertheless, there were no signs in the Canadian provinces of the same lottomania that existed in the United States around the time of the War of 1812. This does not mean that people did not play other games in the Canadian provinces. In 1817 the assembly of Lower Canada passed a law outlawing gambling. The reason given for this law was, again, to prevent *lower-class people* like workers and servants from ruining themselves.[76]

One form of lottery that continued to flourish in Lower Canada during this period was the raffle, especially for charitable purposes. Canadians who wanted to participate in lotteries could also buy tickets in American lotteries. But the 1840s saw the beginning of the disappearance of these lotteries as one American state after another outlawed them. Seeing a good profit opportunity, local promoters of lotteries appeared, and the years 1845–56 saw the appearance of private lotteries in Canada.[77] But, again as in other countries, fraud brought the government's attention to this activity, and in 1856 a law was passed outlawing lotteries and forbidding the selling of foreign lottery tickets. This was the end of legal lotteries in the whole of Canada, except Quebec, until recently. In Quebec, under pressure from the Catholic Church, the law was amended to permit lotteries for charitable purposes in which the prizes were objects but not money.[78] In 1890 the provincial government created a provincial lottery with cash prizes. At the same time, private lotteries flourished, using loopholes in the amended law. But in 1892 the federal government amended its criminal code to outlaw lotteries. This development spelled the end of lotteries even in Quebec.

3. The rebirth of lotteries

Thus lotteries were outlawed in France, England, the United States, and Canada. Belgium outlawed them in 1836 and Sweden in 1841.[79] In Sweden, however, they were reintroduced in 1897 and pari-mutuel betting on soccer games was legalized in the 1930s. Elsewhere a few lotteries survived during the nineteenth century. The Spanish lottery, founded in 1763 in order to build the Madrid hospital, was never outlawed.[80] In 1769 Spain created the Lottery of New Spain, later renamed the Lottery of Mexico, which still survives.[81] Portugal has had a lottery since 1783, when a royal charter created the Santa Casa da Misericordia, an institution charged with collecting money for charitable purposes, in part by means of lotteries.[82] Italy never outlawed lotteries, and, as we saw, the pope sponsored a very successful lottery in the Papal States. Germany has had lotteries since the Middle Ages, and in spite of calls for abolition during the nineteenth century, the German states continued to promote them for fiscal purposes, as did the Netherlands.[83]

The trend changes with World War I, after which governments were left with empty coffers and huge debts. In order to attract subscribers to state loans, the governments of Austria, Belgium, France, Germany, and Italy introduced variations on premium bonds, which had the characteristics of a lottery. (They had not been used prior to the war except in Austria.)[84] It was also the burden left by the conflict that spurred France to reintroduce a lottery in 1933 in order to pay the pensions of war veterans.[85] Belgium introduced a national lottery in the following year. The Irish Sweepstakes had its origin at the end of World War I too, when a ship sank off the Irish coast leaving the families of the drowned sailors destitute. A special lottery organized for their benefit was so successful that it led to the foundation of a permanent lottery.[86]

Although there had been discussion about introducing lotteries in England during the war, the decision was made to avoid them.[87] Following the outlawing of all but a restricted category of lotteries in the 1820s, all categories of gambling were eventually restricted by the Street Betting Act of 1906, of which the avowed goal was to outlaw all betting by the lower classes.[88] Only in 1956 did the Macmillan government introduce a lottery in the budget in the form of premium bonds (an echo of the scheme earlier introduced in France, Germany, and Italy). All other forms of betting, including lotteries and casinos, were legalized in 1960 but were heavily taxed and regulated.

Although during the Depression and World War II many states in the United States considered propositions for introducing lotteries, they were defeated.[89] (Discussion of these events appears in Chapter 3.) In 1963 New Hampshire became the first state to introduce a state lottery, followed by New York in 1966. Since then each election sees a spate of legalization as administrations try to resolve their financial woes; by 1985, 58 percent of the U.S. population lived in states with some form of legalized lottery.[90]

The correlation between governments' increased deficits and the decision to offer lotteries also comes to the fore in Canada.[91] After the outlawing of lotteries in 1893, lotteries went underground. But in 1929 the mayor of Montreal, Camilien Houde, began to lobby for the establishment of a lottery in order to deal with the accumulated deficit of the city. He was backed in the city of Quebec and by the Catholic population, but opposition from the Anglo-Protestant establishment defeated his lobbying. In 1967, facing massive deficits after Expo 67, Jean Drapeau, the mayor of Montreal, decided to create a "voluntary tax" that was a lottery in disguise.[92] In spite of Drapeau's and Montreal's best efforts, this voluntary tax was decreed a lottery by the courts, which abolished it. But lotteries were finally legalized in 1970. Since then all Canadian provinces have introduced lotteries that have prospered.

Why? Some answers are given as the more detailed story unfolds.

2. Why do people gamble?

When Plenty smiles – alas! She smiles for few –
And those who taste not, yet behold her store,
Are as slaves that dig the golden ore,
The wealth around them makes them doubly poor.
George Crabbe

Why do people buy lottery tickets?

At first sight, the answer seems misleadingly simple. They would like to become richer, and they don't see other opportunities open to them. Are there any other means by which one can win a million dollars or more with an investment of only a few dollars, even if the chances are small?[1]

If this were the whole answer, it would be difficult to explain the frequent public condemnation of lotteries, condemnation that has led many times in the past in many countries to their being outlawed. To understand these more complex events – the ban, the violent condemnation, occasionally a permissive attitude toward lotteries – one must first understand why people play these games and whether some groups in society are more likely to play them.[2] Only by examining these questions in detail can one hope to shed light on the broad issue of changing attitudes toward gambling and on pragmatic matters of public policy (for example, the revenues governments can expect from selling lotteries).

We shall mainly discuss participation in games of chance like lotteries, where there is a probability of winning a large prize, and not others, like playing cards with friends, spending hours at bingo games, or going to the casino during vacations in Las Vegas, Atlantic City, Monte Carlo, Deauville, or any of the other less-well-known peaceful French resorts in the Alps or near the Riviera. The narrow focus in this chapter is not a sign of today's dangerous trend of intensive specialization in the social sciences. Rather, as we looked more and more closely into the history of games of chance, we discovered that assuming that participation in them represented just one facet of human nature – that of people's attitudes toward taking risks – was dangerous. People play some games to pass the time, for entertainment. But they play other games for the chance of becoming significantly richer. The groups who play the two types of games are different, and so are, at times, the attitudes toward them. As will be shown, legislation has sometimes made a distinction among the various forms of gambling. In general, attitudes have been more tolerant toward games where limited sums could be lost and gained and that were played for entertainment, and less tolerant toward games where significant sums of money could be won or lost. Why would one expect the two groups to be different? Why would one expect different attitudes toward various games of chance?

An answer to the first question is presented in this chapter; answers to the second will come later.

1. What are people's motivations?

A number of attempts have been made to understand gambling behavior. A few are briefly discussed here; others that have taken a broader look at the issue are examined in the following chapters. Economists have looked at all games of chance as if they belonged to one category – whether the prize was one dollar or a million – and decided that gambling is a matter of taste. Those who like risks gamble, whereas those who do not like risks do not. Although this viewpoint has led to the development of numerous mathematical models developed in esoteric depth, it could not shed the slightest light on any facts.[3] (See Appendix 1 to Chapter 2.)

Freud explained gambling differently. He once wrote that a gambler is a man who, because of his death wish toward his father – quite a taste – has developed guilt feelings. In order to punish himself, he gambles, unconsciously wishing to lose. This seems like a rather strange theory (and one that cannot be falsified), but it should be noted that, to his credit, Freud ultimately discarded it in a letter to Theodor Reik.[4] Psychoanalysts have either related gambling to the Oedipus complex (another taste?) or dealt mainly with the behavior of compulsive, neurotic gamblers, a subject we do not intend to cover, since only a tiny fraction of the population exhibits such behavior.[5]

In contrast to the economic and psychoanalytic literature, in which few attempts have been made to relate gambling to social conditions, sociologists have done just that.[6] Devereux (1980) and Tec (1964), among many others, have argued that when conventional avenues for social mobility are closed, people will find nonconventional ones, which may include crime and gambling.[7] Whereas evidence exists to support this view, evidence also exists that contradicts it. There have been numerous very inegalitarian societies where there was no social mobility and yet there was not much crime and not much gambling either.[8]

Gambling will not be examined here through the prisms of these rigid approaches. We shall suggest, rather, that one can examine both gambling and the confused attitudes toward it by first making a distinction between two types of games. One type, where both stakes and prizes are relatively small (small relative to one's wealth), reflects a choice of leisure activity. Both the poor and the rich are expected to gamble, although, of course, not on the same games. The poorer may play poker, whereas the richer may go to a charity ball where the (tax-deductible) contribution includes participation in a lottery, or spend their vacations in Monte Carlo, where one day they may rent a yacht and another day go to the casino or watch horse racing and bet on it. The "losses" incurred from such games can be compared to the price one pays for other types of entertainment and have less to do with people's willingness to take risks than with how they choose to entertain themselves.

In contrast, other types of games do not take time to play. Thus they do not represent an opportunity for spending one's leisure time. In this case, people's willingness to risk their money for the chance of winning prizes should shed light on their spending patterns. It is people's willingness to take risks in order to try to become richer that is the major subject of this and the following chapters. That is the reason why we focus here mainly on lotteries rather than on games of chance, where only small sums can be won.

Why do people then take such risks? An answer (translated into mathematics in Appendix 1) suggests that shifts in relative wealth influence people's willingness to take risks and to deviate from traditional behavior. When people are suddenly outdone by their fellows, they pin their hopes on undertaking risks they shunned before: Some play games of chance and others venture into entrepreneurial or criminal acts.[9] Exactly the opposite reaction occurs when people outdo their fellows: They stop gambling and insure themselves instead, and avoid taking risks.[10] To put it simply, "too much" wealth and security breed laziness and "stupidity" (in the sense in which Milan Kundera used the word, referring not to ignorance but to the acceptance of received ideas), whereas some types of insecurity breed effort and ingenuity. Since certain groups fall behind and others outdo their key referent groups when the status quo in society is destroyed, one would expect to finding contradictory tendencies: Some people start to gamble, gamble more, and take more risks, and others try to restore stability, advocate insurance, and make bad decisions. This is a sketch (details can be found in Appendix 1), but we shall see later on how one can understand some historical changes by keeping in mind this fixed backdrop of human nature.[11] First, however, let us examine in its light the narrow picture concerning predictions linked with gambling only:

- That a chance to win the big prize will be one of the main reasons for lottery-ticket buying
- That the relatively poor will plan to spend a greater fraction of their wealth on lotteries than the relatively rich
- That people of all classes who have not previously gambled may decide to do so when they suddenly lose part of their wealth (for example, when they are fired, fear the increased probability of being unemployed, and so on)

By the term "relatively poor" we do not mean only people who have lower money incomes. The reason is that a $15,000 income for a fifty-year-old is a different indicator of wealth than the same income for a twenty-year-old. The older man realizes that he can no longer become significantly richer by pursuing opportunities in the labor market. Yet he may still hope that by gambling he can become a rich man. Thus one would expect that older, rather than younger, people with the same measured income will gamble. Too, for a person with one child, a $15,000 income assures a higher position in the distribution of wealth than it does for one with four children: on the same income, the greater the number of children, the poorer the family. Thus we would expect that people with the same measured income who have more children will tend to gamble more.

These statements already suggest why some studies of gambling may have been misleading.[12] In them, information was gathered on the income of the buyer or of his or her household without looking at either the gambler's age or family structure. Sometimes the information on income seemed sufficient only to reach the conclusion that lower-income groups tend to spend a greater fraction of their income on lotteries. At other times, the income of the gambling population seemed, at first sight, too high to support this claim. However, as is pointed out above, income may provide very biased information about changes in one's position in the distribution of wealth, and additional considerations must be made to correct the bias. We shall make them below and check each of the predictions made above.

2. Some stubborn facts

The attraction of big prizes

If people want either to become richer or to restore their wealth after losing a significant part of it, games of chance giving away small prizes will not be perceived as attractive, but others giving away big ones will. Indeed, most market researchers of lotteries in the United States found that "while people like to be winners, they also want to win 'a lot of money.' This is a universal dream, and apparently is the primary reason why people buy lottery tickets."[13]

A survey done by the New York State Lottery found that the typical ticket buyer was motivated by the hope of winning a big prize, and another done by the Massachusetts State Lottery Commission found that the public overwhelmingly favored a single top prize of $100,000 over a large number of top prizes of $1,000.[14] A U.S. government report on gambling found that 77 percent of the people polled gambled in order to get rich, and Landau, in his guide on how to create a successful lottery, concluded that experience shows that there must be a prize that will improve people's circumstances in a way they cannot achieve otherwise.[15] Rubner too, after examining a number of lotteries in several countries (England, Colombia, Spain, Australia, Ghana, West Germany), reaches the conclusion that "it is mainly the size of the top prizes that determines their success" and that "the number of small prizes is being constantly cut down to make way for even bigger top prizes."[16] And both a report of the Royal Commission on gambling carried out in the United Kingdom in 1951 and a 1977 market research study for Loto-Québec reveal that the expectation of a large prize is the main reason given for purchasing lottery tickets.

Lotteries characterized by many unequal prizes – some of which are very large – are not inventions of our times. This has been one of their characteristic features since the seventeenth century. Although the difference between the largest and smallest prizes has varied across countries and time, Sprowls speculated that these differences depend on the discrepancy between being poor and being rich in the particular country at the particular time.[17] For example, he found that the largest prizes in England in the late eighteenth and early nineteenth centuries were greater than in the United States in the same period, and he links this with the fact that discrepancies in wealth in England at that time were also greater. It may not be accidental that since 1980 first prizes in the United States have reached the level of tens of millions, and that several recent proposals for multistate lotteries talk about even larger prizes.[18]

Whereas many lotteries give away large prizes, some do not. In the traditional bingo game the maximum prize is around $5,000. However, the fact is that bingo, which requires one's presence during the game, is viewed by the participants as a way to spend their time rather than as a means of getting rich. The 1976 U.S. government report *Gambling in America* states that "middle-aged and elderly women, widows, and those earning under $5,000 a year are highly represented among the 'heavy' bingo players.... Bingo is viewed more in 'social' terms than other forms of gambling; most players play to have a good time" (p. 163; and see Table 2.1 on the different characteristics of lottery and bingo players).[19]

One can still raise two questions concerning the prize structure of lotteries. First, why isn't there just *one* large prize and sale of fractional tickets? Such a feature would allow buyers to build any portfolio of prizes they wanted and would increase the attractiveness of the game. If the prize was $10 million and the price of the ticket $10, you could buy either a whole ticket or just one-tenth of one, in which case your expected prize would be $1 million rather than $10 million. Instead, what one typically finds is a number of large prizes and no sale of fractional tickets. The reason is that in England and the United States the sale of fractional tickets – called insurance – became illegal, as we saw in Chapter 1.[20] When such legal constraints

Table 2.1. *Percentage of income bet per capita by lottery and bingo participants as a function of family income*

| | Family income | | | | | |
	Under $5,000	$5,000–10,000	$10,000–15,000	$15,000–20,000	$20,000–30,000	Over $30,000
Lotteries	0.3%	0.23%	0.13%	0.06%	0.06%	0.02%
Bingo	0.49%	0.64%	0.18%	0.07%	0.06%	0.04%

Source: Gambling in America 1976, pp. 156, 163.

exist, people may prefer the somewhat greater chance of belonging to the "middle classes" (with, let us say, five prizes of $100,000 and one of $500,000) to the smaller chance of jumping higher (with just one prize of $1 million) and the greater one of staying where they are – at the bottom.[21] It should also be noted that the fact that fractional tickets are not sold does not mean that no substitutes have been found. People frequently buy in groups, cooperating either with members of the family or with co-workers.[22]

The second question is: If it is true that large prizes make lotteries attractive, why do small prizes exist? If one assumes with Sprowls[23] that these small "consolation prizes are essentially refunds which are an inducement to try again" in hopes of winning in the future, we should find both that small winnings are frequently rebet and that people often stop gambling on lotteries altogether when they win larger prizes. This is indeed the pattern that the data reveal. More will be said on this point in section 3.

The poor and those falling behind

Many surveys have found that poorer people spend a greater proportion of their income on lotteries. This was the conclusion reached by Rosen and Norton (1966), who examined the buying patterns in New Hampshire; by Brinner and Clotfelter (1975), who did the study of Connecticut, Massachusetts, and Pennsylvania; by Clotfelter (1979), who did a study of Maryland; by Lemelin (1977) and McLoughlin (1979), who did studies of Quebec and Ontario respectively; by Heavey (1978), who did one of Pennsylvania; and by Clotfelter and Cook (1987), who have done studies of California and Maryland.[24] In the analysis of Maryland's lottery buyers, Clotfelter and Cook found a negative relationship between spending on lotteries and income and education, and discovered that blacks spend more than whites on lotteries. The difference between whites and blacks was most striking for those belonging to the lowest income categories, suggesting that poor whites may believe they have more opportunities for getting richer than poor blacks. The 1976 report *Gambling in America* also showed that families whose yearly income was below $5,000 were spending on average 0.3 percent of it on lotteries and that families in the $5,000–$10,000 income range were spending 0.23 percent of their income on lotteries, whereas those in the $10,000–

$15,000 range were spending only 0.13 percent.[25] These results were obtained without even making adjustments for age and family structure, adjustments that could only have strengthend them, as we shall suggest below.

Examining the British evidence, Newman concludes that, with the single exception of casino gaming, a higher proportion of the mass of wage earners gamble on each of the various gambling activities, and so it "can be stated with confidence that gambling is predominantly a proletarian predilection" (1972, p. 85).[26] Newman also found that single women are relatively less inclined to gamble than married ones: For each ten single female bettors there were fifteen married ones in similar age groups. Too, 30 percent of married men aged eighteen to thirty-four bet on horses, but only 20 percent of single men in the same age group. Although Newman does not present evidence on the number of children, one can speculate that married people, whether women or men, are likely to have more children than the single ones. He also found that betting on football pools and playing bingo are forms of betting that are significantly more attractive to older than to younger people; only in respect of casino gaming is the tendency reversed.[27]

Similar conclusions can be reached when one examines data on Swedes who bet on soccer games. Whereas this game seems at first sight different from a lottery in that it may require both knowledge of the game and information about the teams, the difference disappears if one assumes that all the participants in the betting have access to the same information (that is, if no behind-the-scenes deals among teams are made).[28] Thus participation in soccer pools and lotteries can be compared, especially when it is recalled that for pools the discrepancy between the price of participation and potential gains is as large as for lotteries.

The information is derived from tables built by Tec (1964) on the basis of answers given to questionnaires by 812 men between the ages of eighteen and fifty-five. The tables give information on their income but do not correlate income with age or family structure.[29] Still, when one looks at classification by occupation, one observes that 60 percent of the working-class respondents are regular bettors, compared with 45 percent of the middle class and 40 percent of the upper class.[30] When gambling is linked with class, it is found that 38 percent of those who come from upper-class homes, 46 percent from middle-class homes, and 61 percent from lower-class origins play regularly. It is also found that among those whose parents own a business, 43 percent gamble regularly, compared with 54 percent of those whose parents do not own a business, and that 43 percent of those with higher education gamble regularly, compared with 55 percent of those who have only finished grammar school. As to age, besides the fact that the sample is biased (people older than fifty-five have been excluded), the way the tables have been put together enables the reader to learn only that 54 percent of those between the ages of eighteen and twenty-four gamble regularly, whereas 58 percent of those between twenty-five and thirty-four do so. Nevertheless, the picture that emerges from these tables seems to be that the relatively poor participate disproportionately in games of chance in Sweden too.

In order to get a clearer, more detailed picture, we examined surveys of the winners of big prizes. One survey was made of the big winners ($1 million or more) in Michigan for the years 1973–80. There were forty-six such winners. The survey included age at the time of winning, occupation, and, for some, the number of children and grandchildren. Another survey found that in New York there were eight winners in 1977–8; for each, age and occupation were given. We compared the winners' sample characteristics with the total Michigan and New York populations as given in the 1970 census.[31]

The average age of the Michigan and New York winners was fifty-four, whereas the average age of the Michigan and New York population above the age of sixteen was 27.9. Among the winners, 10 percent (seven, to be precise) were below the age of thirty-five, whereas 60 percent (thirty-four of the fifty-four) were above the age of fifty. This enables one to reject the possibility that the winners are an unbiased sample of the general population (at the 2 percent level). Further, the winners' average number of children was five (for the twenty-nine winners for whom this datum was given), and the average number of grandchildren was six (and these averages do not even include one winner who had seven children and thirty-two grandchildren). Occupations (when the winner was not retired) were all characteristic of the poor or the lower middle class: The winners were janitors, factory workers, and so forth. In conclusion, the probability that such a sample is a random one for the population above the age of sixteen is very small.

Table 2.2. *Age distribution: lottery winners versus the general public*

Age	Winners Percentage	No.	Total population
New York			
16–30	10	5	31.2%
31–40	18	9	15.9%
41+	72	37	52.9%
New Jersey			
16–30	8	4	30.4%
31–40	14	7	16.4%
41+	78	41	53.2%

Sources: Kaplan and Kruytbosch 1975; U.S. Census of Population, 1970.

Similar evidence was found by Kaplan and Kruytbosch (1975) when they compared the age distribution of winners and the population at large in the states of New York and New Jersey. Persons over age forty-one were overrepresented among winners (72 percent of the winner sample and only 52.9 percent of the New York population, and 78 percent versus 53.2 percent in New Jersey), whereas the age group sixteen to thirty was underrepresented (see Table 2.2).

All the evidence summarized above thus strongly suggests that the lottery-playing population tends to be older and poorer and has more children than the rest of the population. Other evidence, however, seems at first sight to provide a different picture. For instance, in Quebec 63 percent of the people whose annual income is between Cdn. $10,000 and Cdn. $15,000 are occasional or regular players (see Table 2.3). These incomes may be average for a young childless worker, but they are low for an older one with four children. Thus it would be misleading to conclude from the information on income alone that in Canada, in contrast to other countries, the middle class are the major lottery players.

We therefore took a closer look at the data, taking into account education and age. The reason for looking at education is that it is positively correlated with income. If one finds that the lottery-ticket-buying public is relatively less educated, we can conclude that relatively poorer and older people bought the lottery tickets in Canada too.

Table 2.3. *Regular or occasional purchasers of lottery tickets by 1976 income (in percentages)*

Type of lottery	$0–$5,000	$5,000–8,000	$8,000–10,000	$10,000–15,000	$15,000–25,000	Over $25,000
Inter-Loto	41	48	52	63	52	59
Super-Loto	28	36	44	41	40	47
Loto-Perfecta	11	26	23	27	23	28

Source: Robert Sylvestre 1977, vol. 3, Tables 3b, 4b, 5b.

Table 2.4. *Regular or occasional purchasers of lottery tickets by years of schooling (in percentages)*

Type of lottery	0–7	8–12	13–15	Over 16
Inter-Loto	58	53	42	39
Super-Loto	43	38	33	24
Loto-Perfecta	25	20	21	11

Source: Robert Sylvestre 1977, vol. 3, Tables 3b, 4b, 5b.

This is indeed what we found: 58 percent of people polled with up to seven years of schooling, 53 percent with eight to twelve years, 42 percent with thirteen to fifteen years, and 39 percent with more than sixteen years answered that they were regular or occasional buyers of Inter-Loto tickets, and similar trends existed for the other lotteries (see Table 2.4). At the same time, the group aged forty-five to fifty-four and those fifty-five and older represented the highest percentage of the lottery-ticket-buying public. Considered alone, this finding may have two explanations. Either these are the ages when people are at the peak of their earning power, or only when one attains these ages does one finally realize that the only way to procure a fortune is by winning the lottery. Considering the previous data, which show that people with less schooling bought more tickets, the second explanation seems to be the valid one.

This conclusion is strengthened by evidence given in a detailed survey of 93 (out of 190) big prizewinners of Loto-Canada between the years 1974 and 1978.[32] The age group fifteen to twenty-four represents 7.6 percent of the winners but 26.2 percent of the population, whereas the proportion of people aged forty-five and older is 46.6 percent in the sample versus 37.3 percent of the general population. These facts may explain why the average family income of the winners was Cdn. $18,962, whereas the mean Canadian family income was Cdn. $16,095.[33] Although at first sight these numbers do not seem to indicate a poorer population of lottery-ticket buyers, the impression is again erroneous because of the lack of adjustment for either age or the number of children.[34] The mean income of a family whose head belonged to the age group forty-five to fifty-four was Cdn. $21,237 (recall that about 50 percent of the winners were aged

Table 2.5. *Regular or occasional purchasers of lottery tickets by age*
(in percentages)

Type of lottery	Under 20	20–24	25–34	35–44	45–54	55+
Inter-Loto	12	33	46	58	68	59
Super-Loto	11	23	32	43	47	46
Loto-Perfecta	12	12	20	24	25	18

Source: Robert Sylvestre 1977, vol. 3, Tables 3a, 4a, 5a.

forty-five and older, and the average family income of all winners was Cdn. $18,962).[35]

But we do not wish to press this point any further, since it should be recalled that we expected *two* groups to gamble. Not only did we expect the poorer and the older to play more, but also others whose realized wealth suddenly turned out to be significantly less than expected owing to illness, accident, loss of job, and so on. The resulting decision to purchase lottery tickets, a reaction to a sudden loss and less security, will not be a regular, planned one, but rather a spontaneous one. But this kind of reversal of fortune can happen to anybody, rich or poor, young or old, with or without schooling. Thus, if one puts together the two categories of people – the poorer who plan, and the unfortunate who may decide suddenly to buy lottery tickets – one may misinterpret the data and recommend wrong policies. Just how misleading such aggregate data might be depends on the percentage of people who decide to buy spontaneously relative to the percentage of people who plan to buy tickets. We have found only one survey that raised this question;[36] it found that 50 percent buy them spontaneously and the rest plan to purchase them (see R. Brenner 1985, Table 2.5, p. 62). This evidence may suggest only that something under 50 percent of the lottery-ticket buyers may be old and poor. The rest may be young or may have no children but may have just been subjected to an unexpected, unfortunate event (losing a job, not getting the significant raise expected, and so forth). Devereux suggested in his massive classic study on gambling that "the well adjusted middle class salaried employee may lose his job for a variety of causes that lie partially or wholly beyond his control ... [and] ... gambling may appear as one of the by-products of this sequence,"[37] whereas Scodel (1964) labels gambling a safety valve for that fraction of the middle class who are afraid of losing their position or, in the case of upwardly mobile ethnic minorities, insecure about their "social insurance" as Americans. Anecdotal evidence on this point was revealed in a poll in Quebec (where unemployment had reached an all-time high of 15 percent): People reported that the money they had previously allocated to beer and wine was now allocated to lottery tickets.[38]

Additional evidence supports this interpretation. Tec (1964) found that in Sweden gambling behavior was well correlated with a person's dissatisfaction at work, and Brunk (1981) concluded that in the United States dissatisfaction with current income was a strong reason for lottery-ticket buying. In the already mentioned detailed survey of ninety-three big prizewinners of Loto-Canada in 1974–8, the winners were asked whether or not before they won their prizes they thought they could still advance in their careers. Of the sixty-eight winners who answered the question, 51.5 percent said no. Moreover, 41.6 percent answered that they expected their situation either to stay unchanged or to deteriorate. To the question "Would you choose the same job again?" 29 percent answered no, and 36 percent answered that they would not like to see their children do the kind of work they were doing. Only 19 percent answered that they would. These answers suggest two things. First, the winners come from both groups (the poor who planned to spend relatively large amounts on lotteries and those who suddenly became poorer and dissatisfied and decided to gamble). Second, the winners are relatively old: It is hard to believe that 51.5 percent of the working population consider themselves as already being at a dead point in their careers. (In the numerous works summarized by Campbell and Converse, the percentage of dissatisfied workers varied between only 11 and 23.)[39]

Further evidence suggesting that there is a positive relationship between the propensity to gamble and being relatively poor and frustrated also comes from another direction. Numerous studies have found that French Canadians earned less than English Canadians (although the difference narrowed in the 1970s).[40] Thus one would expect that French Canadians would gamble relatively more and be disproportionately represented among the winners. Indeed, out of the ninety-three winners in the sample above, forty-five (or 48.9 percent) were Francophones, whereas in 1975 they represented only 25.6 percent of the population.

But one must be careful with the interpretation of these data. One also finds that 67.8 percent of the winners were Catholics, whereas 28.9 percent were Protestants. Yet in Canada in 1976, 47.3 percent were Catholics and 43.4 percent Protestants. Thus Catholics are overrepresented among the winners. Two interpretations can be given of this fact. First, the Catholic Church has tended to be much less disapproving of gambling than the Protestant churches,[41] and one may thus expect that people belonging to the former will gamble more than those belonging to the latter. (Among the winners, 62.3 percent of the Catholics and 50 percent of the Protestants stated that their religion was either "very important" or "important" to them.)

The second interpretation of the nonproportional participation according to religion is linked to the previous information on Francophones and non-Francophones. Since the overwhelming majority of Francophones are Roman Catholics, and since Francophones are disproportionately represented among winners, one would expect that Catholics would also be overrepresented in the sample. However, there are more Catholic winners in the sample (61) than there are Francophones (45). Since in Canada Catholics have lower average incomes than other religious groups,[42] one could predict that they will tend to spend relatively more on lottery tickets and thus be disproportionately represented among the winners. There are not enough data to be able to say which interpretation (the religious or the one based on the Catholics' lower wealth) has the greater predictive power.

This same survey also reveals that two regions – the Maritimes and Quebec – that had relatively lower incomes were overrepresented among the winners. Among the million-dollar single winners, 50 percent were residents of Quebec, whose proportion of the 1976 population was only 27 percent. The Maritimes were the residence of 40.5 percent of the winners whose residence was neither Quebec nor Ontario, whereas their population represented only 25.6 percent of the Canadian population outside Quebec and Ontario.[43]

Statistical analysis and its pitfalls

Detailed data on lottery-buying patterns are available in Canada. We hoped that with their help we could carry out the best comparison between theory and facts. A closer examination of the data reveals, however, that we were too optimistic. Detailed data are indeed available, but they are quite inaccurate. Yet, as is shown in Appendix 2 to this chapter, with an appropriate statistical procedure a reasonable examination can still be done.

Two samples were at our disposition. One is based on a study commissioned by Loto-Québec in 1980. A random sample of 2,015 Quebeckers were interviewed on their spending patterns in several types of lotteries, on their sociodemographic characteristics, and on their attitudes toward lotteries and gambling in general. When analyzing this sample, we considered only spending on lotteries that had a relatively large prize (Cdn. $50,000 and up). We also had to eliminate some of the observations because of missing variables and were thus left with only 851 usable observations.

The second sample is based on a survey of expenditures of 10,937 Canadian families, made by Statistics Canada in 1982, where one of the items on the list was spending on lotteries. Although these data sets seemed at first sight impressive, we soon discovered that there are a number of problems. First, no distinction is made between expenditures on lotteries that offer a relatively large prize and ones that do not. But this is the least of the problems. We found that if one adds up the sums people said they spent on lotteries (using the appropriate statistical procedure), one comes up with Cdn. $47.3 million for the Atlantic provinces, Cdn. $264 million for Quebec, Cdn. $308 million for Ontario, and Cdn. $137 million for Western Canada.[44] If people's answers were accurate, the sums should more or less equal the respective provincial lotteries' revenues (since, it should be noted, each has a local monopoly). But they are off the mark by 35 percent in Western Canada, 39.2 percent in Ontario, 40 percent in the Atlantic provinces, and 49 percent in Quebec (see Table 2.6).

Although some of the differences can be explained by the fact that foreigners too buy these tickets, they contribute under 10 percent of the revenues.[45] Thus there is a large unexplained discrepancy between what Canadians say they do and what they actually do, at least as concerns their gambling expenditures. The discrepancy may be explained in a number of ways. One explanation is that people simply do not remember well how much they spent during the year, since the sums they spent were relatively small. To compound the effect, older people gamble relatively more and may have even less reliable memories. But this explanation is insufficient: It could as well produce overestimation as underestimation. An additional explana-

Table 2.6. *Actual revenues and sample's estimate of lottery*
purchases from provincial lotteries corporation, 1982

Corporation	Actual revenues (million $)	Revenues estimate (million $)	Difference (%)
Atlantic	78.6	47.3	39.8
Quebec	515.87	264	48.8
Ontario	506.89	308	39.2
Western Canada	210.56	137	34.9

Note: Column 2 is computed with the help of the coefficients given in the survey.
Source: Statistics Canada 1982, *Family Expenditures in Canada.*

tion might be that people do not think about including the small winnings that they rebet on lotteries as part of the income spent on them.[46] Depending on the lottery, 16 to 24 percent of revenues is redistributed in the form of prizes of under Cdn. $100 (between 11 and 17 percent being redistributed in the form of prizes of under Cdn. $10). Suppose that one wins such a prize and decides to spend part or all of it on lotteries in addition to the planned weekly expenditure. When asked about total expenditure at the end of the year, people answer approximately by just multiplying the planned weekly amount by fifty-two and forgetting to declare the small winning. In this case, underdeclaration by the relatively poor should result, since if the poorer spend disproportionately, they are the ones who get, disproportionately, the small prizes. Yet another explanation for the underdeclaration may be that people do not tell the truth about their spending on lotteries, since such spending is open to condemnation.[47] This would not be the first time that, for these or other reasons, people have not made accurate declarations about their expenditures on games of chance.

McKibbin remarks that in 1895 Henry Higgs, a pioneer investigator of people's expenditure patterns, noted that his efforts to collect data gained ground very slowly, since "many people talk about it as being a stomach policy of the bourgeoisie, whereby the bad management of the working classes should be demonstrated."[48] Thus, although Higgs provided data on housing, food, and clothing, there was not much about "pleasures." Indeed, Higgs's American publisher commented that it is strange that he "made no reference to any allowance in . . . budgets for amusement expenditure. The budget of an American workman of the same class would assuredly include a regular weekly outlay for amusement."[49] McKibbin adds that so would the budget of the British workman, even if, for the reason mentioned above, the category "amusement" was not included in the statistical data. More recently, the compilers of a family expenditure survey for the year 1964 report what Statistics Canada does not, that when families are asked to detail their personal expenditures they understate the expenditure on items about which they feel guilty: tobacco, alcohol, and gambling.[50] Thus, it is useful to emphasize that one should not expect too much from the statistical results, no matter how sophisticated is the technique used.[51]

So it was quite surprising that not only the Loto-Québec but even the Statistics Canada data led to results that, on the whole, seem consistent with the picture drawn until now (for the detailed analysis, see Appendix 2), and there were no surprises: The poorer, the older, and those who fall behind play more, and the upwardly mobile play less.[52]

3. Do gamblers spend recklessly? Are they criminals?

Arbiters of morals as well as some social scientists have had rather negative attitudes toward gamblers, arguing that gamblers, in general, overestimate their chances, are unstable, and destroy their family life, and so they recommend outlawing all forms of gambling.

There is no evidence whatsoever to support their view, and thus one must explain the prevalence of such opinions and the regularity of their emergence and impact as disguising something else. What that something else might be is examined later.

First, the previously quoted British Royal Commission on gambling concluded that gamblers were as aware as nongamblers of the unprofitable nature of gambling and did not overestimate their chances to win.

Second, although no distinction has been made between gamblers playing just lotteries and those who played other games of chance, the following information is revealing. According to the U.S. government's report *Gambling in America*, these leisure activities characterize gamblers: They watch somewhat less television than nongamblers, read more newspapers and magazines, and read about as many books. Gamblers devote more time to opera, lectures, museums, nightclubs, dancing, movies, theater, and active sports. They also socialize more with friends and relatives and participate more in community activities. The few things that they spend much less time on include home improvements, gardening, knitting, sewing, and going to church (p. 68). In their book *Gambling, Work and Leisure* (1976), Downes and his co-writers provide little evidence to support the view that the majority of gamblers spend their money recklessly, whether it is money laid out on stakes or money earned from winnings. The facts are that people budget their expenditures and that gamblers use any large win thriftily and sensibly,[53] spending it on home-centered items.[54] Devereux too noted that, in the more stable working-class neighborhoods, gambling takes the form of *disciplined* petty gambling.[55] In betting on horse races, too, small wins are rebet more often than large ones; rebetting is largely confined to regular punters, although even among this latter group three times as many save their winnings or spend them on household goods as rebet them.[56]

A somewhat similar picture emerges from Newman's (1972, 1975) examination of the British evidence. Two-thirds of adult Britons gamble regularly, some more and others less. Manual wage earners, as already noted, predominate, especially among those who play more frequently. But Newman concludes that their "self restraint, exercised in the interest of prolonged participation, reduces their proportionate losses enabling them to recoup a larger proportion of their stakes," and adds that gamblers had a greater budget awareness than nongamblers.[57] He also notes that these regular gamblers are tough-minded, emphasize the virtues of self-interest, personal effort, and independence, and are suspicious of strangers, of outsiders, and in particular of government bureaucracies, displaying a pronounced hostility toward the openhandedness of the welfare state.[58]

A similar picture is revealed by the Swedish survey. Gamblers and nongamblers discharged their familial, occupational, and social duties in a similar fashion. Gambling did not interfere with attempts to advance through conventional channels of social mobility; rather it seemed to provide an additional strategy that served this goal. When gamblers and nongamblers were compared, neither their intention to establish businesses nor their participation rates in training to improve their job differed. Nor was any relationship found between gambling and crime, marital instability, or the degree of participation in community activities. On the contrary, gamblers participated in adult education courses more than nongamblers (41 percent of gamblers versus 33 percent of nongamblers in the same age group).[59]

Igor Kusyszyn found five psychological studies done since 1928 comparing people who gambled with those who did not. The studies reached the same conclusion: The differences were insignificant. Kusyszyn did his own study (in collaboration with Roxana Rutter) in 1978, comparing thirty-five heavy gamblers, forty-two who gambled less, nineteen nongamblers, and twenty-four lottery players. They not only found heavy gamblers to be "as psychologically healthy as the non-gamblers" but also found that light gambling did not lead to more intense gambling (the light gamblers had been playing for fifteen years on average).[60] Thus their conclusion was similar to Weinstein and Deitch's (1974) that light gambling is not a stepping-stone to heavy gambling. Just so, the majority of lottery players persist in their habit of betting small amounts.[61]

The Royal Commission on gambling in the United Kingdom also found that "generally speaking, the average expenditure on gambling must be considerably less than the average expenditure on other indulgences such as alcoholic liquor or tobacco."[62] "The great majority of those who take part in gambling do not spend money on it recklessly and without regard to the effect of their expenditure on the standard of living of themselves and their families."[63] "We find no support for the belief that gambling, provided that it is kept within reasonable bounds, does serious harm either to the character of those who take part in it or to their family circle and the community generally."[64] The report also concluded that "whatever the extent of gambling in this country, we have been unable to find any conclusive evidence to support the view that it interferes seriously with production."[65] "The conclusion we have reached on the whole from the evidence, is that gambling is of no significance as a direct cause of serious crime, and of little importance as a direct cause of minor offences of dishonesty."[66] This study thus reached the same conclusions as those drawn in Britain at the beginning of the century,[67] which found that most of the appalling poverty was due to structural factors (unemployment, family size, bad health, low wages). Gambling and drinking were responsible for the much less significant "secondary poverty" and were "themselves often the outcome of the adverse conditions under which too many of the working classes live."

Neither in Sweden and England nor in Ireland, Gibraltar, or Norway was there any evidence that gambling and crime are related. Nor was such evidence found in the United States, where the myth that gamblers are criminals seems to prevail. The evidence is that the American bettor is not involved in criminal acts other than the placing of the illegal bet itself – an insufficient reason to condemn gambling.[68]

Cornish summarizes additional similar evidence. In England a 1951 study carried out by the principal medical officer in Wakefield Prison showed that out of eight hundred consecutive admissions examined in 1948, in only 2 percent of cases was gambling "a factor in the offender's downfall." Even among this 2 percent, gambling was considered to be merely one aspect of a "generally slack and dissolute life," and in only seven cases was betting a significant factor.[69] Similar studies of criminal populations have been carried out more recently. Sewell (1972) found that the frequency of gambling for a sample of short-term prisoners at Pentonville was not really different from that of comparable groups from national samples, such as those provided in Gallup's (1972) and Borill's (1975) surveys. Of course, if one examines the relationship between crime and gambling when gambling is outlawed, the results would be tautological and could shed no light on the discussion of whether or not gambling and crime are correlated.

The Swedish experience is revealing in this context. When gambling was outlawed (up to 1930), the Swedes gambled on the English soccer games, thereby smuggling out substantial amounts of Swedish currency. But once gambling was legalized, the criminal elements that were involved with smuggling and gambling disappeared. (Recall the very similar French and other experiences presented in Chapter 1.)

These findings are not novel. McKibbin, in the previously mentioned study of working-class gambling in Britain between 1880 and 1939, concluded that even gambling on all games of chance lumped together made few demands on the economy of those who practiced it:

Even at the time no significant material consequences were ever detected, and critics were driven either to untruths or simple ideological statements: "Very likely his house is not broken up, his furniture is not sold, his wife and children never see the inside of the workhouse. He is degraded that is all, and his descent is progressive . . ." Although it was not for want of trying, the various commissions could find no general relationship between gambling and poverty, or between gambling and crime, other than that most gambling was illegal to start with. Witnesses repeatedly confessed that they found poverty or crime unaffected by gambling, and one actually admitted that "there are cases where the prisoner alleges that his downfall is due to betting where the police, on making enquiry, can find no truth in his statement at all." (1979, p. 157)

More on gambling in the past in various countries will be said later.

At first sight, these data concerning the lack of correlation between gambling and crime may be surprising, for two reasons. First, recall that two classes of people are expected to gamble relatively more: the poorer and those who suddenly fall behind. The first group plans participation, whereas the second suddenly decides to participate. The motivation to commit crimes cannot be linked at all to the first group – only to the second.[70] But if the first group represents the majority of buyers, whereas only a small fraction of the second gambles on criminal acts (the rest bet on mere games of chance or on entrepreneurial acts), it should not be expected that, in general, gambling and crime will be strongly correlated. Only some who have suddenly lost a significant fraction of their wealth and see no avenue for climbing back may decide to bet both on games of chance and on criminal acts, and they in turn represent only a small fraction of the people who gamble. Thus the lack of correlation is not surprising, after all, once one takes a second and closer look at the problem.

The second reason, which is more difficult to follow, involves why, in spite of quite clear-cut evidence, popular discussion associates the introduction of gambling with crime.

The easiest answer is that people are ignorant of the facts, and those who preach banning gambling do it because of religious beliefs. Although this answer is not quite satisfying, we shall see later, when we examine gambling in a broader context, how one can understand such reactions and their impact on other people's opinions.

The other answer is that the negative attitude toward gambling in the United States may stem from a reason already mentioned: namely, that during the time it was outlawed, the games were supplied by the underworld. (As will be shown in Chapter 5, this sequence has occurred regularly across countries and time.) However, to condemn gambling on this basis is erroneous; for it was the very fact that gambling was outlawed that created the incentive for the underworld to capture this sector. But, as has already been pointed out, gamblers even then did not commit crimes except to place illegal bets. It is also argued that when games of chance are introduced in a locality, the crime rate will rise because of prostitution, mugging, and so on. This argument seems to confuse as well: The rise of crime in this case seems to be attributed to the increased numbers of expected tourists. The problem may, then, be with tourism rather than gambling. But one must be careful in extrapolating the U.S. experience to other countries: The calm French resorts, where the casino is the center of the town, do not provide the slightest support for making such a correlation. One must even be skeptical in interpreting the U.S. data concerning positive correlations between places where people gamble and crime rates. Recall that in the United States the tax laws allow one to deduct losses from theft up to a certain amount. Why, then, should not gamblers who lose a few hundred dollars go to the nearest police station and announce that they have been mugged? As police everywhere are overwhelmed with work, there is very little chance that they will look for muggers and discover that the declaration was a mere invention.

Briefly, the picture of the typical gambler that emerges from all the evidence presented up to this point is close to a description reported in Campbell:

He is a white employed male . . . earning between five and ten thousand dollars a year. He worked regularly, steadily, dependably, wearing a blue or a white collar. Yet the frontiers of his career expectations have been fixed since he reached the age of 35, when he found that he had too many obligations, too much family, and too few skills to match opportunities with expectations.[71]

4. The behavior of winners

Is it true, what many writers have said, that winners of big prizes waste their money, don't work, gamble more, abandon their families, and generally go to the dogs? The answer is no.

The facts, once again, confirm the boring stable image of the lottery player. Kaplan has done several studies (1978, 1985a). Although in the first, preliminary, one (based on his interviews with one hundred winners), he agreed with the critics of lotteries and concluded that, indeed, the winners stopped working, in the later more precise and reflective study he gives a very different interpretation of the facts. The more recent research is based on information about 576 winners in the United States who won prizes of $50,000 and above: 25 percent of the sample won $1 million and more, 29 percent won between $200,000 and $1 million, 38 percent won between $100,000 and $199,999, and 8 percent won between $50,000 and $100,000.

The average age of the winners was fifty-four, 64 percent being fifty or older, 16 percent being between forty and forty-nine, and only 20 percent being under the age of forty. Thus, it is not surprising that the majority of those who won large prizes either retired early or quit their jobs. What should one expect from people fifty-four years old or more who suddenly become rich and who have worked hard all their lives? The next answers are typical and provide a flavor of what is going on, a flavor hidden by the dry statistics. A fifty-seven-year-old clerk in the New York subway system who won $3.5 million said, "I was able to retire from my job after 31 years. My wife was able to quit her job and stay home to raise our daughter. We are able to travel whenever we want to. We were able to buy a co-op, which before we could not afford."[72] Another winner said, "Since we have raised *eight* children and educated them in Catholic schools in the amount of 112 years tuition paid, it was a help to be able to pay without depriving ourselves for years as we did.... We feel very secure that we can travel more and have helped our family."[73] Yet another said, "My husband retired in 1981, as he had cancer surgery in 1978 and we wanted to enjoy the remaining years of the income. The end of this year, we expect to turn our home over to the ones left at home, travel for six months – which we could never have done." A sixty-year-old woman from Massachusetts said, "A year after I won the money, my sister had an operation and had a year to live. I was able to retire and care for her,"[74] and a sixty-eight-year-old winner said that "winning the lottery was a Godsend for us. My husband was sick for two years ... and passed away this year. I had to close my ... shop and make bedrooms for my mother and sister-in-law."[75] This is an age when one can hardly be expected to start a new career; anyway, 45 percent of the winners were only high school graduates and another 25 percent not even that, and the majority of the winners were laborers who had put in long hours of work for years. Their retirement should not be viewed as an example of "erosion of the work ethic" or be interpreted as a sign that this group of players was in any way predisposed toward unstable participation in the labor force. At the time of winning, these people had worked at their jobs an average of thirteen years, 25 percent of the winners for twenty years or more. (In contrast, the American labor force as a whole has an average job tenure of four years.) This is, of course, a sign of stability, but it can also be interpreted as a block to career opportunities. Kaplan also found, as one would expect, that the higher were a winner's education and income, the more likely it was for him or her to continue to work.

What did the winners do with their money and the leisure it bought? Eighteen percent gave more time to their family and children, 32 percent worked more on their houses (for, as one would expect, a large percentage of the winners bought a house, made improvements to the one they owned, bought furniture, and so forth), 5 percent did more volunteer work, 4 percent did graduate study, and 32 percent devoted themselves to various leisure activities. Indeed, after reviewing this evidence, Kaplan calls into question the popular myth about marriages or family lives being destroyed after winning. On the contrary, winning seemed to stabilize them. Although there were a few divorces, the respondents admitted that their home lives were boring and bad before they won (winning, in fact, "stabilized" husbands and wives through enabling them to live apart after years of not getting along). But it is the stronger ties reflected in the previous quotes that were typical. And what else did the winners do with their money? As noted, they spent it on housing and travel – but less on gambling.[76]

In conclusion, none of the evidence presented so far lends the slightest support to the rationale for which lotteries are condemned today. Indeed, Rubner had already noted that "gambling, particularly in Britain, is clouded by hypocrisy, cowardice, and sanctimoniousness.... Like Anthony Crosland [a once well-known British politician], I, too, have come across this mixture of puritanism and paternalism so curiously common among the British intelligentsia, which is exemplified in the 'pubs, pools, and prostitutes' argument. It combines a belief in the moral virtues of abstinence with the conviction that the working class wastes all its surplus income on alcohol, tobacco, and gambling, if not actually women. Crosland defiantly says this of himself: 'If I suddenly had a large increase in income, I have no doubt that I should spend a large part of it on smoking, eating, drinking, gambling, and similar deplorable recreations; and I decline to debase myself on that account.' "[77]

It is this wrong-headed extrapolation of the relatively fortunate – their inability to enter into the minds of the relatively poor or of those who fall behind – that explains, in part, their biased attitudes toward lotteries. For, as we have seen, the unfortunate do not think at all in these terms when they buy lottery tickets. They think about educating their children, buying a house, and buying household products; and when they win the big prize, this is indeed what they do with their money. Recall the eloquent articulations of the benefits of winning quoted earlier and contrast them with the benefits perceived by Crosland. The latter captures the view from above, the way some of the fortunate may think: When they already have their cottage, when they have already provided for their children's education, for their retirement, for their vacations, then what will they do with still more money? The fortunate may attribute the negative effects of being bestowed with sudden large unearned income to their own experience of similar events, like suddenly receiving a large inheritance when they are already accustomed to a comfortable life. But such a situation should not be confused with that of the less fortunate, who can better appreciate the value of money and decide to husband sudden winnings.

Perhaps George Bernard Shaw in *Pygmalion* captures best, in words, the different attitudes (the facts captured them here). Devereux (1980) recalls the scene in which Eliza's father accepts from Professor Higgins only five pounds instead of ten, on the ground that, with the smaller sum, "he would feel free to treat himself to a glorious 'binge,' whereas with the larger sum he would feel constrained to use it sensibly" (p. 796n) – as indeed he later does when he gets an even larger sum. (Then he even stabilizes his family life and marries his mistress.) Shaw's assessment, which is consistent with the facts, contrasts with Crosland's, which is not.

This contrast is illuminating for an additional reason. Note that Shaw distinguishes between the effect of obtaining a relatively small sum and a relatively large one. The unexpected small sum received from Professor Higgins cannot move him up in society, and is spent

on insuring friendships, on strengthening already existing social con-
tacts through inviting others for drinks at a pub. However, when he
gets the large inheritance, he decides to manage it prudently. Of
course, what is large for Mr. Doolittle may not be large for somebody already comfortably established in the middle class.

Getting a sudden $250,000 inheritance when one expects an
annual income of $50,000 or more is not bad, but it is insufficient
to move one into a higher class, and it may be spent as recklessly
as Mr. Doolittle spent his five pounds. A case known personally to
Devereux and described by him, may be revealing: "A college student
inherited a modest fortune of $250,000 on his twenty-first birthday,
and set about quite deliberately to spend it all within a year. He
rationalized . . . that the fortune was too trivial to live on permanently, but that its presence would . . . deflate his motivational drives
toward academic and pecuniary success, would 'ruin his character'
and spoil his life. So he took the year off, with a few college friends,
and 'blew the works' in riotous living" (1980, p. 785). (We could find
no systematic evidence showing how typical such behavior is.)[78]

5. Compulsive gamblers – in parentheses

As the data clearly show, compulsive gamblers are a tiny fraction of
the gambling population – the majority of those who gamble do so in
hopes of becoming richer – and those who commit crimes an even
smaller fraction of this subgroup.[79] Yet, obviously, they are the ones
who capture the writers', the journalists', and the filmmakers' attention. Ashton's *History of Gambling in England* (1898), Chafetz's *Play
the Devil: A History of Gambling in the United States* (1960), and
Sullivan's *By Chance a Winner* (1972) are full of stories about compulsive gamblers, and Dostoyevsky's *The Gambler* is about a man
who left his mark on people's imagination.

However, such histories can hardly be viewed as attempts to
understand gambling. The authors have chosen *interesting* stories,
and such stories are not provided by the lives of moderate, average
people but by those who in one way or another have deviated from
the norm. Although Dostoyevsky's book certainly captures one side
of human nature, his own life reveals that the picture is more complex and not necessarily consistent with the moral of his book. His
brother's death, the demise of the review he had been editing, and his

passion for gambling left Dostoyevsky bankrupt (by the way, he immediately and voluntarily assumed the care of his brother's family). To cope with these burdens, Dostoyevsky did not commit crimes but worked feverishly, and his most famous works, *Crime and Punishment* (1866), *The Gambler* (1867), *The Idiot* (1868), and *The Possessed* (1872), were, according to Nabokov (1981), written under constant stress. Dostoyevsky worked in a hurry to meet deadlines with hardly any time to reread what he had written.[80] But with the help of his stenographer, whom he married in 1867, he met his deadlines, and gradually, between 1867 and 1871, they achieved some financial security. Thus *The Gambler*, telling the story of the weak schoolteacher who promises himself every evening to abandon his addiction, reflects a possibility. Dostoyevsky's life reflects another.

Still, we do not doubt that compulsive gamblers impose a cost on their families and thus on society. But can the existence of such a tiny minority be used as an argument against lotteries and gambling? There are compulsive eaters, compulsive drinkers, compulsive workers, compulsive watchers of television, compulsive womanizers. Their lives and their families' lives may be as miserable as those of the compulsive gamblers', and they too impose a cost on society. But prohibitions on drinking are rare. And whereas eating, drinking, working, and watching television are activities recommended to be carried out in moderation, excesses are not legally forbidden.

6. Conclusions

What then makes gambling on lotteries an act that has frequently attracted special condemnation?

These gamblers are poor or fell on hard times and would like to be richer.[81] They are not criminals, they do not spend recklessly on games, they do not seem to differ significantly from nongamblers in their leisure activities, and they do not seem to be ignorant of how small is their chance of winning big prizes. (How can they be when articles on the winners of big prizes are front-page stuff and always point out the precise tiny probability of winning?) These facts, then, cannot explain the special indignation. Neither can it be explained by the fact that a tiny minority of gamblers are compulsive players, considering the fact that heavy drinking, although it has consequences similar to heavy gambling (destroying family life, crime), is not condemned today in such severe terms. Few recommend banning all drinking because of the small percentage of heavy drinkers.

So what makes lotteries with big prizes so special? Answers to this question are given in the following chapters, where lotteries and gambling, and the attitudes toward them, are examined in a historical context.

3. Why is gambling condemned? Words, facts, and the discrepancy between them

As we have seen, two things may induce noncompulsive players to play: entertainment or the chance to become rich. Entrepreneurs aware of these two motives will invent and bring to life a variety of games of chance to satisfy such desires, employing people and resources. The entrepreneurs will sell the games, others will buy them, and the losers will both pay the winners and cover the entrepreneurs' costs and profits. A sector like any other commercial sector in society?

Opinions have varied. Since antiquity, people have frequently made a distinction between the two types of games of chance: one that represented a social pastime, a game among family and friends, an entertainment, and one where the possibility of getting rich existed. The first type of game was viewed as part of the recreation business. So, although such games have at times been condemned – as singing, dancing, sports, and spending time and money in taverns have been – the condemnation was not related to the fact that people played a game of chance or that they took "unnecessary" risks, but to the fact that they spent their time in a way judged unproductive by others. The idea was that if gambling (or any other recreational activity) was outlawed, and the laws were enforced, people would spend their time and money in more "productive" ways. Those who shared such opinions perceived that during the game wealth was redistributed but was not created. Therefore, if the people and resources used in this activity (time spent included) were reallocated, society would benefit. Wouldn't it?

Before answering this question – in the negative – it should be noted that the accusation of diminished productivity has also been made when time spent playing was not the issue. The point made was, rather, that by playing such games people would develop a "getting something for nothing" mentality and would thus make less effort. It was also argued that once people believed in the idea that chance played a significant role in human affairs, the legitimacy of some institutions, religious in particular, would be questioned. Such skepticism, claimed members of these religious institutions, would have a further negative effect on society.

As was pointed out in Chapter 2, there has been no evidence since the late nineteenth century to support these opinions. Although compulsive gamblers have posed problems for society, they apparently represented, in the more distant past too, a tiny fraction of the gambling population. This can be inferred from the fact that among the many reasons put forward for condemning and outlawing gambling since antiquity, reference to compulsion is rare. The main reasons for the negative attitudes were different.

The evidence interpreted in this chapter suggests that one of the reasons for the negative attitude was that people disagreed about the ways in which humanity's optimism could be ritualized. Some thought that religious institutions must provide the answer. Others sought solutions in gambling or in looking for activities offering opportunities for spending leisure time and ritualizing people's hopes. The two types of solution seemed incompatible to some, and gambling was condemned by those who thought that institutions based on religious beliefs should provide the proper ritual. The criticism was especially severe during periods when the influence of traditional religion was declining and either new beliefs or entrepreneurs offering new options for spending time made their appearance. We document this experience across countries and time.

Additional broad consistency is documented despite the fact that the past and the present are very unlike. It is shown that during periods when the status quo is changing and people are moving up and down the social ladder, gambling regularly takes some blame. However, as has already been suggested, gambling is really a symptom rather than the disease.

The selection of countries and periods for making these and additional points has been guided in part by the availability of documents and data and in part by our assessment of when gambling was an issue and when it was not.

The chapter starts with evidence from antiquity and then examines in detail the events surrounding changes in attitudes and in legislation concerning gambling in England and in the United States. It shows how these changes were linked with both class distinctions and fluctuations in the influence of various groups.

1. Gambling and religion: chance and providence

In ancient Jewish law, the negative attitude toward systematic and excessive gambling was due to a number of opinions. One held that taking money from another without giving valuable consideration in return was like larceny; another held that wasting time and money in gambling, instead of using one's time to study or work, for example, ignored the "general welfare of the world" (*yishuvo shel olam*).[1] Last, but not least, the condemnation was linked with the deeper issue concerning the contrasting notions of chance and divine will discussed in Chapter 1. Let us recall briefly the main argument.

"The lot is cast into the lap; but the whole disposing thereof is of the Lord" was the biblical explanation of the casting of lots in Proverbs 16:33. This statement was the focus of the theologians in their attacks on gambling. Whenever this technique was used, the outcome was interpreted not as a matter of chance but as a revelation of the divine will. The association with the heavens implied that the throwing of the dice should be treated seriously, with proper ritual and respect, and used only in cases when men were incapable of making decisions based on precedents. The outcome of the casting of lots was thus perceived as being determined by some supernatural force that was "just." Yet such religious beliefs associated with the throw of the dice were shaken from time to time, and it is during such periods that surviving documents reveal a severe condemnation of gambling. The condemnation should not be surprising. The belief that the throw of the dice is determined by a supernatural power is consistent with the existence of religious institutions and their hierarchy. (As Voltaire said, "Our priests are not what simple folk suppose; their learning is but our credulity" [*Oedipe*, 4.1].) In contrast, the belief in chance may be perceived as being less so, and seems more consistent with the existence of gambling palaces in Las Vegas and Atlantic City and entrepreneurs à la Donald Trump. People's increased willingness to gamble may thus be viewed by some as a symptom of the decline of the power of religious institutions. One possible response to such a sequence of events on the part of the religious hierarchy may be to invent false accusations in attempts to impose restrictions on institutions viewed as symbols of a belief in chance.

In ancient Greece, the worship of fortune and of fate started only when belief in the Olympian religion collapsed.[2] Pliny (23–79 c.e.) relied on Greek sources when he made this observation and compared patterns of behavior in ancient Greece with those of his times:

Throughout the whole world, at every place and hour, by every voice, Fortune alone is invoked and her name is spoken: she is the one dependent, the one culprit, the one thought in men's minds, the one object of praise, the one cause. She is worshipped with insults, counted as fickle and often as blind, wandering, inconsistent, elusive, changeful, and friend of the unworthy.... We are so much at the mercy of chance that Chance is our god.[3]

Some writers went so far as to say that it was the "poisonous notion of chance [that] was weakening the fibre of the Roman."[4] Perkins contrasts the widespread belief in luck and worship of the goddess Fortuna with the fact that the familiar word "fortune" cannot be found in the New Testament:

It would appear that the life envisaged by the New Testament writers had no place for gambling or the acknowledgement of luck. As the years passed, the Christians were influenced to some extent by the prevailing Roman customs, for we find Tertullian writing in the second century: "If you say you are a Christian when you are a dice player, you say what you are not, for you are a partner with the world." (1958, p. 8)

Islam too condemns gambling, the ban again being related to a basic tenet of monotheism, that blind fate was not the governing force of human destiny. According to Rosenthal (1975), the assertion of purposeful divine control as against the belief of pre-Islamic Arabs in a capricious fate was the main theme of the divine revelation received by the Prophet and the prime cause of Islam's initial spiritual success.[5] Early Muslim theological thinking used gambling as a metaphor to illustrate the concern with free will against predestination. At that point, the discussion was still conducted in neutral terms. Nard (a version of backgammon), invented in the pre-Islamic period, was contrasted with chess. Nard, according to this discussion, had been invented to show that no worldly goods are gained through cleverness and skill. The invention of the game was a response to a perception that the world bounces human affairs around capriciously. Chess was then invented in order to counter the ideas suggested by the existence of nard, since it showed that success went to the clever individual with a will to succeed. With the success of Islam, however, nard – and gambling in general – was severely condemned, since the Prophet's vision seemed to convince people that they lived in a world with a definite purpose, from beginning to end completely determined by God, a purpose that did not permit anything to be left to chance.

In which circumstances did these views gain currency? In Mohammed's time, Arabia was divided among warring tribes, some nomadic and others settled in agricultural oases or towns. These latter groups, whose numbers were apparently increasing, found themselves in an ideological vacuum, since the traditional tribal customs, fitting smaller groups and a nomadic way of life, were weakened. The theological simplicity and relative legal precision of Mohammed's message, combined with the Arab's pride in not accepting foreign ideas, helped the early and relatively quick and widespread acceptance of the new faith. Within two decades all Arabia was united into a new religious–political community, and in the twenty years following Mohammed's death it seized the richest provinces of the Byzantine empire and destroyed the Sassanian state, an achievement that cannot be explained by any military innovation but by the confidence inspired by the new religion.[6]

Once Islam became established, the many lists of minor and major sins that were condemned by Islamic writers either disregarded or devoted very little space to gambling – much less than to alcohol, for example, which was also prohibited. Still, this literature reveals that gambling was viewed as a contemptible *lower-class* pastime to which only the economic and spiritual dregs of society would devote themselves, whereas chess apologists contended that their game was played by persons of high standing in society.[7]

The early church fathers and councils clearly condemned gambling among all Christians. Canon law forbade games of chance from the very beginning: Two of the oldest church laws threatened excommunication of both clergy and laity found gambling.[8] The Council of Elvira (ca. 306 C.E.) decreed that if guilty of gambling, one could, however, be reinstated after suspension for one year. Clement of Alexandria, Tertullian, and others condemned gambling on the grounds that it reflected an interest in material things, in being a "partner with the world," and seemed in contradiction with the striving for a blissful afterworld, required behavior from a Christian. (Compulsion does not seem to be the writer's concern.) Yet during medieval times the distinction between magic and religion, and between providence and chance, was blurred, and in spite of condemnations of gambling, the medieval church did not deny the claim that people were able to manipulate God's grace for earthly purposes. Aquinas, Boethius, and Dante all stressed that the notion of divine providence did not exclude the operation of chance or luck. It was during the turbulent sixteenth and seventeenth centuries when the power of the church was declining and new beliefs tried to establish themselves that these latter views came under severe attack, in England in particular.[9]

As Keith Thomas remarks, if there was a common theme that ran through the writings of Protestant theologians during these centuries, it was the denial of the very possibility of chance or accident. In his *Institutes of the Christian Religion* (1559), Calvin condemned the widespread belief in chance:

For what would you be more ready to attribute to chance, than when a limb broken off from a tree kills a passing traveller? But very different is the decision of the Lord ... Who, likewise, does not leave lots to the blindness of fortune? Yet the Lord leaves them not, but claims the disposal of them himself.... To the same purpose is another passage from Solomon: "The poor and the deceitful man meet together: the Lord enlighteneth the eyes of them both." For although the poor and the rich are blended together in the world, yet, as their respective conditions are assigned to them by Divine appointment, he suggests that God, who enlightens all, is not blind, and thus exhorts the poor to patience.... Those who have learned this modesty will neither murmur against God on account of past adversities ... like Agamemnon in Homer, who says, "The blame belongs not to me, but to Jupiter and Fate." Nor will they ... put an end to their own lives.... But they will rather search the Scripture to learn what is pleasing to God. (Cochrane and Kirshner 1986, pp. 368–9)[10]

To make fortune into a goddess was a grave mistake, emphasized the Anglican *Homilies*, and "that which we call fortune," wrote the Elizabethan bishop Thomas Cooper, "is nothing but the hand of God, working by causes and for causes that we know not. Chance or fortune are gods devised by man and made by our ignorance of the true, almighty and everlasting God."[11] Every Christian had to know that life was not a lottery, but reflected the working out of God's purpose: The events of this world were not random, but ordered. Lewis Bayly, in the influential devotional guide *The Practice of Piety* (1613), blamed fires on people's practice of making preparations for market day on the Sabbath. Sickness too was attributed to God's will, and it was argued that "health came from God, not from doctors."[12] Such were the teachings of most theologians and moralists, at least until the later seventeenth century, although there were exceptions.

Thomas Gataker, a Puritan divine, in his treatise *Of the Nature and Use of Lots* tried to eliminate objections to the use of lotteries and to justify their use in routine, secular contexts. He argued that whereas God determined all events, the fall of the dice was no more an immediate providence than the daily rising of the sun. He also distinguished between the two types of games of chance, one where large sums were at stake and others played for entertainment. He concluded that wasting one's estate on games was to be avoided, but the use of lots in games of recreation, including card games, was legitimate.[13] When stakes were so small in proportion to the player's wealth that loss would not cause anxiety and gain would not constitute a source of "unearned" income that would be more than trifling, Gataker did not condemn the game. Yet his views were contested, the objection to games of chance lingered, and as late as 1687 Gataker's ideas were discussed as unrepresentative of the main body of theological opinion.[14]

2. The English background

In what circumstances were these debates in England taking place? England's population as a whole had been increasing significantly since 1520, although the growth was erratic. According to Stone (1972), the doubling of the population in the 120 years before the Civil War was the critical variable of the sixteenth and seventeenth centuries. Its ramifications affected every aspect of society, leading to major changes in agriculture, trade, industry, urbanization, education, social mobility, and overseas settlement.[15] For example, from 1650 there had been a dramatic growth in trade with America and the Indies; consumption of sugar, tea, coffee, and tobacco soared; the import of new textiles from the East increased and led to outcries from the defenders of English woolens, who predicted the ruin of the English economy because of this new addiction to luxury. There had been innovations in agriculture and in the way estates were managed. Indeed, according to Plumb, much that was regarded by Lord Ernle or Sir John Clapham as new in the eighteenth century – the growing of root crops, the introduction of clover and new grasses, systematic crop rotation, and beneficial leases – was well established in East Anglia and elsewhere by the reign of Charles II.[16] The sixteenth and seventeenth centuries also saw an unprecedented ferment of scientific and intellectual activity. Yet Lawrence Stone emphasizes that in order to understand the political history of the period, less attention should be paid to absolute increases in wealth due to the aforementioned innovations and to changes in the ways one came to own it, and more to changes in the distribution of wealth due to changes in the numerical proportions of the various strata of society. The period between 1540 and 1640 saw the growth of wealth and of the size of the landed classes and of the professions, and a massive shift of relative wealth away from church and crown and away from the very rich and the very poor toward the upper-middle and middle social strata. Such relative shifts always lead to aggression, with the help of swords as well as with the help of words. It is, therefore, not unexpected that men in seventeenth-century England killed, tortured, and executed each other for political beliefs; sacked towns; brutalized the countryside; and were subjected to conspiracy, plot, and invasion.[17] This uncertain political world, notes Plumb, lasted until 1715 and then began rapidly to vanish.

While these changes were taking place, it was also estimated that about a third to half of the population were at the bottom. These were the "cottagers, paupers, labouring people and outservants. Many of these were copy-holders occupying their own small tenements, but even more were wage labourers, for the decline of the English peasantry was already under way."[18] Life expectancy was still short; even among the nobility, life expectancy at birth for boys born in the third quarter of the seventeenth century was about thirty years. (Today it would be around seventy.)[19] Bubonic plague was endemic until the last quarter of the seventeenth. In 1563 some 20,000 Londoners, in 1593 some 15,000, in 1603 some 36,000, in 1625 some

41,000, and in 1666 some 68,000 died.[20] Along with helplessness in the face of disease, fire was, according to Keith Thomas, the greatest single threat to one's security and wealth.

It was during these two centuries of contrasting changes – the rising number and wealth of professional groups of lawyers, clergymen, merchants, and officials on one side, and the continuing or even worsening poverty of other people on the other side – that the heated debate about providence versus chance was taking place and comments on people's increased propensity to gamble were being made. Chance and gambling were perceived as God's and the church's competitors. Why was this debate so important? When a long-established and firmly held belief is shattered, all hierarchies may feel threatened. If one "truth" is discarded, then who knows what others may follow?

Not surprisingly, as Keith Thomas points out, belief in providence and in the idea that people usually get their just rewards made its greatest appeal to members of the rising groups, to those with the opportunity to better themselves: the merchant, the shopkeeper, the aspiring artisan.[21] Lower down the social scale, the doctrine of providence, the teaching that the poor had only themselves to blame, that it was their idleness that had landed them where they were, was less likely to find acceptance.[22] For the believer in luck could account for misfortune without jeopardizing self-esteem. A secular notion of chance explained any apparent discrepancy between merit and reward and helped to reconcile people to the environment in which they lived. "Since the World is but a kind of Lottery, why should Gamesters be begrudged the drawing of a Prize? If . . . a Man has his Estate by Chance, why should not my chance take it away from him?" wrote Jeremy Collier in "An Essay upon Gaming" (in *A Dialogue between Gallimachus and Delomedes*, 1713).[23] It is not surprising that many poor turned not only to gambling but also to nonreligious modes of thought – be it a belief in magic, witchcraft, and methods of divination – which offered, among other things, more immediate explanation than religious beliefs of why it was that some men prospered while others suffered; and to drink, which could momentarily anesthetize them in adverse circumstances.[24] It is not surprising either that such beliefs and activities were continually condemned by religious institutions and continual attempts were made to discredit them.

Yet it is misleading to conclude that attacks on gambling were made in England by religious groups only. There were other groups who feared falling behind if people preferred to gamble rather than spend their time differently. We shall go on to reveal how additional accusations too played roles in shaping antigambling legislation in England and the United States and brought us to the incoherent set of laws that not only the gambling but some other industries too face today.

English gambling laws – who passed them and why

English statutes on games of chance reflected two distinct attitudes, the change taking place toward the end of the seventeenth century. Before that, gaming per se was not viewed as unlawful. The law did not prohibit games, but rather some of their negative consequences, decreased military preparedness being claimed as a major one. Apparently, instead of spending money on bows and arrows and time on mastering their use, people preferred to play at dice. Consequently, in 1388 Richard II secured the passage of a statute that forced people to buy items necessary to pursue the martial arts and stop spending on "tennis, football, coits, dice, casting of stone kaileg, and other such importune games."[25] But the accusation was made by the military lobby, and one may doubt its truth. Remark that once again no reference is made to compulsion.

A statute of Edward IV in 1477 forbade the use of houses for games of chance, since such games were perceived as leading to riots by members of the army that Edward IV disbanded after returning from the expedition to France. A statute of Henry VIII in 1541 repeated the arguments found in the two previous statutes: Popular gaming was condemned, since it was claimed to diminish military ability (apparently gaming continued to substitute for archery as an occupation for people's leisure time) and to disrupt public order.[26] But this statute too was passed on petition of the bowyers, fletchers, stringers, and arrowhead makers, and was called an "act for maintenance of archery and debarring of unlawful games." The petition mentioned that people were every day inventing new games, such as "logating in the fields" and "slide thrift, otherwise called shove groat," and emphasized that these inventions might cause the loss of trade in archery to Scotland "and other places out of this realm."[27]

The reason one must be skeptical of the accusations that gambling was harmful is that it is well documented that competitors who fall behind frequently make false accusations and invoke patriotism and nationalism to restore their position with the help of protective legislation.[28] In this particular case, the military perceived the gambling industry as its competitor, whereas above the clergy perceived the same industry as their rival.

Except for a brief reference to games of chance in the *Case of Monopolies* (1603) (where it was noted that the common law did not prohibit the playing of games), no significant changes occurred in English gaming law until 1657. Legislation enacted during this year allowed any loser in a gaming transaction to sue for the recovery of twice the sum lost. The statute also declared all gambling debts arising after June 24, 1647, to be "utterly void and of no effect." Although this legislation as such did not survive, its content foreshadowed subsequent civil law on gambling in England.

Maintaining the status quo

A statute of Charles II in 1664 aimed to limit fraudulent and excessive gambling.[29] Whereas punishment for cheating or fraud is not surprising, the reasons for condemning "excessive" gambling and the nature of the punishment may be and should be noted. Gaming debts secured on credit in excess of £100 were judicially unenforceable if incurred "at any one Time or Meeting." Contracts relating to the payment of these debts were "utterly void and of no effect." Any securities conveyed in relation to such debts were also declared void. In the case of "excessive gaming," any person could sue the winner for a penalty similar to the one imposed for cheating. Thus, the law tried to prevent the redistribution of significant amounts of wealth by gambling. As such, it seemed to protect the relatively rich, since obviously only they could lose relatively large amounts.

"An act for the better preventing of excessive and deceitful Gaming," passed in 1710 under Anne, shows this intention clearly. The first section of the statute made "all Notes, Bills, Bonds, Judgements, Mortgages, or other Securities or Conveyances Whatsoever" given in payment of gambling debts "void, frustrate, of no Effect to all Intents and Purposes." The statute diminished the sum for which a loser could sue to £10, and it even allowed anyone not in collusion to sue for treble the amount lost. Also, in order to prevent the quarrels that apparently regularly arose from gambling during this period, a section in the statute provided that any person instigating such a quarrel would forfeit all of his worldly possessions to the crown and serve two years in prison. Blakey (1977) concluded that since gambling resulted in large transfers of wealth, it might have added to the disruption already taking place in England's land-based society. The purpose of the statutes might have been to eliminate at least this source of instability, although, as noted above, the major source of instability lay elsewhere. According to the statistical information presented in Stone's works, the period between 1540 and 1640 was unique in English history between 1080 and 1880 for the speed with which manors changed hands, there being more gentry rising and falling then than at almost any other time in English history.[30]

Games of chance were condemned for additional reasons linked with matters of status. Malcolmson (1973) notes that until the eighteenth century, the distinctions among social strata were blurred when sports and games of chance were played during holidays. This reflected in part the upper classes' membership in the community, in part a recognition that such rites served to dissipate frustrations and maintain the existing local hierarchies, and in part that the upper classes, who had the right to start and stop the games, were still in charge. During the seventeenth century there were changes in this customary, understanding attitude toward such practices, and gambling was condemned *because of* the relative ease with which people from a lower class interacted during games with those from a higher, because winners from the lower class seemed to be accepted, because of the bad example the upper classes gave the lower, and because these changes were interpreted as reflecting the diminished power of the established classes:

Lantrillou is a kind of republic very ill-ordered, where all the world are hail-fellow well met; no distinction of ranks, no subordination observed. The greatest scoundrel of the town, with his money in his pockets, shall take his turn before the best duke or peer in the land, if the cards are on his side. From these privileged places not only all respect and inferiority is banished, but everything that looks like good manners, compassion or humanity. Their hearts are so hard and obdurate that what occasions the grief of one man gives joy and satisfaction to his next neighbor.[31]

Similar condemnations of gambling can be found repeatedly during the eighteenth and nineteenth centuries. The next two, one written in 1784 and the other in 1870, are typical.

There is a turn of thought suited to each rank singly, which leads a man to act in it habitually with a certain prosperity and decency. And a person of high rank can scarcely degrade himself to those who are greatly his inferiors, and admit them to a constant familiarity, without at the same time degrading his mind to the level of their ideas, or at least sinking it much below the level proper for his own.[32]

It is a melancholy truth, but confirmed by the history of all nations, that the most polite and refined age of a kingdom is never the most virtuous.... Distinction of personal merit being but little regarded – in the low moral tone that prevailed – there needed but to support certain "figure" in life (managed by the fashionable tailor), to be conversant with a few etiquettes of good breeding and sentiments of modern or current honour, in order to be received with affability and courteous attention in the highest circles. The vilest sharper, having once gained admission, was sure of constant entertainment, for nothing formed a greater cement of the union than the spirit of *high gaming*. There being so little cognizance taken of the good qualities of the heart of fashionable assemblies, no wonder that amid the medley of characters to be found in those places the "sharper" of polite address should gain too easy an admission.[33]

These English attitudes do not seem unique. In the New World too, perceptions of games of chance and of sports and their value depended on who was playing them. Both Fabian (1982) and Findlay (1986) wrote that the planters of Virginia, striving to set themselves apart and being concerned with establishing status, may not have welcomed cockfights to the colony, since the contests served to blur class distinctions. But during the mid eighteenth century, the growing appeal of cockfights reflected the Virginia gentry's increased confidence in their social position. By then, the gentry presided over audiences at cockfights and horse races and dominated in the betting that accompanied all sporting events.[34]

Lotteries and legislation

Lotteries were subject to other legislation. As mentioned in Chapter 1, the first recorded lottery in England was launched in 1566 in order to raise money for the repair and maintenance of harbors and other public works, and later lotteries were used to raise money for the English plantations in Virginia (1612), to finance the bringing of fresh water to London (1627, 1631), to repair damage done to the fishing fleet by the Spanish (1640), and to aid poor and disabled soldiers (1660).[35] Since the prices of tickets were relatively high and the prizes took the form of plate and tapestry as well as money, the relatively rich were expected to buy tickets in these lotteries.[36]

The facts that lotteries were first played by the rich and that "excessive" gambling on other games was their problem can be inferred not only from the earlier-mentioned evidence but also from both the reasons mentioned in 1699, when private and public lotteries were suppressed, and from the writings of Sir William Blackstone, a leading commentator on English law in 1769. In 1699 it was noted that promoters of lotteries "most unjustly and fraudulently" got themselves great sums of money from the children of "gentlemen, traders and merchants," whereas Blackstone much later wrote:

Taken in any light, [gaming] ... is an offense of the most alarming nature.... Among persons of a superior rank, it hath frequently been attended with the sudden ruin and desolation of antient and opulent families, and abandoned prostitution of every principle of honour and virtue, and too often hath ended in self-murder.... It is the gaming in high life, that demands the attention of the magistrate; a passion to which ever valuable consideration is made a sacrifice, and which we seem to have inherited from our ancestors.[37]

At the end of the seventeenth century, control of lotteries passed from the crown to Parliament. The statute of 1699, which prohibited all lotteries, stated that in future the only legal lotteries would be those authorized by Parliament. During the first half of the eighteenth century, a number of such special lotteries were authorized, among other things to raise funds for the construction of Westminster Bridge in 1739 and to establish the British Museum in 1753. Opposition to lotteries began in the second half of the eighteenth century, not only because of some fraudulent practices but also more and more because they were declared to be "injurious to the commerce of the kingdom and to the welfare and prosperity of the people."[38]

There were still commentators in 1754 who advocated abolishing all antigambling laws, since they perceived them as protecting the wealthy and the status quo rather than the poor. One noted that "Gaming . . . abhors Perpetuities. Property is in constant circulation, but then, like the Sea, what it loses on one Shore, it gains on another."[39] But such voices were rare. One reason may be that it was exactly this feature of gambling – the reallocation of property by chance – that went against a main feature of the Protestant ethic, which fitted the continuing expansion of the entrepreneurial middle classes. The typical views among the influential groups whose comments survive held that the poor "were weak enough to trust the improvement of their lot to schemes which depended upon mere chance, instead of employing it in [skilled] trade,"[40] and that statutes were necessary to preserve the distinctions of rank and quality. When state lotteries were outlawed in 1826, the epitaph written for the occasion, as noted in Chapter 1, emphasized that

> . . . it was found that their
> continuance . . .
> encouraged a spirit
> of Speculation and Gambling among the *lower*
> classes of the people . . .[41]

Why speculation and gambling were linked and condemned together will be explained in Chapter 4. The next section examines why gambling was condemned along with various other pastimes, and how these broader condemnations, too, were related to threats to the status quo, the established ways of making class distinctions.

3. Gambling and other pastimes

Gambling in general and lotteries in particular were not the only activities condemned during the eighteenth and nineteenth centuries. Cruel sports, drinking, and a wide variety of other leisure activities were also condemned. The preoccupation with them was such that some writers were led to identify the choice of what to do with leisure time as one of the great problems England faced during the nineteenth century. Just as during the sixteenth and seventeenth centuries, contemporary commentators paid relatively little attention to the fact that behind this problem lurked continuous demographic change. Later historians have emphasized that population growth and its increased mobility continued to be "the elemental fact which conditioned so much of English history in the nineteenth century."[42]

What did people perceive as problematic? Working-class leisure was perceived as a threat to ordered society.[43] The concern was with "crime" rates and idleness. Gambling was linked with both, and with more. The gathering of a great number of people who attended lottery drawings was feared by the propertied classes as providing the starting point for riots and revolutions.[44] Another issue was the choice between pursuing social harmony by means of traditional cultural homogeneity and pursuing it by competition, an unfamiliar option that led to the invention of a wide variety of leisure activities perceived by some as undermining the harmony they were seeking rather than promoting it. The choice of leisure activities – the opportunity to spend time gambling in particular – was linked to this debate too. Let us see how.

Rivalry among the innovative leisure industries

The very essence of our laws has been against the social meetings of the humble, which has been called idleness, and against the amusements of the poor, which have been stigmatised as disorder.

Bulwer Lytton

Popular culture rooted in villages of the eighteenth and earlier centuries was characterized by festivals and holidays that were linked with the seasonal work of an agricultural society, when recreation and work were not always separated. Hunting and fishing in groups for both profit and pleasure were typical. Storytelling accompanied the work of spinners and servants; one member of such groups of workers was appointed to read aloud to the others. Women gossiped over their sewing or at the communal water source. The year was broken by festival days and fairs, and the working week was irregular, work being concentrated in its latter part, leaving time for days rather than hours of leisure at the beginning of the week. Rituals that we now view as brutal and excessive were common: Sports using animals were popular and during holidays "excessive" drinking, eating, and fighting were tolerated. As was shown in the preceding section, on such occasions, and at other times when some games of chance were involved, the distinction between social strata was blurred, although who was at the top of the social pyramid was not forgotten.[45] Criticism of how poorer people chose to spend their leisure was, however, common. Medieval preachers denounced some festive gatherings and sporting contests, since many such popular diversions occurred at times when people were supposed to be practicing their religion. Also, as noted, there had been restrictions on gambling but no special attacks on it. Instead, regulations were imposed either in order to diminish the risk of rioting and fighting when games were played and crowds were present, or to make class distinctions, gaming being permitted to the rich at all times but limited among commoners to the twelve days of Christmas.

The increased population of the eighteenth and nineteenth, with the resulting enclosure movement, growth of cities, and the types of constraint imposed by the new industries, which differed from those required in agriculture, led to the breakdown of many traditional pastimes and gave incentive to the discovery of new ones. Simultaneously, as one might expect, recreation and work, which previously frequently intermingled, separated. When there are more people, there is a greater variety of tastes to satisfy, and specialization follows. Impersonal market exchanges substitute for exchanges previously carried out within the family or among kin or other local groups. Exchanges in the recreation industry were no exception.[46] This change did not occur either uniformly or smoothly; the traditional pastimes mixed with work survived for longer periods of time in the countryside than in the new cities. Full acceptance of new pastimes fitting the new industries had to wait until regular working hours were established. The employers of the Industrial Revolution first complained about irregular work patterns due to customary holidays and habits of drinking and larking on the job, although by the eighteenth century it became customary to think of a normal working day (a "fair day's work") as ten hours with two hours left for meals.

Whereas work thus became more clearly separated from recreation, those working in the new industries in the cities at the end of the eighteenth and the beginning of the nineteenth century could not, anyway, have either much time or space to enjoy the traditional recreations. The number of traditional full-day holidays taken by clerks and workers had fallen significantly. Bank of England staff, for example, had enjoyed forty-two holidays in the eighteenth century. By 1830 the number was down to eighteen, and by 1834 only Christmas Day and Good Friday were allowed, in order "to prevent the interruption of business." A Saturday half-holiday was being introduced in many factory towns only from the mid nineteenth century, and the number of public holidays was not increased until passage of the Bank Holidays Act of 1871. By this time attitudes toward the new recreations had changed, and the *Times* of August 6, 1872, praised the new legislation with these words: "Rational, sober, and modest amusements are more and more supplanting all others, and the riot which made some old-fashioned folks doubt whether Holidays could do people any good has become all but a thing of the past."[47] But much discussion and legislation expressed exactly such doubts.

The timing of the disappearance of traditional recreations was affected by laws and regulations and by the encouragement of voluntary organizations, the temperance movement being the most prominent among them, which saw the old pastimes as being inconsistent with the constraints imposed by the new organization of industry.[48] Such regulations and encouragements were viewed as necessary for additional reasons too, since, as one writer put it,

the lower class of people are at this day so far degenerated from what they were in former times, as to become a matter of astonishment.... And if we take the judgement of strangers ... we shall find them all agreed, in pronouncing the common people of our populous cities, to be the most abandoned, and licentious wretches on earth. Such brutality and insolence, such debauchery and extravagance, such idleness, irreligion, ... and contempt of all rule and authority, human and divine, do not reign so triumphantly among the poor in any other country.... And the reason for this...: Our people are *drunk with the cup of liberty!*[49]

This increased liberty was due to the breakdown of custom, of previous forms of social control. This breakdown in turn was linked to the significantly increased population and its increased mobility.

While he remains in a country village, his conduct may be attended to, and he may be obliged to attend to it himself. In this situation ... he may have what is called a character to lose. But as soon as he comes into a great city, he is sunk in obscurity and darkness. His conduct is observed and attended to by nobody, and he is therefore very likely to neglect it himself, and to abandon himself to every sort of low profligacy and vice,

wrote Adam Smith of the laboring man.[50] It is this perception of the disappearance of the customary sources of discipline and not just reluctance to accept innovations in recreation that explains the alarm of the new middle classes when they looked at either the traditional or the new recreational choices of the working classes, gambling among them.

During the eighteenth century intensified attacks were made against blood sports. Opposition to cockfighting, bull baiting, and throwing at cocks reached a peak with a series of local acts against these sports. Walvin (1978) and Elias (1986) have written extensively on these changing attitudes and explained them, along with others, as the result of social awareness that blood sports and other turbulent pastimes were inconsistent with the new more controlled and orderly attitudes to work. The campaign against violent and bloody recreations had its class undertones. Whereas the violent and bloody activities of the poor were under attack (cock, dog, and bear fighting), fox hunting was not. Throughout the eighteenth century many laws were enacted to protect the hunting rights of the rich; the game laws provided legal immunity to the landed hunter but imposed penalties of death, transportation, or imprisonment on the poor crossing the recreational divide. To shoot foxes was strictly forbidden (the killing was done by the hounds), and the farmers had to comply, although foxes were stealing their chickens and geese. In 1809 an article in the *Edinburgh Review* remarked:

A man of ten thousand a year may worry a fox as much as he pleases, may encourage the breed of a mischievous animal on purpose to worry it; and a poor labourer is carried before a magistrate for paying sixpence to see an exhibition of courage between a dog and a bear! Any cruelty may be practised to gorge the stomachs of the rich, none to enliven the holidays of the poor.[51]

Such restrictive legislation had a long history in England. In 1671 an act had disqualified all except the landed classes from game hunting, and another act in 1692 further added that "inferior Tradesmen, Apprentices, and other dissolute Persons neglecting their Trades and Employments should not preserve to hunt, hawk, fish or fowl." A century later, in 1796, William Pitt, the prime minister, defended similar exclusive legislation, arguing that "by too liberal an indulgence in this amusement [referring to competitive shooting of game], they [the poorer classes] might be diverted from more serious and useful occupation."[52] Such evidence has led some historians to the conclusion that shooting represented just one of the ways by which the aristocracy and the gentry collaborated, but that such collaboration was a hindrance to local harmony.

In 1833 the *Quarterly Review* criticized such legislation on exactly this ground and argued that racing could promote harmony, since thousands of the less fortunate could participate. Yet attempts were made to prevent even this participation:

The Act of 1740 "to restrain and prevent the excessive increase of Horse Races ..." was passed, amongst other reasons, because "the great number of Horse Races for small Plates, Prizes or Sums of Money, have contributed very much to the encouragement of idleness, to the Impoverishment of many of the meaner sort of the subjects of this Kingdom,"... The Act confined matches (as opposed to races) to two locations, New Market and Black Hambleton in Yorkshire, exclusive venues for the rich.[53]

Once again, just as for laws regulating gambling and shooting, the same perceptions are reflected: fear of the idleness of the poor if they win, and lack of confidence in the judgment of members of this class to choose their recreations.

Another type of recreation under attack was associated with drinking. Although people always drank, during the eighteenth and early nineteenth centuries drinking became especially widespread among the poor. Why? A great number of factors interacted to produce the phenomenon, factors that seemed to escape the attention of most of the contemporary critics.[54] Alcoholic drinks had few substitutes as thirst quenchers. Even in the countryside, safe drinking water became scarcer with the rise in population. Even with increased investment in water companies after 1805, London's water was still unpurified, and London hospitals gave alcoholic drinks to their patients, not just because they were painkillers but also because they were safe. Milk was not only double the price of beer, but also dangerous to drink (it was not yet pasteurized, and its relative anonymity in urban areas facilitated adulteration), and tea became popular only after 1830, when the price fell sharply. But increased consumption of beer and other alcoholic beverages was due to many more things, the most important being that the pub, where people drank, gambled, and watched "cruel" sports, was one of the central places around which working men's social life turned. The rise of the pub has been documented by many historians, but the authentic voices of the nineteenth century come to us through a series of articles in the *Morning Chronicle*.[55]

On October 18, 1849, this newspaper announced that it would publish "a detailed description of the moral, intellectual, material, and physical condition of the industrial poor throughout England."

It did so for the next eighteen months, and the survey revealed the numerous subtle ways in which customary ways of life, and of spending one's leisure time in particular, were breaking down. One article refers to the effects on family life of women working in factories from adolescence. Being less capable of looking after their families, they encouraged their husbands to spend more time outside the house, in the pubs in particular. Of course it was not only the women's lack of domestic competence that led them there. Lack of light, heat, furniture, and space did not make the house a very comfortable home to live in:

> One of the worst features attending the system is the cheerlessness with which it invests the poor man's house. On returning from work, instead of finding his house in order, and a meal comfortably prepared for him, his wife accompanies him home, or perhaps arrives after him, when all has to be done in his presence. . . . The result is that . . . he goes to the nearest alehouse. . . . A great deal is lost also through the unthrifty habits of his wife. Her experience at out-door labour has been acquired at the expense of an adequate knowledge of her in-door duties. She is an indifferent cook – a bad housewife in every respect.[56]

(So now one can speculate and blame the Industrial Revolution for the origin of not-so-palatable English food.) Again the difference between the poorer and the richer people's outlook and the latter's lack of understanding come to the fore. The middle classes advocated domestic pleasures and valued privacy and family autonomy, one moralist writing that "men understand the nature of pleasure so well or possess it so much as those who find it within their own doors"; and they were suspicious of assemblies, public gatherings, crowds.[57] But they failed to understand that whereas the poor had houses, they could not be transformed into homes with the money that could be saved by avoiding gambling, drinking, or occasionally dressing up.

Thus for the poorer, pubs were the focus of entertainment and betting; in the nineteenth and twentieth centuries these drinking places served as working people's meeting places and recreation centers. But those who objected to working-class drinking rarely understood that what they attacked was not just drinking but much more. In 1858 a temperance reformer captured what this "much more" meant, but her comprehension was, as she herself admitted, a rarity:

> Sociable pleasures were precious to working men for whom alternative recreations were scarce; to abandon drink was to abandon society itself, unless

some alternative grouping were provided.... "I saw the hard struggle to give up all," wrote Mrs. Wightman,... [the] temperance reformer, of a working man taking the pledge in 1858, "for I knew not till then, that, with the working man, signing the pledge involves nearly everything included in the world..."[58]

But Harrison warns that the protest against working-class drunkenness may be as much an indication that the customary inseparability of work and recreation had become inconvenient as an indication that drunkenness had perhaps become more prevalent.[59]

The new opportunities for spending time that were lacking when Mrs. Wightman, the temperance reformer, made her statements were coming, but slowly, owing to misunderstanding of the changes that were taking place.[60] The fact is that up to the mid nineteenth century, as population continued to rise, as cities grew larger, and as land was being taken over for housing and commercial purposes, many traditional places used for sports or walking were eliminated. It was only in the second half of the century that parks and playgrounds became widespread. Railways, which enabled excursions, bicycles, music halls, journalism, and organized sports were some of the innovations that became common.[61] Alternatives were even coming from religious institutions. At first, finding themselves operating in a competitive leisure market, they attacked the competition. But as the secular world offered a greater variety of entertainment, religious picnics ceased to satisfy, and the churches, trying to recruit and hold members, began to tolerate what they had previously condemned; outdoor games and dancing began to be admitted by 1890.[62] Moreover, innovations were also made in the chapels, which by 1880 had better music and also organized sewing classes, bazaars, concerts, drama, and cricket and football clubs.[63]

Attacks on the new forms of recreation of the working classes were fueled by secular ideologies too.[64] Although toward the end of the eighteenth century Adam Smith argued that no society can be "flourishing and happy, of which the far greater part of the members are poor and miserable" (p. 88), many still believed in mercantilist ideas, "the doctrine of the utility of poverty," inherited from previous centuries. Viewed through such a lens, having a large low-wage economy was perceived as beneficial, for otherwise the country could not export. High wages were believed to threaten England's competitive position, since they were assumed to make workers lazy – just like the windfall of prizes in games of chance. Poverty, rather than the provision of opportunity to innovate and thus obtain the means to rise within a hierarchy, was perceived as giving the main incentive for both greater effort and less spending on "nonproductive" activities. Avenues for getting richer that did not require making an effort were viewed with suspicion. William Temple, in *Reflections on Various Subjects Relating to Arts and Commerce* (1752), suggested that "to hold the lower Orders to Industry, and guard the Morals of the Poor, on whom all Nations must rely for Increase and Defence, is the truest Patriotism."[65]

This view of how the relatively poor would behave if they got higher wages reflects the same misunderstanding as the one discussed in Chapter 2 in connection with the behavior of people who get a windfall too small to change their status significantly. The resulting pattern of expenditure seems frivolous to the middle classes; but, as was pointed out, the poor who spent the money could have a different perception. The expenditure, be it on a "glorious binge" or a fancy dress worn on some occasion, "insured" the spenders, since they acquired prestige and honor among members of the group with whom they interacted on recreational occasions. Remember Mr. Doolittle's response when Higgins gave him a small sum. "Dressing up and spending freely for a holiday were relatively accessible means of winning approval," writes Malcolmson when examining English recreational patterns, and he concludes that "many other channels through which status might ... have been achieved, especially those which the middle class favored, were in practice blocked off by the completely unrealistic economic capabilities which they assumed.... What seemed rational from the people's point of view was regarded by middle class observers as criminally extravagant and irresponsible."[66] And yet it was frequently on the basis of such incorrect opinions that laws concerning recreational opportunities were passed, the advocates believing that people would spend their money more "rationally" if some recreations were legally forbidden.

These confusions are typical of members of societies that, during periods of larger demographic change and consequent innovation, bet on ideas, some accurate, others not, in search of explanations. One such inaccurate idea reflected some groups' lack of understanding about the appearance of new recreations. Leisure and work became more and more separated, a consequence of rising population, the increased size of markets, and the resulting specialization. This meant, however, that what was previously informal leisure activity now provided business opportunities. (Gambling was just one such industry – one in which both the owners of establishments and the employees came from the lower classes.)[67] But this was not the way the adjustment was perceived in those times. The poorer people's involvement in the new leisure industries seemed unjustified, for leisure could respectably be enjoyed only when work was put first. Involvement with gambling, new sports, and other innovations in the emerging business of recreation, even if one was a proprietor rather than a customer, was not viewed as work but as idleness and waste. Thus, the poor were left bitter and suspicious. It seemed that no matter what they did, whether they tried to stick with customary recreations, adapt them, or bet on new ones, they could do no good.[68] The condemnation of gambling was linked with this debate over the proper nature of leisure and recreation, and not just with either the Protestant outlook and the role of chance in society or the fact that some traditional recreational sectors hoped to maintain their profits or to get ahead if gambling was prohibited. The discussions surrounding legislation against betting, which culminated in the Betting Act of 1906, show how.

4. Prohibitions on betting

Whereas lotteries were outlawed in the first half of the nineteenth century, both on- and off-course betting flourished, the latter appealing to the working classes.[69] Off-course betting shops were numerous, carrier pigeons relayed the results from the meetings, and, before the widespread use of the telegraph, avid punters – working-class entrepreneurs – hung over bridges to catch the name of the big race winner from the fireman as the train flashed through.[70]

Simultaneously with the increased betting, all the customary objections were expressed again, and remedy for them was sought in the 1853 Betting Houses Act that prohibited the use of "a house, office, room or other place" for betting. Since the act did not forbid betting, lawyers, with their characteristic skill, interpreted it as implying that betting transactions could still take place in *public* places. So the bookmakers found themselves in the streets, where betting flourished. Thus legislation meant to eliminate the working classes' daily betting (on-course betting on credit, confined to the upper classes, was still permitted) turned out to have no impact. According to all surviving documents (numerical evidence, as pointed out in Chapter 2, is not available), working-class betting flourished – it was now even more visible – and newspapers commented frequently that the betting mania was all-pervasive.

There is little doubt that since population was rising, more and more people were playing and that the betting transactions mainly took place in the streets. There must be little doubt too that the poorer people were playing.[71] As was pointed out in the preceding section, drinking and betting being linked with the poorer people's few available opportunities for leisure activity and with their hopes of getting richer, the increased participation should not be surprising. However, there is considerable doubt about the worth of accusations that gambling was a major source of social evil.

McKibbin (1979) and Dixon (1980a) both conclude that gambling made few demands on those who practiced it and that no significant material consequences were ever detected; critics of gambling were driven to untruth and ideological statement. McKibbin also remarks that in spite of accusations of the contrary, various commissions at the end of the nineteenth century could find no causal relationship between gambling and poverty or gambling and crime (other than the fact that gambling was illegal to start with). What they found was that poverty led people to gamble and to drink.[72] Expenditures on gambling and drink, however, did not represent a severe strain on their resources, but, in general, were strictly controlled. Yet several influential authors treated gambling not just as a greater problem than drinking (viewing drinking as destroying the individual by slow degrees, whereas gambling wrecked the whole family in a single throw) but also as a *cause* of drinking, and others claimed that gambling could not be controlled the way drinking could be.[73] Others made attacks on gambling on customary grounds: Seton Churchill's *Betting and Gambling* (1894) insisted on the pressing need to control working-class gambling, since "law of labour . . . one of the most obvious of God's laws" was being disturbed by gambling.[74] Others, as Dixon notes, repeated the well-known arguments for "legitimate" modes of getting richer: inheritance, gift, or return for labor and the rendering of service. "To deal with property on the principle of chance, which is non-moral, must be immoral because it involves the false proposition that property itself is non-moral."[75] What are the explanations for these attacks?

These attacks, as well as some of the previously described trends in leisure patterns, took place during the era frequently called a "Great Depression," when not only did the rate of growth in the United Kingdom's industrial production drop to 20.8 percent between 1870 and 1880 and to 17 percent between 1880 and 1900, from 33 percent in 1860–70, severely setting back segments of the population, but Britain's competitive performance in the markets of industrial countries was also particularly disappointing. Britain was falling behind the Americans and especially the Germans.[76]

The loss of industrial preeminence provoked a number of reactions, from the protectionist "fair trade" movement of the 1880s to public discussions of what made Germany click and Britain fall behind.[77] One conclusion was that redistributive policies could lead to greater social harmony, diminishing the workers' discontent and increasing their productivity. This was also the period when part of the "propertied classes who were not moved by conscience . . . [were] moved by fear of social explosion from below"[78] and favored redistributive policies. The riots of the unemployed in London in 1886 and 1887 helped bring about this new frame of mind. (The *Times* of February 9, 1886, had reported that the West End "was for a couple of hours in the hands of the mob.")[79] The Fabians demanded the restitution to public use of all rent and interest, rents being perceived as the result of social factors (one should add demographic ones) and not the result of the efforts of owners.[80] Another conclusion of the debate was that "Fair trade, Commercial Consuls, Technical Colleges – good and necessary as they are – will not avail to stem the inroad of the German, unless our manufacturers and merchants brace themselves."[81] (Does all this sound familiar?) But how to make the working class work harder, become more productive, and restore Britain to its previous glory?

Prohibiting gambling was perceived as a step in that direction, since the "law of labor" was viewed as being violated by gambling. Dixon quotes testimony before the 1901–2 select committee on gambling in which a magistrate worried that "if the betting craze goes unchecked, the sober youth of Germany will take the reins of the commercial world,"[82] and notes that such opinions were "corroborated in 1906 by Arthur Shadwell's *Industrial Efficiency: a Comparative Study of Industrial Life in England, Germany and America*, in which the English working class was presented as the most indolent and degenerate section of 'a nation at play.'... Money that the workers should have 'invested' in British industry by buying goods ... was instead being wasted in betting, and so, if there was unemployment, the workers had brought it on themselves."[83]

The British did not seem to be paying attention to the quite characteristic decline of the entrepreneurial spirit among the established classes in countries that happened to be, for a while, "on top," or to the significant drop in birth rates and the longer life expectancy since the 1860s as being related to the relative slump and the structural changes that occurred as the century neared its end.[84] Instead, the frequently repeated idea that gambling caused idleness passed for evidence among the influential professional classes, leading to attacks that culminated in the 1906 prohibitive Street Betting Act. Behind it were the nonthought of traditional ideas of religious groups, the fear of competition from innovations in recreation that the working classes chose to enjoy and that other classes were suspicious of, and the fact that the debate was taking place in the shadow of alarming signs of Britain's relative decline in the world.[85]

At this point, one cannot help recalling one of J. M. Keynes's remarks in *The Economic Consequences of the Peace*: that great events of history are often due to changes in the growth of population that, because of their gradual character, escape the attention of contemporary observers and are attributed to the follies of statesmen or the fanaticism of atheists. The continuing debates about gambling seem to be a good illustration.

The 1906 act – an additional angle

It is not true, as one might have expected, that only the interests representing the upper classes, the racecourse owners, and some racecourse bookmakers were behind the prohibitive legislation. This "class law," as it was then called, which banned one of the working classes' choices of entertainment and one of their avenues for sustaining the hope of becoming richer (whether through prizes or the provision of entrepreneurial and employment opportunities), but which did not impose constraints on richer people's betting, was passed with the support of key members of the *labor* movement too; the members of Parliament from the new Labor Party voted for the bill.[86] How can we explain such support?

Closer inspection reveals that such attitudes are not unusual and should be expected.[87] The leaders of the Labor Party thought what religious leaders thought in previous centuries, that if the poor spent time drinking, gambling, and reading racing papers, their instruction in "moral" behavior on the one hand, and in political activism and the benefits of socialism on the other, would be slowed down. Thus, if gambling were prohibited, the poorer people's willingness to turn to politics was assumed to be greater. The labor leaders' opinion was possibly shaped by the fact that the demand for tips and racing news played a large part in the development of the popular press (half of the evening papers started in the 1870s and 1880s had a close association with sports and gambling).[88] To think that, if betting were prohibited, instead of reading racing news the working class would choose to read or listen to political treatises may sound unlikely. Yet labor leaders apparently acted upon it.[89]

The thought, however, was not new, not even among labor leaders. Whereas, as we have seen, the established classes were at first alarmed when they encountered the masses' new forms of leisure activities, by the mid nineteenth century many seemed to accept that leisure for the masses was legitimate (though they were still disagreeing on the content of this leisure). The change in outlook was probably influenced by the idea expressed in 1833 that "it was well known that healthy, happy men were not disposed to enter into conspiracies. Want of recreation generated incipient disease, and disease, discontent; which, in turn, led to attacks upon the Government."[90] But it is exactly this fact, that more and more new forms of leisure came to be tolerated, that led to fears by spokesmen of the working class in the second half of the century of "the displacement of political energy into apolitical and hence conservative leisure."[91] Such ideas seemed to be lurking behind the vote of the leaders of the Labor Party in 1906; the prohibitive legislation was perceived by them as just part of a much broader agenda for social reform.[92] Such a line of thought also recalls that of labor leaders in Prussia who opposed Bismarck's social legislation.[93] In that case, social security was perceived by labor leaders as a serious threat to the solidarity of the labor movement; it would weaken the workers' revolutionary ardor (which, of course, Bismarck realized).

The legal prohibition on working-class betting continued until 1960, when the Betting and Gambling Act legalized betting shops.[94]

Why did attitudes toward gambling change in England during the twentieth century? A number of factors interacted. Increased emphasis was placed on unemployment and health rather than on gambling and drinking as causes of poverty. The changed ideology led to redistributive policies and increased government welfare programs, which required additional revenues; gambling was perceived as a possible source of such revenues. The changed ideology also led to a more widespread recognition that the 1906 "class law" was outdated. Last, but not least, it was acknowledged that the law was ineffective: People continued to gamble and the police were unable to enforce the law.[95] What happened during these decades of prohibition is summarized in the documents of the 1978 Rothschild Commission, which, commenting on the 1906 act, concluded that the intention was to restrict off-course betting to the wealthier section of the population. But "in practice, [the law was] hopelessly ineffective. Bookmakers satisfied the wish of the ordinary British punter to stake a few shillings on a horse either by operating illegal betting offices or employing a runner to secure illegal cash bets in the street. Instead of suppressing betting among poorer people, the law produced resentment and attempts to corrupt the police, contempt for authority and a bookmaking trade operating outside the law, prey to protection rackets and gang violence."[96] More will be said in Chapters 4 and 5 about the effects of prohibitive gambling legislation.

The evidence presented and interpreted up to this point has highlighted a few broad recurring trends in attitudes toward gambling and changes in such attitudes. Although the background is different, major episodes in the history of opinion about gambling in the New World, presented next, provide further evidence concerning these trends.

5. Law and gambling in the New World

Antigambling legislation eventually became a feature of all states in the United States during the nineteenth century. But the reason for its adoption differed from region to region. What the settlers first found was a sparsely populated wilderness where a new society was to develop. But according to whose vision should it be shaped? How was gambling perceived in the different visions?

The Puritans who settled in the area that is now Massachusetts condemned gambling because they opposed "idleness."[97] The Massachusetts Bay Colony in its first year of existence outlawed not only the possession of cards, dice, and gaming tables, even in private homes, but dancing, singing, and all unnecessary walking on Sundays too. All capital crimes listed in the Massachusetts Code of 1648, with the exception of rape, cited the Bible as their authority. The Blue Laws of Connecticut, 1650 Code, followed this example and denounced game playing because it caused "much precious time to be spent unfruitfully." The Great Migration (1630–40) and the rising merchant class (gradually converted to the more liberal Unitarian faith) led to the gradual transformation of the interpretation of the criminal law from God's punishing sin to the state's maintaining public order. In 1737 the Massachusetts legislators amended the antigambling law by noting: "All lawful games and exercises should not be otherwise used than as innocent and moderate recreations, and not as trades or callings, to gain a living or make unlawful advantage thereby."[98] Still, as late as 1748, a New Jersey act equated idleness and immorality with fraud and the corruption of youth. Thus, one must be careful in interpreting references to gamblers as criminals. Their only *crime* may have been that they gambled.

In spite of such statutes, lotteries were authorized during the eighteenth century and were, in general, successful. There could be several reasons. The century saw the decline of Puritanism and the rise of the merchant middle class. As important, however, may be the fact that the banking system was undeveloped and local governments could not easily borrow against anticipated revenues. As noted in Chapter 1, before 1790 there were only three incorporated banks in the New World.[99] Since taxation was poorly organized too, lotteries were perceived as the alternative. An additional reason might be that, as in England, the proceeds from the early authorized lotteries went to worthy causes, and the price of tickets was relatively high. The Harvard College lottery sold 25,000 tickets at $5 each, when per capita annual income for the white population was about $60 – it is as if the price of today's ticket were $1,000.[100] The launching of these lotteries might not have been, therefore, different from today's occasional New York City bash to benefit a charity, a museum, or a library. In 1892 a historian remarked:

Lotteries organized for public projects . . . were not regarded at all as a kind of gambling; the most reputable citizens were engaged in these lotteries, either as selected managers or liberal subscribers. It was looked upon as a kind of voluntary tax for paving the streets, erecting wharves, buildings, etc., with a contingent profitable return for such subscribers as held the lucky numbers.[101]

Indeed, between 1744 and 1774 the colonies sanctioned approximately 158 lotteries. A third financed the building of canals and roads and 27 the building of churches; 13 helped educational institutions; and 5 financed the start of new industries. The prices of these tickets too continued to be relatively high, occasionally $10.[102] These lotteries were, in general, respected: Community leaders promoted lotteries instead of promoting charity drives. George Washington promoted lotteries to finance westward expansion, Benjamin Franklin launched one to erect a steeple at Christ Church in Philadelphia and another in 1748 to buy cannons for the city; John Hancock was behind one in 1762 that helped rebuild Faneuil Hall; and we recall that Thomas Jefferson saw lotteries in a favorable light. Eventually, as in England, entrepreneurs came up with the idea of "insurance": accepting less than the ticket price to bet on a certain number and returning to the bettor, if he won, a corresponding fraction of the prize. With the introduction of this practice, critics started complaining that the lotteries had become a "burden" on the *poor*.[103]

In other parts of the colonies, perceptions of gambling and of lotteries were different. In the South, the British 1710 statute was adopted; it did not prohibit gambling but protected the losers of more than £10. The law thus did not reflect a work ethic or an ideology; rather, as Blakey (1977) and Fabian (1982) both note, it tried to prevent disruptions caused by large losses and the upper classes giving a bad example to the lower ones. In the South too, lotteries were seen as a case apart, but for reasons different than those in the Northeast. The need to pay taxes regularly, when crops were not regular and banking institutions were not developed, led to the view that lotteries could provide the solution by being an irregular form of taxation, authorized when crops were sold and cash was available.

Legislators in both the Northeast and the South became, however, aware of the fact that lotteries could substitute for taxation only if competition were restricted. That is why private lotteries were banned whereas those run by the states were not, and why lotteries were discussed separately from other games of chance. In the North-

east an additional reason for the ban was the occurrence of fraud.
Ezell remarks:

To understand why authorities began licensing lotteries rather than abolishing them altogether, it is necessary first to remember that the people as a
whole wanted them, believing that the drawings could be kept honest. Most
vocal opposition ceased with the assumption of governmental regulation;
it was one's own affair if he risked his money in an honest lottery. (1970, p.
77)

But licensing and the restriction of competition led to additional
problems. By 1790 the institutions in whose name the lottery was
launched no longer handled ticket sales. Instead, a few brokers, like
security underwriters today, bought up the tickets at a discount and
marketed them at face value in all the states. It may not be accidental
that the Chase National Bank and the First National Bank of New
York City were founded by lottery brokers. The lottery brokerage
firm of S. & M. Allen not only transformed itself into a banking and
stock brokerage firm, but also served as the place where Enoch W.
Clark, a relative of the Allens who later established E. W. Clark &
Co. of Philadelphia (which became the largest dealer in domestic
exchange in the 1840s and 1850s), started his career. In New York,
by 1823 two entrepreneurs, John B. Yates and Archibald McIntyre,
had the privilege of handling nearly all the sales of the New York
authorized lotteries.[104]

That lotteries provided an avenue for some of the rich to get even
richer not by winning prizes but by being granted the monopoly
power to sell tickets, that the businessmen associated with their sale
formed a strong lobby for the financing of public works through
lotteries, that lotteries lost their local, prestigious charitable character, that the poor bought the tickets and could get rich by chance
rather than hard work, and that there were a few cases of much-
publicized fraud were among the factors that led, during the first half
of the nineteenth century, to increased opposition and to an eventual
ban.[105]

In parentheses, one should add that attitudes toward gambling
and lotteries in the Midwest were different. By the time midwestern
towns needed capital for major improvements, the newly chartered
banks of New York and other eastern cities could provide the necessary loans. Lotteries thus lost one of their benefits as perceived by
local governments.[106] As for the West, before 1850 taverns, casinos,

and bordellos were the entertainment fixtures of the new small towns, and nobody objected to gambling. But during the second half of the nineteenth century many of the western states passed comprehensive antigambling laws under the influence of either farmers or the laws drawn up in the eastern states.[107]

Beneath the surface: changes in the status quo

Opposition to conferring privilege and concern about the fact that some of the rich were getting richer while others were falling behind (even if not absolutely) were reflected both in opinions concerning lotteries and in many other ways during the nineteenth century. At the beginning of the century, Andrew Jackson attacked the banks on the ground that their stock was largely owned by foreigners and the "rich," and in a message to Congress he emphasized that the bank owners' fortunate situation was due to privilege rather than superior talent:

When the laws undertake to add to these natural and just advantages [superior industry, economy and virtue] artificial distinctions, to grant titles, gratuities, and exclusive privileges, to make the rich richer and the potent more powerful, the humble members of society – the farmers, mechanics, the laborers – who have neither the time nor the means of securing like favors to themselves, have a right to complain of the injustice of their Government.[108]

Although there were rich people in the United States even before the Civil War (Stephen Girard, John Jacob Astor), great fortunes were rare. It was only when railroads, coal, steel, timber, manufacturing, meatpacking, and big-time finance became more and more important that a caste of entrepreneurs became prominent for living the way the nouveaux riches always do. At the same time, millions of European poor were flooding off the immigrant ships and into the factories.[109] "Who could admire such drones while people of equal or greater innate virtue and promise were working long hours in sweatshops and steel mills and living in fetid slums along the back alleys of industrial America? The answer is, precious few," concludes Hughes.[110] He shares the opinion of Robert Wiebe, who, in *The Search for Order: 1877–1920* (1967), argued that during the entire period after the Civil War, the social structure was undergoing upheaval. Small-town and rural America tried to maintain power at a time when power was shifting toward the new middle classes in urban areas.[111] Cedric Cowing, in *Populists, Plungers and Progressives* (1965), makes a similar point, emphasizing that the first rural reactions to the concentration of money in the cities were Greenbackism, Grangerism, and antimonopoly, and when "the farmers' economic position, worsened by the droughts after 1886, had been declining ... the result was the 'Populist Revolt.'"[112]

Changing attitudes toward a number of channels through which people could get rich (gambling being one; speculation, as is shown in the next chapter, another) have been examined with this background in mind. Although traditions and the historical background were different in England, the United States, and elsewhere, the same pattern of reactions when relative shifts in wealth and power took place seems evident. Moral and legal reforms were advocated as the means of restoring and preserving the status quo of those falling behind.[113] With the diminishing deference to the clergy, gambling was attacked. When the uneducated and the urban working classes were viewed as the rising social group who rejected both the social status and the political power of the entrepreneurial middle classes as well as some of their leisure activities, gambling, drinking, and other recreations were condemned. When the farmers were falling behind and the influence of urban groups was growing, urban pleasures and the sins of gambling, of drinking, and of speculation were condemned. Inventing moral issues seems to be one of the preoccupations of members of powerful groups whose power is declining. Gambling became a moral issue when such a sequence of events took place. But the accusation that it was a major cause of poverty, of laziness, and of instability seems erroneous – although the accusation that those who get the power of a monopoly in selling lotteries become rich is not.

The invention of such accusations should not be unexpected. When people are outdone and some rise farther above others than is customary in the game, even if that happens to be an entrepreneurial game, the relative shift will either provoke fear or excite the envy of those falling behind. This emotional reaction during such trying times leads to bad decisions, their justification being articulated in endless imaginative ways and the naked truth being hidden behind accusations, slogans, the invention of moral issues, and the heavy, dense curtain of language. More will be said on these points in the next chapter.

6. Gambling during the Great Depression . . .

The Great Depression of the 1930s in the United States sees the rise of gambling fever; churches and charitable organizations were reaping rich dividends from it. Although the condemnations of earlier ages were not forgotten, one could read more and more frequently about good reasons for tolerating gambling and even making it legal.[114] The Reverend Francis Talbot, a Catholic priest and editor of *America*, wrote:

I cannot grow frenzied with the puritanical precisionists who rate the bourgeois pastime of bingo as a major sin. . . . Played under proper auspices [the church?], with petty stakes, the worst harm that bingo causes is a sore throat. Church bingo parties are a healthy substitute for gossip teas, lovesick movies and liberal-minded lectures.[115]

As one would expect, Protestant churches were less open to gambling.[116]

In many states, the first form of gambling to be decriminalized was bingo, run by charitable and religious organizations. The first step toward its legalization occurred in Massachusetts in 1931; in 1937 Rhode Island followed. Pari-mutuel betting was next, New Hampshire, Ohio, and Michigan legalizing it in 1933.[117] Bingo became extremely popular at amusement parks, firemen's carnivals, grange suppers, and church socials. Its popularity during this depressed era was, as one would expect, the result of what many commentators critical of the game described as "the hope of being able to win something for nothing."

Of course, not everybody was concerned with discussing morality or religious beliefs when advocating legalization of lotteries. Some did it in pragmatic terms: It would prevent the flow of American money into foreign lotteries or untaxed underworld coffers, and it would supplement significantly diminished government budgets, thus providing relief to taxpayers. *Time* magazine (April 20, 1936) wrote about the efforts of Mrs. Oliver Harriman, the head of an organization called the National Conference on Legalizing Lotteries, Inc., to legalize lotteries. She stated that there were no moral issues involved, that taxation had reached its limits, and that revenues from lotteries were needed to help the poor, who were suffering more than ever before.[118] During the 1930s, when interest in lotteries was at its height, the legislatures of New York, New Jersey, Massachusetts,

Pennsylvania, Maryland, Louisiana, Illinois, Maine, New Hampshire, Connecticut, California, and Nebraska all considered bills legalizing them. (In Massachusetts in 1935 the bill was rejected on a tie vote of 110 to 110.)[119] A bill was even introduced in the House of Representatives, sponsored by Edward A. Kenny, who died in 1937 just before the matter was brought to final action. No other political entrepreneur pushed the project, and, although the interest in legalizing lotteries continued (almost every subsequent session of Congress discussed the issue), the war started, and more important issues were now on the legislators' minds.[120]

Additional information on the increased interest in gambling during the Depression comes from various polls. In October 1935 *Fortune* gave the results of a national poll answering the following question: "Do you think that lotteries similar to the Irish Hospital Sweepstakes and conducted only for charity or taxation should be allowed in this country?" Fifty-five percent answered yes, 33 percent no, and 12 percent answered, "Don't know." There were wide regional variations in the answers. On the industrialized, urbanized Pacific Coast 79 percent, and in the northestern states 58 percent, favored it. In 1936 the Gallup poll provided similar results: 59 percent said yes and the rest no. However, in April 1938, when "the depression-born lottery craze" was past and the United States was slowly starting to recover from the slump, 49 percent were in favor and 51 against. Still, in this last poll, 55 percent of the poor wanted lotteries and only 45 percent of those with "average and over" income favored legalization.[121]

Although lotteries were forbidden, substitutes were invented. The Great Depression was the period when contests swept the country. The game involved buying a relatively cheap product, which gave the right to participate in the lottery (yes, legally they were called "contests"), with prizes varying between $25 and $100,000. (How these contests satisfied the laws prohibiting lotteries makes interesting reading, for once again it shows how people, especially lawyers, with great imagination use their essential skill of playing with words to circumvent laws and regulations. And if you ever wondered why even today in order to participate in a contest you must answer the question how much is two plus two, the answer is that the origins of this practice are in the manufacturer's having had to prove that the "lottery" in fact required skill.) For the poor, slot machines became the most important form of betting. One contemporary observer estimated that in 1939 the national take from these machines exceeded $500 million, and a Gallup poll taken in the same year indicated that one out of three adults took an occasional chance at winning the jackpot.[122]

Contests in various forms already existed in the eighteenth century both in England and the United States. But it was during the Depression that they became most widespread. Three thousand contests were sponsored and some hundred million entries were submitted. After 1933 the volume of contest business leveled off and then slowly decreased in the last years of the decade. Contests were, however, still very popular as late as 1941.[123] As one would expect, most sponsors offered one large prize, in general a monetary one, although contests offering to sponsor the college education of the winner's child were widespread. Contests offering radios, cars, fur coats, and diamonds of similar monetary value were less so.[124]

The last observation is important, since it shows how biased the condemners of lottery players are when they accuse players of irresponsibility toward their families. The fact that contests where the children's education was the prize were among the most popular complements and is consistent with the picture of lottery players drawn earlier, which showed that they are, on the whole, a poor but quite responsible group. This conclusion is further strengthened by considering the fact that elsewhere, too, successful lotteries frequently distributed as first prizes the following items: commodities in Denmark's lottery for agriculture, housing in Israel's state lottery, cars in Ghana, and books, sewing machines, plots of land, and journeys abroad in communist countries.[125] Of course some of these prizes could be sold (and thus such lotteries are not different from ones with large monetary prizes). But some prizes either could not be sold (education of children, trips abroad) or could be sold only at substantial cost. The fact that such lotteries were nevertheless successful suggests that the players were interested in prizes like these. This interest reveals a motivation for gambling that can hardly be condemned.

The Depression years also brought in their wake the chain-letter craze of the 1930s and other variations of the numbers racket. Another invention of the Depression was the movie house "bank night": Tickets bought not only admission but also a chance to win prizes. Horse racing and gambling on races prospered during this period, for laws prohibiting racing and bookmaking went largely unenforced.[126] Charity organizations and private businesses devised schemes whereby they gave away cars, refrigerators, and stoves as prizes, and some Chambers of Commerce, representing a majority of the merchants in a town, engaged in these enterprises. Whereas in the 1920s business looked down on contests, considering them "cheap" and "circus-y," during the Depression years the contests became respectable, said a contemporary commentator.[127] Many writers gave, and still give, negative connotations to such practices: Devereux, for example, remarks that it "was essentially a form of bribery, in that it offered an artificial incentive, in the form of dazzling prizes, to induce the public to buy a given brand of product."[128] But this view misunderstands: During the Depression both the poor and those who suddenly became so *wanted* to spend more on lotteries, but entrepreneurs were legally banned from offering them. The right to participate in lotteries, that is "contests," had to be sold jointly with another product. (In other words, the incentive for a tie-in arrangement was given by the law, and it was the law, therefore, that gave some monopoly power to all the producers who could merchandise their product with a lottery, even if it was not called that.)

But does such a joint offer necessarily increase the price of a product? The answer is no, not necessarily. Assume that during normal times a brand of cigarettes is sold for $10 a dozen, and $10 million is spent on advertising. With the introduction of the contest, a firm decides to spend $5 million on expenses involving the lottery (prizes and administration costs) and only $5 million for advertising in the media. Since lotteries became more attractive to the public during the Depression, the smaller expenditure on customary advertising and larger expenditure on lotteries could be more useful than the larger expenditure on customary advertising before. Indeed, by 1931 contests were rapidly displacing "special offers" and "premiums," and in 1932, remarked Eric Bender in 1938, "the nation went contest-crazy."

Of course, numerous industries may dislike the new way of selling – newspapers, radio, television. Their revenues from advertising diminish by the $5 million that is now spent on increased administration within firms and on direct redistribution to the public. So one should beware of the negative editorials about contests then and today. Once again, they may disguise self-interest and not be a matter of morality.

Instead of being entrepreneurial and recommending canceling the legal ban on lotteries and games of chance by pointing out that maybe circumstances had changed or that the initial ban might have been an error to start with, the courts tried to stick to the letter of the law.[129] It is ironic that the invention of some marketing techniques during the Depression (contests, giving "gifts," bank nights, etc., invented by small businessmen to prevent bankruptcy) was condemned in the name of legislation passed by Jacksonians a century before – legislation that at that time was perceived as protecting those falling on hard times.

The fact that during the Great Depression people gambled more was not lost on observers in England. Whereas the twentieth century saw a slow but steady decline in the proportion of income spent on drink, the reverse is true for betting and gambling, expenditures on the latter growing enormously during the Depression. An inquiry concerning office and warehouse workers in a number of firms in the city of Birmingham found that 80 percent were gambling regularly, legally or illegally.[130] Others noted that gambling increased during the period of economic and industrial depression between the wars "when the fascination of possibly winning something by luck did undoubtedly make its appeal to men and women who were living under conditions of financial stringency."[131] It was, in part, the proliferation of dog tracks, following their establishment in the 1920s, and the gambling opportunities they offered to the depressed urban workers that led to the investigation of the 1932–3 royal commission into the whole issue of gambling.[132] Another reason for convening it was that in 1930 the Irish Free State began to promote the Irish Hospitals Trust Sweepstakes both in Ireland and in the United Kingdom.[133] The royal commission seriously considered the revival of state lotteries, and also recommended the legalization of off-course cash betting.[134]

Not surprisingly, the most eloquent view of gambling comes from this period. An anonymous article, entitled "Chance," published in the English journal the *New Statesman and Nation* (June 6, 1931) seems to capture accurately the view from below:

The next best thing to a fortune is the chance of a fortune.... To purchase a ticket in a lottery, indeed, is to buy a kind of fiction in which oneself is the hero. It is to see oneself, in one's mind's eye, happy and rich, free from all the cares and anxieties involved in earning a living, able to buy a cottage in the country, to take as long a holiday as one wishes.... It may not be the most heroic of ideals, but it is among the most innocent.... Besides this, the desire for money won without labour does not exclude dreams of a nobler kind. It might even be maintained that anyone who longs to lead a noble life should wish to obtain money without labour so that he may be released from the material struggle for gain and be able to devote himself to loftier pursuits.... Getting and spending we lay waste our powers, says Words-worth, and getting wastes even more of our powers than spending. Day after day, hour after hour goes wastefully by in the effort to provide our families and ourselves with the necessaries of existence.... It turns most of us inevitably into materialists. Let one of us win a first prize in a sweepstake, however, and he will have time to sit down and read the philosophers.[135]

This is certainly one possible interpretation for the ancient Latin proverb that could so well describe the majority of gamblers, "Pri-mum vivere, deinde philosophari," or, as Brecht put it more recently, "Food first, ethics later."

7. . . . and today

Crises such as the Great Depression and World War II generated proposals for national and state-run games. As in England, tra-ditions, religious ones in particular, weakened (even if one takes into account some well-publicized recent revivals linked with TV preaching), the view of what causes poverty changed, and govern-ments' need for revenues was perceived in a different light. Still, one heard less about lotteries, contests, and other games during the relatively calmer 1950s and 60s when conventional thinking held that those in power knew how to secure full employment and raise living standards. The rise of lotteries and of the popularity of gambling is correlated with the shattering of expectations after more than a decade of inflation, recession, rising unemployment, and high income mobility – upward and downward.[136] In the early 1970s, a thirty-year-old college graduate earned only about 15 to 20 percent more than a thirty-year-old male high school graduate. This gap held steady to the end of the 1970s. But during the 1980–2 recession the gap between college and noncollege graduates began to grow until in 1987 it reached 49 percent – $26,250 for the college graduate versus $17,250 for the high school graduate. Another factor that explains increased insecurity and downward mobility is the growing number of families headed by single women. In the early 1970s, one in nine families with heads under the age of sixty-five was headed by a single woman; in 1987 one family in six was, the average income being $13,500. The Census Bureau sampled 60,000 homes in 1986 and reported that average family income, including Social Security, was $34,924, or $1,000 more (adjusted for inflation) than in 1979. Yet the gain reflected that of top earners. Among the richest 20 percent, average income grew from $70,260 to $76,300 (in 1986 dollars). Among the poorest 20 percent, it fell from $8,761 to $8,033. In a 1987 survey, when asked whether it was more or less difficult for middle-class people to maintain their standard of living relative to five years before, 65 percent answered that it was more difficult.[137]

One result of increased insecurity, the increased threat of shuffling across income ranges, seems to be a flourishing conviction that luck and not only insight or hard work determines whether one strikes it rich. This belief is reflected only in part in the fact that by now lotteries are legalized and that they, along with other games of chance, are extremely popular. Games, contests, and sweepstakes are becoming more and more popular: According to some studies, sweepstakes are today the most successful advertising tool.[138] A new state lottery in Massachusetts has drawn thousands of players by offering subsidies for daytime child care among its prizes, and in Rockford, Illinois, the "garbage lottery," encouraging citizens to recycle their garbage by awarding prizes of $1,000 and up, has proved very successful.[139] Dog fighting has moved during the seventies from rural to urban areas, appealing to the disenfranchised and the unemployed.[140] And one of the most visible of all signs: Game shows on television that distribute large prizes are tremendously popular. Forty-three million viewers tune in to see "Wheel of Fortune" each day, making it the highest-rated syndicated series in television history.[141]

So now one can speculate on the popularity of Vanna White, whose job consists of nothing more than silently turning letters on a board to form names, phrases, and so forth on the aforementioned program – her compensation for this arduous job running well into six figures. Her popularity may be due in part to beauty, talent, and personality. There is little doubt, however, that in part her popularity is a sign of increased willingness by some of the public to fantasize about getting rich by chance during less secure times.

4. Gambling, speculation, insurance –
Why they were confused and condemned

When I was young, people called me a gambler. As the scale of my operations increased I became known as a speculator. Now I am called a banker. But I have been doing the same thing all the time.

Sir Ernest Cassel, private banker to Edward VII

To gamble.
To bet.
To speculate.
To invest.

All these terms and others ("to take a chance," "to take risks") have been used when people played the futures markets or bought and sold houses, stocks, or other assets. Nevertheless, there are significant differences in meaning among these terms, although they are sometimes confused. This chapter discusses what the differences are, what the sources of the confusion are, when they were confused, and how the confusion led both to additional prejudice toward gambling and to erroneous legal decisions. In spite of emphasizing the differences, the similarities between gambling and speculation will be discussed too; one of them being that they stabilize rather than destabilize society.

1. Gambling and speculation

If names are not correct, language will not be in accordance with the truth of things.

Confucius

The word "gamble" refers to an act where the participant pursues a monetary gain without using his or her skills. It is therefore appropriate to use this word for games of chance only. If one uses it to describe business transaction or transactions in the stock market, the writer implicitly makes a value judgment implying that the actor in the transaction did not and could not have any specific skills or use either superior judgment or special information when carrying it out.

"Speculation" does not apply to a game of chance. It refers to carrying out an act where one backs one's own *opinion* against the established one or against "the market's." The act may be a scientific debate as well as the purchase or sale of a stock, real estate, or any other financial or nonfinancial asset. The reason for using the word "speculation" (or "betting on an idea") is that when individuals carry out the act they do not have enough evidence available to prove whether they are right or wrong.[1] This situation is in contrast with a gambling situation. The latter refers to situations that have been and can be repeated many times, and where the probabilities, as well as the monetary gains and losses, are the same for everybody and well known.

Thus, when people say to one another that they gamble on the stock market, they are biased and make value judgments. For they view the actors in the stock market as possessing neither special skills nor backing for their opinions, but just playing "thoughtlessly," as if they were participating in a lottery. This may be the reason why when poorer, younger people, viewed as inexperienced, buy stocks – as the epigraph to this chapter suggests – they are said to gamble. The commentator implicitly suggests that these people lack judgment. (Well, if they had, why are they poor? Or, as some Americans say, "If you're so smart, how come you're not rich?") A further difference between gambling and speculation concerns the commentators' evaluation of the initial sums needed for being involved, gambling requiring smaller sums than speculating. By taking into account these differences in the meanings of the words, one can conclude that speculation refers to a noncustomary act, a deviation from the majority's opinion, when relatively larger sums than in gambling are at stake. The opinion and the act are noncustomary because there is no evidence at the outset for justifying the speculators' opinions and their actions: They go against "the market."

But there are similarities between gambling and speculation when one looks at them from other angles. If one raises the question as to what motivates gamblers and speculators, the answer is simple and the same: the hope of getting rich and doing so quickly. And if one raises the question as to how gambling and speculation are different from other channels of getting richer, the answer is again simple and the same: Although to start speculating requires a greater sum of money (today) than to start gambling, both channels are characterized by the fact that relatively unimportant sums of money can be increased through them to important ones. Whereas large sums of money may be earned by some entrepreneurs, some professionals, and some who excel in sports or entertainment, speculation in commodity trading is, with gambling, one of the very few roads to big money that are open to the shoestring financial entrepreneur.[2] As one can infer from the story told in the preceding chapters, it is precisely this feature of speculation that leads to the cynical and condemning attitude toward speculators – when they turn out to be right and become rich.

It was not always the case that speculation required greater sums than gambling. In the now outlawed "bucket shops," which flourished between 1816 and 1905 in the United States, one could have speculated with one, two, or five dollars on price fluctuations in commodity markets. These sums were not larger than those required for participation in games of chance. Bucket shops were disapproved of by the Chicago Board of Trade (which in 1905 won a legal battle against them) because of the fear that they would bring into general disrepute the legitimate exchange, since trade in futures would be viewed as mere gambling. As we shall show later in this chapter, the board's concern seems legitimate, although the evidence is insufficient to determine whether the board's goal was to restrict competition or whether it had a genuine fear that trade in futures might be prohibited unless a sharp distinction was made in the public's mind between gambling and speculation.[3]

The Board of Trade's declared attitude had precedents. Miers and Dixon remark that in England

respectability had to be acquired by a commercial world too closely associated with the problems of gambling. In the eighteenth century it was not only that stockbrokers sold lottery tickets along with shares; their whole business was regarded as a type of gambling. Scandals like the South Sea Bubble, and Acts penalising stock-jobbing and declaring public companies common nuisances were only the clearest signs that both institutionally and in public opinion, legitimate insurance and share dealings were little different from gambling. In much the same way as the Gaming Act of 1845 reinforced the integrity of the law of contract to protect genuine capital transactions, so the abandonment of the lotteries brought legitimation and respectability to genuine capital investment.[4]

Speculation and investment

What are the differences between speculation and investment?

In general, by the term "investment" economists refer to abstaining from current consumption in order to use the freed resources in ways to increase future consumption. This definition, however, cannot distinguish between the terms "saving," "investment," "speculation," and "gambling." The last two strategies are also used in pursuit of the same goal. The distinction seems to be elsewhere.

"Investment" refers to the spending of money and other resources (time, for example) in activities that have already been carried out in the past. Such expenditure patterns are thus linked with customary ones perceived to carry smaller risks than speculation, since past experience is a guide.

Another difference between speculating and investing is linked with the length of time the buyers are expected to hold onto their purchase: If it is shorter, some people call the purchase speculation; if it is longer, they call it investment.[5] Yet another difference is linked with these two combined, and is related to the different motivations of the speculators and investors as the writer making the distinction sees them. Let me elaborate this point.

We have seen that by gambling a few people get rich, but that, on average, the players expect to lose relatively small amounts. By investing in a well-diversified portfolio, one may expect a reasonable return, a more or less steady income. By speculating, one may earn more than by investing, but one has to put at stake larger amounts per unit of investment than in gambling: One may gamble with a dollar and get rich, but one cannot speculate on the stock market with a dollar. Looking at the distinction from this angle, it becomes evident that one may become significantly richer by either gambling or speculating, but not by investing. Since investing is associated with traditional, established industries, the expected returns on stocks should, over the long run, roughly equal interest rates.[6] But if future incomes are discounted by interest rates, such investing cannot change one's wealth; only people's consumption patterns are altered over time.

Once this additional observation is made, it becomes clearer why the terms "gambling" and "speculating" have, for some, a negative connotation, whereas "investment" has a positive one.[7] By gambling and by speculating, the poorer try to become richer. The fact that luck or chance plays a role in an eventual success is evident. In contrast, continuous repetitive investment maintains stability, and people who grew up viewing this activity around them are less likely to perceive that chance or luck has anything to do with the higher income of the conservative businessman or banker. Those whose interest is in maintaining stability will thus condemn speculators, gamblers, and reliance on chance, but praise "prudent investment." It is thus not surprising to learn that the attempt to distinguish between investment and speculation seems to be traceable to the Puritan work ethic.[8]

One reason for confusing gambling and speculation thus becomes clear. Gamblers and speculators try to do the same thing – become rich quickly – and some try it feverishly. The fact that a few succeed and do so without any physical or special visible intellectual effort[9] (in the case of speculation in futures in particular) may be perceived by some groups as sinful. Whereas conservative businessmen and bankers can frequently make a steady income from their investments, so that by starting out being relatively rich they stay so, a few speculators are likely to go from rags to riches in a short time. Also, the role of the banker in the community of providing credit and liquidity is evident, but the fact that speculators fulfill precisely these same roles as well as that of providing insurance against fluctuations in prices in futures markets is less obvious and more difficult to prove.[10] The fact that the outcomes of the speculators' actions are beneficial, even if their motivation is nothing more than getting richer, is from time to time lost when passions stirred by the envy of others run high.

These arguments and those advanced before explain why many writers have said – wrongly – that both gambling and speculation have destabilizing effects on society.[11] These writers have made the accurate observation that in times of social instability more people gambled and speculated. But their perception of the causal link was wrong; it was not people's gambling and speculation that caused the instability. Gambling and speculation were symptoms and not the disease. The status quo was already upset, for one reason or another, which led to more gambling and more speculation, with traditional industries (and fortunes associated with them) falling behind and new ones emerging. Gambling and speculation were in fact stabilizing; they diminished uncertainty already and inevitably existing in society. Providing these options has a calming effect, sustaining people's hopes during difficult times. If people cannot hope to get richer through institutions permitting gambling and speculation, who knows on what revolutionary, ideological, or religious institutions they will make a bet instead? Or in what destructive ways their desperation will show?

Thus what seems to be hiding at times behind the torrent of words about the destabilizing effect of speculation are not well-thought-out arguments about effects on trade, but the same ones that led to the condemnation of gambling: envy of the fact that others are getting much richer without any special visible talent.[12] Yet nothing illustrates better the stabilizing role of the speculator than some events that took place during the 1848 revolution in France.[13]

Stabilizing speculations

The head of the House of Rothschild in Paris was asked why he was buying French government bonds when the streets of Paris were running with blood. His reply was that he could buy the French bonds at twenty-five cents on the dollar only *because* the streets of Paris were running with blood. Was the impact of the Rothschilds' act stabilizing or destabilizing? By buying the bonds they showed confidence in the eventual restoration of stability in France. By this expression of confidence they checked the panic selling, prevented the price of bonds from falling further (thus having a positive effect on people's savings), and may even have had a broad impact on people's expectations as to France's future in general. Some people may have thought: If the Rothschilds have confidence in the future of France, maybe so should we. The question is then: Who helped to restore the country's stability, the few speculators who believed in its future or the majority who did not?

Was the Rothschilds' monetary success due to "avoidable ignorance" (a term that some economists use today to imply that if information were diffused, more people would become somewhat richer, rather than a few becoming significantly richer)? The answer is no; they just believed in a future that the majority of Frenchmen did not. And, as in bets on football games where those who win large prizes are always those whose predictions are out of line with the other forecasts, the Rothschilds won the large prize for backing their own opinion.

Were the Rothschilds "taking advantage" of the French terror when buying the bonds at panic prices? The words "taking advantage" have a negative connotation, suggesting that somehow the Rothschilds could be sure that they would profit, rather than lose, by spending their money in this manner. But this way of posing the question is erroneous, confusing consequences with expectations. Yes, it turned out that they profited handsomely from their belief in the future of France, a belief that most other Frenchmen who were getting rid of their government bonds apparently did not share. (So who was the greater patriot?) But no, they did not "take advantage" of anybody, since they could not be sure of the future course of events. So no, their courageous speculation was not destabilizing the economy, but stabilizing it, whether one looks at the narrow effect of their actions on bond prices or at the broad one of having an impact on people's belief in a more stable future.[14]

Less dramatic examples of the stabilizing effect of speculative markets, in a narrower sense, are not hard to find. An example is the development and demise of the onion futures market in the United States. The market was active from 1949 to 1958. It was killed that year when trading was banned by law. An index of seasonal price variations for a period of active trading before 1949 and a four-year period following the prohibition of futures trading reveals that the before-and-after indexes were nearly identical, ranging from a harvest low of about 75 to a spring high of about 145. In contrast, while the futures market existed, the index had a harvest low of 87 and a spring high of 118. Seasonal variations in cash onion prices were thus greatly reduced during the period of futures trading and went back to earlier levels when the market was killed.[15]

Boyle found similar evidence when he compared fluctuations in the price of wheat before futures trading was started with fluctuations afterwards (although other factors than the mere existence of futures trading must be allowed in this case).[16] His finding is that price fluctuations before futures trading were more than twice as great as the fluctuations afterwards. He also found that complaints that futures trading changed the average price level of a traded commodity were not better grounded than charges about increased fluctuations. In the 1890s at a large and representative meeting of farmers, a resolution was passed condemning futures trading in wheat on the ground that it lowered the price of wheat. Three weeks later, five hundred members of the National Association of American Millers met in convention in Minneapolis and passed a resolution condemning futures trading on the ground that it raised the price of wheat. The correlation between the specific accusation and these groups' interest is evident.

But the best example of the beneficial effect of speculation, in the narrow sense of price fluctuations only, is given by the brief German experience at the end of the nineteenth century when futures trading was prohibited.[17] The law was passed in 1896 by the Farmers' Party, which claimed that speculation depressed prices. The law prohibited all dealings in futures and punished speculators severely. What were the consequences? Some speculation still took place illegally in restaurants and streets. Commercial experts writing on this episode assert that the prohibition kept the price of wheat in Germany for a while at six to ten dollars below where it would have been otherwise and thus first caused excessive exports. Afterwards the shortfall had to be made up by imports, at heavy cost to all Germans. The statute also rendered the farmers subject to the whims of local millers and small traders, since they lost much information on which to base decisions concerning the production of grain. The Berlin merchants were subject to the whims of bureaucrats. For, with the tacit approval of some members of the German government, who realized that the prohibition was foolish, some merchants speculated through agents in Liverpool, New York, and Chicago. These and other destabilizing effects led to a rather rapid change of mind; on April 2, 1900, futures trading in Germany was reopened. There is little doubt, therefore, that the proposition that speculation is always destabilizing is wrong. What people may mean by the statement that speculation is sometimes destabilizing is made clear in the next section.

2. What does "destabilizing speculation" mean?

Anyone taken as an individual is totally sensible and reasonable – as a member of a crowd, he at once becomes a blockhead.

Schiller

When a few are wrong and the multitude are right, the few will lose significant amounts of wealth, and each member of the crowd may gain an insignificant amount. But what if the multitude turn out to be wrong and the few turn out to be right? Then the few may get very rich, and prices will fluctuate significantly. When the latter event takes place, some people label it an impact of destabilizing gambling and speculation.[18]

Thus, some writers have argued in retrospect that speculation has a negative effect due to the "herd instinct," and that the chief evils of speculation flow from the participation of the general public, who lack special knowledge and enter the market purely in a gambling spirit. According to these writers, the evils of speculation are particularly acute when, as generally happens with the investing public, the forecasts are not made independently: "Were it true that each individual speculator made up his own mind independently of every other as to the future course of events, the errors of some would probably be offset by those of others. But ... the *mistakes* of the common herd are usually in the same direction. Like sheep, they all follow a single leader.... A chief cause of crises, panics, runs on banks, etc., is that risks are not independently reckoned, but are a mere matter of imitation," wrote Irving Fisher.[19]

In these phrases Fisher condemns a belief in mistaken ideas when they are shared by many people. Yet if this is what people sometimes mean by "destabilizing speculation," one cannot arrive at the conclusion that things would improve if speculation were forbidden. For the term refers to judgment gained through experience, experience that the speculators could not possess. If used in this sense, the term does not imply that without the specific speculation society would be better off. When people fall behind or others leap-frog them or they do not achieve the wealth they expected, they will deviate from their traditional beliefs and bet on new ideas. But only some people's ideas will turn out to be useful (in which case later generations will not talk about speculation), whereas others turn out not to be (in which case later generations may include the episode in the history of speculations). Yet a priori one cannot say who will turn out to be right, and thus prevent the "destabilizing speculation."

Let me make these arguments clear by examining a few examples. The tulip mania, Mackay remarks in *Extraordinary Popular Delusions*, had its following among the ambitious, upwardly mobile Dutch middle classes.[20] For them, tulips became the ultimate status symbol, much like anything signed by Picasso, Rothko, or Gucci today. The large fluctuations in prices had to do with the fear of members of this class that they would not be perceived as belonging to the class unless they possessed tulip bulbs. The mania was thus due to the belief that the tulip would permanently remain a status symbol, the center of attention in the richer people's foyers.

Suppose that such expectations turned out to be accurate; that is, suppose that tulips and some paintings did not continue to be mere "flowers" or "art," but symbols of status. Then there would have been no significant fluctuations in their prices, and episodes linked with a change once and for all in the price of tulips and of paintings (when they turned out to be symbols) would not have been included at all in histories of destabilizing speculation. Only because the idea turned out to be wrong and many people lost their wealth once such a turn of events took place did these episodes appear in histories of destabilizing speculation.[21]

Or, for further illustration, consider the Rothschilds' speculation examined before. There is little doubt that their act cannot be perceived as other than an example of stabilizing speculation. Suppose, however, that the Rothschilds made a mistake and the political situation in France was not stabilized as they expected. Then the value of bonds, after first going up when the Rothschilds and their followers made the purchase, would have come crushingly down, and both the Rothschilds and their followers would have lost their wealth. If this had happened, the episode might have been introduced in the history of destabilizing speculation of the "march of folly."[22]

Thus, to the question "Was the belief in tulips being an eternal symbol of wealth erroneous?" the answer, in retrospect, is yes. But to the question "Was the belief at the time destabilizing?" the answer is no. For the Dutch upper and ambitious, upwardly mobile middle classes were then looking for a symbol of wealth, and if they did not bet on the tulip, they would have made a bet on something else: Seventeenth-century portrait painters or musicians? Astrologers? Who knows? Would such beliefs and subsequent actions necessarily have fewer destabilizing consequences than the belief in tulips being a symbol of wealth? The answer is, once again, no. Instead of fluctuating tulip prices, the salaries of astrologers, painters, and musicians would have come crushingly down once their services were no longer perceived as the means of showing off one's wealth. As to the third question ("Did the belief in tulips *eventually* have destabilizing effects?"), the answer is yes, in the sense that when it turned out to be erroneous it led to loss of wealth.

As a final example, consider the answer to these same three questions with regard to astrology, which several societies used for a long time for forecasting. Was belief in astrology erroneous? The answer is yes. But was the belief destabilizing? The answer is no, not necessarily. For who knows on what other follies, absurdities, or other methods of divination people would have bet instead? Did the belief *eventually* have destabilizing effects? The answer is yes, in the sense that when people discarded those beliefs, "wealth" that depended on such beliefs was lost, and institutions whose existence depended on such beliefs lost their roles too.

There are therefore two different ways to interpret the term "destabilizing speculation." The first suggests that the term just disguises the envy of those falling behind during periods of social instability, which, however, is caused not by speculators but by events not under their control. The accusation is made by those who fell behind, hoping for a redistribution of wealth from those who got richer. The second interpretation refers to the impact of beliefs held by crowds when they turn out to be erroneous. But it should be made clear that labeling some acts destabilizing, and even agreeing with the statement that speculation is sometimes destabilizing, does not imply either that speculation should be banned or that one could necessarily have offered a better idea at the time when people first came up with one that later turned out to be erroneous. The statement just implies the obvious: When an idea is found to be wrong, those who committed the error will pay a price for it; that is, they will lose wealth.

There is another, trivial context in which the "evils of speculation" are mentioned, namely when fraudulent acts are involved. Yet the use of the term in this context is inaccurate. The South Sea Bubble and some other financial fiascoes like the recent one-day mini-bubble linked with Paul D. Herrlinger cannot be used as examples to prove the evils of speculation, although they are mentioned in such a context.[23] For the fluctuation in prices was due to fraud, to a criminal act. Fraud and crime should not be confused with speculation, even if their impact on prices is similar.

3. More on the distinction between gambling and speculation

As the discussion in Chapter 3 and the section above shows, ideas, both erroneous and correct, have long lives. As late as 1898, when

Ashton summarizes contemporary views he remarks that

paradoxical as it may appear, there is a class of gambling which is not only considered harmless, but beneficial, and even necessary – I mean Insurance. Theoretically, it is gambling proper. You bet 2s.6d. to £100 with your Fire Insurance; you equally bet on a Marine Insurance for the safe arrival of your ships or merchandise; and it is also gambling when you insure your life. Yet a man would be considered culpable, or at the very least, negligent and indiscreet did he not insure.[24]

What Ashton failed to see, though the arguments in the preceding section and in Chapter 2 make it extremely clear,[25] is that there is a sharp distinction between gambling and insurance. By gambling, people have tried either to restore or to increase their wealth, whereas by insuring themselves they have tried to protect what they have already achieved or customarily can expect. Thus, although there is a sharp distinction between the two, there is no inconsistency in one's being involved in both acts. What led writers like Ashton and others to make the confusion is discussed in the next section.

Here it should be pointed out that Ashton is by no means the exception who could not see the distinction between gambling and insurance. Even today many economists do not seem less confused. Most see the difference between "insurer" and "gambler" as a matter of taste[26] rather than as depending on one's wealth and social rank. According to this so-called risk-aversion theory, those who gamble like risk, and those who insure themselves are averse to risk, and thus, goes the prediction of this theory, one cannot both gamble and insure oneself. Friedman suggested that the "natural bias" of the academic student against gambling and in favor of insurance,[27] which is reflected in both elaborations of this theory and in negative attitudes toward speculation, is due to the fact that

It is natural for [the academic student] to regard a futures market ... as a market in which a "legitimate" producer hedges his risks by transferring them to a "speculator"; the producer is viewed as buying "insurance" from the speculator. But granted that this is a possible and indeed likely interpretation of an actual futures market, it is not the only possible one. May such a market not be one in which the "legitimate" producer engages, as a side line, in selling "gambles" to speculators willing to pay a price for gambling and knowingly doing so? And if so, putting moral scruples about gambling aside, is any economic loss involved?[28]

Friedman puts his finger on the right point when he uses the word "legitimacy." For, as we saw in Chapter 3, it was precisely the legitimacy of some markets, where social ranking and the allocation of property could be altered by chance and by speculation, that was questioned from time to time. This was another source of the confusion: the perception that only the actions of producers who wanted to maintain their wealth were viewed as legitimate, and not those of the speculators who wanted to get richer.

Inability to make this distinction also seems to be the source of another error made in discussions of gambling and speculation. Irving Fisher, for example, wrote that "the distinction between a speculator and a gambler . . . is usually fairly well marked. A gambler seeks and makes risks which it is not necessary to assume, whereas the speculator is one who merely volunteers to assume those risks of business which must inevitably fall somewhere."[29] This argument is not useful, because both the speculator and the gambler assume a risk that falls somewhere. For the gambler, the risk fell on him; he finds himself at the bottom of a social pyramid. As we have seen, the propensity to gamble is linked with both one's social rank (and with having a lower rank) and fluctuations within the social pyramid. The gambler did not create additional risks; he responded in one particular way to the risks inherent in all societies. If he did not gamble, who knows how he would maintain his hope for a better life? By consulting an astrologer?[30] By believing in a blissful afterworld? By betting $5 on TV evangelists? By betting on revolutionary ideas? Or would he simply lower his aspirations and either morosely reconcile himself to a mediocre fate or become desperate and take out his anger in destructive ways? One cannot say, therefore, that a gambler "seeks and takes risks which it is not necessary to assume." The risks inherent in the social pyramid will be assumed anyway; if not by gambling, then through other channels. *Thus, the distinction between a gambler and a speculator is not that one takes and the other volunteers to assume risks, but that the gambler assumes risks linked with social ranking, whereas the other assumes risks linked with trade.*[31] This distinction may explain why, although both gamblers and speculators have frequently been condemned, speculators were still sometimes tolerated even when gamblers were not. At least the former, when climbing up the social ladder, did so through a channel linked with trade. The gamblers' hopes and success were viewed as symbols of a lack of belief in the legitimacy of the existing social order.

4. Gambling, speculation, and insurance and the confusion among them

The confusion among gambling, speculation, and matters related to risk taking in general, and to insurance and commercial decisions in particular, has ancient roots and has been reflected not only in the everyday use of words but also in court decisions, academic discussions, and government policies. The German experience at the turn of the century was just one extreme example.

One of Demosthenes' orations condemned with aristocratic contempt the manner in which the Greeks of his time insured marine cargo. The insurer advanced somewhat less than the value of the ship and its cargo. He received back, when the voyage was successfully completed, a much larger sum.[32] The difference – call it "reward for risk," "interest," or part of one's profits – only suggests that either over a longer period of time with fewer ships, or over a shorter period of time with more ships, the lender could make up for occasional losses and stay in business, because enough ships completed their trips successfully. However, the commentators whose writings survive from antiquity and through the Middle Ages felt uncomfortable with such practices, with the idea of lending money in general, and with taking interest – viewed for a long time as usury – in particular.[33] Daston (1987) notes that Pope Gregory IX's thirteenth-century decree Naviganti prohibited the most popular form of maritime insurance as usurious. This prohibition led jurists to discussions about the distinction between insurance and usury on the basis of risk, and among various forms of investment, some where gains were obtained with labor and others where gains were perceived by some as being obtained without labor. With the expansion of commerce during the next two centuries, civil and canon lawyers used the notion of risk to defend suspicious commercial practices. They had to prove that the risk was large enough so as to avoid suspicions of usury, but not so large as to bring about suspicions of gambling. By the mid sixteenth century, it had become customary to argue that those who shared risks deserved a share of the profit as much as those who shared labor. Yet the aforementioned ideas about risk and usury continued to impose constraints on the insurance industry. It should be recalled that the usury legislation of 1777 in England made any loan for interest greater than 5 percent illegal unless it involved some "genuine risk." According to Daston such laws explain, in part, the insurance companies' initial reluctance to use probability theory, since "the quantification of risk seemed to presume too much certainty for the venture to be genuinely risky" (1987, p. 247).

Navigating between these notions, marine insurance developed in fourteenth-century Italy and, according to Thomas (1971), had taken root in England by the mid sixteenth century. Other types of enterprise linked with the notion of risk fared less well. The 1570 Code of the Low Countries outlawed both gambling and life insurance, putting them in the same category; insuring the lives of persons and "wagers . . . and similar inventions" were banned. All ordinances regulating insurance prior to 1681 that mention life insurance prohibit it, and usually prohibit bets on lives in the same clause; this was the case in Amsterdam (1598), Middlebourg (1600), Rotterdam (1604), and Sweden.[34] Life insurance remained illegal in France until 1819.[35] In addition to the general problem linked with the notion of risk, there are additional explanations for this stance.

Daston (1987) shows that until the sixteenth and seventeenth centuries the notion of probability was linked with gambling devices like dice and lotteries. Even the mathematicians who developed probability theory up to the eighteenth century – Pierre Fermat and Jacob Bernoulli, among them; John Grant, who built the first mortality table in his *Natural and Political Observations . . . upon the Bills of Mortality* (1662) – did not explain how the notion of probability applied to mortality. (Wasn't that a matter of divine will?) In fact, great mathematicians, Leibniz among them, objected to such an application. Thus, the fact that historically the notion of probability was linked only with gambling may explain why insurance and gambling were at first classified under the same heading.[36]

An additional reason for putting the two in the same category is that early insurance schemes were, in fact, not different from gambling. The popular tontine, for example, was a type of annuity shared by subscribers to a loan, the shares increasing as the subscribers died, till the last subscriber got all that was left. Such schemes provided the opportunity of sudden upward social mobility, just like lotteries.

In spite of all these confusions and reservations, the insurance industry was expanding rapidly in England between the sixteenth and eighteenth centuries.[37] As noted, marine insurance was first prominent, although the law relating to arbitration of insurance

disputes remained unsatisfactory (and merchants insured themselves
by dividing both the ownership of the ship and the value of transported goods among a number of individuals). The situation changed
in the early eighteenth century with the development of Lloyds coffee
house as a regular meeting place for underwriters and the foundation
in 1720 of two substantial joint-stock companies devoted to marine
insurance, the London Assurance and the Royal Exchange. Fire insurance first emerged in London in 1680, and the Amicable Society
for mutual insurance of lives was established in 1706 (although its
scheme provided a tontine-like arrangement). This was the only
insurance company, from among fifty established between 1699 and
1720, that survived the crash following the South Sea Bubble.

This rate of failure should not be surprising. The years between
1690 and the middle of the eighteenth century saw in England not
only a society swept by the gambling craze, but also one that went
through its Industrial Revolution, with innovations rapidly being
made in commerce, technology, law, the arts, and literature.[38] The
insurance industry was no exception, and, as one would expect, some
innovations turned out to be successful and many others did not.
Some innovative companies tried to sell insurance against cuckoldry
and lying – and went bankrupt.[39] It was not just the burst of the
South Sea Bubble that put an end to such insurance schemes. Legislation passed in 1764 and 1774 (the Gambling Act) made insurance
contracts illegal as wagering agreements unless the policyholder had
an "insurance interest" under the contract.[40] The interest had to be
in proportion to the amount insured; otherwise the policy would be
declared null and void. At the same time as this legislation was
passed, the literature on insurance was full of attempts to distinguish
sharply between insurance and gambling. Daston remarks:

The extraordinary success of the Equitable [insurance company] is the result
not only of its exploitation of the regularity of the mortality statistics and the
mathematics of probability to fix premiums ... but also of its creation of an
image of life insurance diametrically opposed to that of gambling. ... Long-
term life insurance was aimed at a growing middle-class of salaried professionals – clergymen, doctors, lawyers, skilled artisans – who were respectable but not of independent means. In a world where apparently even a
clergyman could not count upon commercial charity, the sudden death of the
provider could topple the family from the middling ranks of society to the
very bottom. Such reversals of fortune were the proper fate of the gambler,
not the good bourgeois. (1987, p. 248)

In other words, whereas in the past tontine schemes offered the hope of moving up the social ladder, the new life insurance played on the fears of sudden downward social mobility of the new and expanding middle classes.

There is a further question that the reader might have asked: Why did insurance companies appear so late in history? How did people deal with misfortune during earlier times? The answer is that when populations were smaller, more isolated, less mobile, when warfare, pirates, plagues, and other diseases were the main sources of misfortune, family, kin, and community charity were the main sources of insurance. Additional insurance was provided by a wide range of beliefs – in magic, in witchcraft, in some divine power – that fulfilled, among others, the role of forcing the relatively fortunate to redistribute wealth toward those who suddenly became less so.[41] Keith Thomas in his book about the decline of magic concludes that "at a lower social level, the eighteenth century saw the launching of pioneer insurance schemes by industrial firms for their employees and the proliferation of working-class friendly societies. Nothing did more to reduce the sphere in which magical remedies were the only form of protection against misfortune" (1971, p. 659).

Insurance thus gained ground at the expense of both charity and magical beliefs, and, echoing Adam Smith, it was perceived as a "precise, scientific, and at the same time practical form of that unconscious solidarity that unites men."[42] By the third decade of the nineteenth century, the divorce between insurance and gambling seemed final. Gambling was, to a large extent, outlawed, whereas insurance became a pillar of social order, guaranteeing that "a man who is rich today will not be poor tomorrow."[43]

5. Legal confusions and political debates about gambling and speculation

Contracts under which one party agreed to take on himself the risk of variations in the price of stocks between certain dates without transferring the stocks were never regarded as contrary to the common law. Yet by the nineteenth century opposition to such contracts grew particularly severe in Germany and also in the United States and England.

In *Rumsey v. Berry*, the Supreme Court of Maine held:

A contract for the sale and purchase of wheat to be delivered in good faith at a future time is one thing, and is not inconsistent with the law. But such a contract entered into without an intention of having any wheat pass from one party to the other, but with an understanding that at the appointed time the purchaser is merely to receive or pay the difference between the contract and the market price, is another thing, and such as the law will not sustain. This is what is called a settling of the differences, and as such is clearly and only a betting upon the price of wheat, against public policy, and not only void, but deserving of the severest censure.[44]

Similar judgments were frequently made in other states too. But in 1865 the Indiana Supreme Court held that dealing in futures was not illegal gambling. Later, however, that same court changed its opinion and declared that commodity speculation was illegal gambling if at the time of making the contract neither party intended actual delivery.[45]

The courts seemed to struggle with the problem of permitting futures contracts but prohibiting gambling and speculation, without apparently understanding that without speculation such contracts cannot exist. An 1887 statute in Missouri tried to make the distinction, but a statute in Michigan in the same year banned all futures contracts.[46] In 1867 the Illinois legislature passed an act declaring that participants in futures contracts, referred to in the act as gambling contracts, should be fined a thousand dollars and imprisoned for up to one year in Cook County jail. Seven members of the Chicago Board of Trade were arrested under this act.[47] The act was repealed one year later, but in 1874 all futures contracts were again banned in Illinois. In 1875 the prohibition was cancelled, but in 1889, in *Schneider v. Turner*, the court once again held that all option contracts were unlawful, stating explicitly that the rationale for the decision was to "break down the pernicious practice of gambling on the market prices of grain and other commodities."[48] Apparently the statute was not effective, for a year later, in *Soby v. People*, the court stated that the practice was becoming more widespread. Only in 1900, in *Booth v. People*, was it finally explicitly stated that the prohibition of market gambling (by which term reference was made to bucket shops) need not embrace all contracts for options to buy or sell, but only contracts that threatened the public safety and welfare.[49] With this vague statement, open to any interpretation – like any statement where the word "welfare" appears – much of the legal uncertainty surrounding the development of a commodities market in Illinois was eliminated. Discussions of a similar nature were held in Canada in both Quebec's Court of Appeal (*Forget v. Ostiguy*, Sept. 27, 1883) and later, on appeal to the Imperial Privy Council, in the House of Lords (1895).

The confusion in the public's mind, and in that of judges, between gambling and speculation, and the fact that gambling contracts, as we have seen, were not enforceable, also explain why the stock exchanges spent great sums of money and effort to make the distinction as sharp as possible.[50] Otherwise the fate of the institution might have been in doubt.[51]

The debates and confusion surrounding futures markets were apparent in political discussions too. Over a hundred bills were introduced in the U.S. Congress to abolish futures trading. In 1893 a bill recommending a prohibitive tax on all futures trading in farm products failed to pass only because final action before Congress adjourned required a suspension of the rules of the House of Representatives, and the necessary two-thirds majority vote failed by the margin of 172 to 129. A similar bill in 1894 passed the House but failed to gain approval in the Senate. The attacks on futures contracts reflected the same confusion that marked the legal decisions.[52] A Kansas representative described futures markets as follows in 1890:

Those who deal in "options" and "futures" contracts, which is mere gambling, no matter by what less offensive name such transactions be designated, neither add to the supply nor increase the demand for consumption, nor do they accomplish any useful purpose by their calling; but on the contrary, they speculate in fictitious products.[53]

And in 1892 one senator declared that

at least 95% of the sales of [Chicago Board of Trade] are of . . . fictitious character, where no property is actually owned, no property sold or delivered, or expected to be delivered but simply wages or bets as to what that property may be worth at a designated time in the future. . . . Wheat and cotton have become as much gambling tools as chips on the taro-bank table. The property of the wheat grower and the cotton grower is treated as though it were a "stake" put on the gambling table at Monte Carlo. . . . Between the grain producer and the loaf eater, there has stepped in a "parasite" between them robbing them both.[54]

Yet it should be noted that Cowing, who examines the attitudes toward stock and commodity speculation in the United States during the nineteenth century, views all these discussions within a broader framework and concludes that "the anti-futures campaign was . . . a relatively obscure part of the larger Populist program that aimed, by the use of agrarian ideology, to regain some politico-economic power for the farmer" (1965, p. 258).

Briefly, the role of futures markets in providing both insurance against fluctuating prices and liquidity for the participants in these markets may not have been recognized by some vocal fraction of the population.[55] But behind the apparent misunderstanding lurked the envy of successful speculators and resistance to providing a channel for social mobility through which a new class of people were becoming rich when others were falling behind. This is the only interpretation that one can give to Wilson's lament on passage of the Limited Liability Act in England in 1862.[56] Before that date, he wrote, gambling in stocks had been confined to a limited class of the wealthy. But after 1862, with the significantly lower prices for shares, speculation gradually became the fashion with classes of people hitherto unfamiliar with it, and by 1870 "education came to the help of the share manufacturer, and by and by, the financial newspaper, the professional tipster and the 'bucket-shop' agencies outside the Stock Exchange, conducted with the avowed purpose of guiding the play so as to bring wealth to the gamblers, exercised their malign influence."[57]

6. Giving futures markets a chance

As we have seen, some people's special condemnation of gambling was on the ground that money spent on gambling was not spent on "necessities." Thus the poorer people's expenditure patterns were under particular scrutiny. The attitude, however, also reminds one of the advice given by brokers to their somewhat richer clients, namely, to invest as much money as one can afford to lose, but not more. "Speculate only with your genuine risk capital," they say; that is, "Speculate only when you have met your financial responsibilities with regard to living expenses, retirement and insurance plans, and education for children."[58]

But if the poorer and the somewhat richer were to adjust their behavior to these opinions, gambling and speculation would disappear. Those whose incentives to gamble and to speculate are greatest are expected to change their attitude. If one already has the "necessities" (a relative term),[59] or all the things the brokers are talking about, why bother with speculation? It is getting these things – the comfortable retirement, the better education for children and postponing a meal, a drink, the buying of a house in hopes of having more and better meals and drinks and a finer house in the future, that gives the incentive to gamble and to speculate. These are the hopes and ambitions that are taxed when prohibitions against gambling and speculation are in effect. There is no doubt, however, that a price must be paid for maintaining such hopes and ambitions; one price is that at times the hope of boundless wealth and the fear of falling behind one's speculating fellows may lead to fraud and to "bubbles." Hope and optimism, envy and fear, like anything else, do not come free. Yet, there is little doubt that, to paraphrase Mandeville, "Envy itself, Hope and Vanity/Are the Ministers of Industry."

The discussion in this chapter does more than satisfy one's curiosity about the distinction to be made between gambling and speculation. It has practical implications. As we have seen, some people genuinely believed that the elimination of futures markets could stabilize prices and the incomes of farmers, or even raise the farmers' income. (Although one can doubt the sincerity of both the politicians' word and their support of some causes, there is no reason to be skeptical of the motives of the many judges who wanted to prohibit trading in futures.) It is clear, from the evidence and arguments presented here, that there is no way that government officials speculating on a prohibitive strategy could achieve the proposed goal.

Those who sincerely favored the prohibition of futures thought that gambling and speculation would be eliminated, and with them that the "haphazard" and "irrational" operation of commodity markets would disappear. In other words, an implicit claim behind their policy was that the administrators of bureaucracies – be they Wheat Boards, Onion Boards, or the administrators of buffer stocks – could distinguish better than anybody else between long-term trends and what these administrators perceived as arbitrary changes in the sentiments of speculators and gamblers.

Needless to say, this claim is not a speculation, but an error; the facts go against it. The administrators had no way of telling better than the rest of the public whether a price change would be followed by further movement in the same direction, let alone by how much or for how long, and whether a fluctuation was of shorter or longer duration. Not only did the administrators have no advantage over the speculators in making predictions; they were worse at it. They had less incentive to make an effort. Hidden in the anonymous labyrinth of a government bureaucracy, they had neither reputation nor money at stake. In contrast, the opportunity cost to the speculator of making a bad prediction was higher: either to lose wealth or miss the opportunity of accumulating it.

Yet the prejudice against speculators continues today. The same restrictions that were imposed on gambling and futures markets during the nineteenth and early twentieth centuries are now imposed in many Third World countries. Instead of encouraging the use of forward markets by small producers and traders, and the development of organized commodity markets and banks in local centers, these countries support national and international "stabilization" measures, such as buffer stocks and regulations like price floors, price ceilings, and crop quotas, the constantly pathetic performance of some of them notwithstanding.[60] The sometimes costly and disastrous consequences of such intervention are well documented.[61] An alternative to these erroneous strategies is the promotion of banking and other modern financial institutions and reliable communication facilities. Unfortunately, instead of pursuing this strategy, Third World governments severely limit the range and scope of these institutions.

Their attitude may not be surprising in light of what has been presented and discussed in earlier chapters. What is surprising even in the United States today is that in a major article in *Newsweek* entitled "Thatcher's Two Britains" one can find the following sentence: "And although a few of the new middle class have made it as entrepreneurs, many have simply followed the upper classes into lucrative but unproductive fields such as law and banking."[62] The statement implies that financial entrepreneurship (for which legal expertise is necessary) is somehow always unproductive. This sentence, just like the opinion of judges in earlier times, may reflect either genuine confusion or disguised envy.[63]

If it reflects confusion, economists are to be blamed in part. For nowhere in their teaching do the great majority deal with innovation and entrepreneurship in general and in financial markets in particular, or with how people's hopes of becoming richer have an effect on various markets. Since all these elements are absent in economic theory, the policies advocated by economists do not take them into account either.[64]

Now that we have discovered why people gamble and who the gamblers are (in Chapter 2), and then why gambling was condemned and to what poor policies and legal decisions the condemnation has led (in Chapter 3 and in this chapter), the next chapter will examine the options that governments have today for regulating gambling.

5. Governments, taxation, and the impact of prohibitions

The mode of taxation is, in fact, quite as important as the amount. As a small burden badly placed may distress a horse that could carry with ease a much larger one properly adjusted, so a people may be impoverished and their power of producing wealth destroyed by taxation, which, if levied in another way, could be borne with ease.

Henry George, *Progress and Poverty* (1879)

Widespread legalization of lotteries and other games of chance in recent times is not just a sign that some government officials and other people recognize the fact that previous prohibitions were wrong-headed, that gambling is not a cause of either poverty or diminished productivity, and that the poor have a right both to choose their recreations and spend their money the way they want. It also reflects a need to finance sudden increases in government expenditures.

Government officials correctly perceived that there was an unexploited opportunity to raise money by legalizing gambling. There was clearly latent demand for games of chance; people gambled illegally, and the revenues from such illegal expenditures were untaxed; and enforcing prohibition involved expenditure. As a result, some governments decided to venture into the business while maintaining monopoly power, realizing that they could obtain the highest revenues by banning the sale of substitutes.

But it would be a mistake to conclude that unexpected increases in government expenditures or deficits in state budgets have *necessarily* led to the legalization of lotteries and other games of chance. Although the potential for raising revenues by this method was recognized, decisions were frequently made to maintain the ban. In England, in spite of the Treasury's interest since the 1920s in imposing a gambling tax and in suggestions concerning the state control of gambling and sale of lotteries, all proposals were rejected until the 1960s. And, as we have seen, similar decisions were made during the depression of

113

the 1930s in the United States.[1] What had changed when some games
of chance were legalized was not only that governments' expenditures suddenly increased and that the alternatives of raising taxes or
of lowering expenditures seemed unfeasible, but also that views of
what causes poverty and what the remedies are had significantly
changed, that religious convictions had weakened, and that attribut-
ing a significant role to gambling in determining the productivity of
workers had all but disappeared. At the same time the desire to
gamble did not diminish. Movements up and down the social ladder
continued and not only fueled the desire to advance, but were also
behind the weakening of customs, of traditional ways of thinking,
and of the conviction that luck, and not only ingenuity and hard
work, determines whether or not one will strike it rich.

Although some of the old influential views about the detrimental
effects of gambling have thus been discarded, new ones condemning
gambling on other grounds have been invented. These newer views
concentrate on the relationship among governments, taxation, crime,
and games of chance. Whether they are erroneous or not will be
examined in this chapter.

But first let us take a glance at the magnitude of the sums we are
talking about and whether or not there is regularity in revenues from
lotteries when they are legally permitted and no changes in the law
occur. In England between the years 1802 and 1826, net revenues
from lotteries represented between 0.3 and 1 percent of the government's net revenues (the gross share being between 1 and 2 percent).[2]
In France between 1815 and 1828, net revenues hovered around 1
percent of the government's total receipts. More recently, in the
United States between the years 1978 and 1983, net revenues from
lotteries, as a percent of the respective state's general revenues, were
between 3.7 and 5 percent in Maryland, 2 percent in Connecticut,
and 1.5 percent in Massachusetts.[3] As for a pattern in revenues from
their sales, the evidence presented in Chapter 2 leads one to expect
that revenues from lotteries should be countercyclical; that is, increase during recession and turbulent periods and diminish during
stable and good times. For during recessions people become suddenly unemployed, and frustrated expectations become the rule rather
than the exception. In such circumstances, as we have seen, people
are more likely to gamble; implicitly, both the statistical evidence
presented in Chapter 2 and the more qualitative evidence presented

later seem to confirm this statement.[4] It may be useful to emphasize the implications of this correlation for pragmatic reasons.

It is during recessions that governments experience relatively high expenditures because of commitments made when better times were expected, combined with suddenly diminished revenues, and face difficult choices. Imposing additional taxes, increasing debt, and revising previous commitments – none of these are very attractive. Lotteries and other games of chance are among the few items whose sales may rise during recessions, thus providing revenues for governments. Increased willingness to spend on games of chance also provides opportunities for entrepreneurs and for employment. Banning this sector not only makes the potential buyers, those already falling behind and the poor, even unhappier, but it also gives incentives to illegal entrepreneurship, thus cutting governments off from additional revenues. Moreover, the governments' expenditures must even rise, since law enforcement costs money. But, as can be inferred from the arguments presented earlier, there is more hiding behind the apparently simple recommendation "let your people gamble" (honestly, of course) than just the consideration of creating employment.[5] The question should be viewed in a much broader context: a policy that favors change and facilitates adjustment to it.

1. Games of chance and taxation

Many social scientists condemn the government's monopoly of the sale of lotteries today on grounds of some vague and totally wrong new arguments. Lotteries are condemned because revenues from their sale are viewed as a form of regressive taxation; that is, on the ground that the poorer are spending a greater percentage of their wealth on lotteries than the relatively rich.

Why is condemnation on these grounds wrong? By examining facets of this question and discussing the evidence, we shall gain a still better understanding of the confusion that continues to surround the issue of games of chance in general and that of lotteries in particular.

Why is regressivity bad?

The foundations of the traditional theory that perceives regressivity as bad, as diminishing happiness in a society, are so weak that they are hardly worth criticizing.[6] One of the assumptions behind it is that if the government redistributes wealth and achieves greater equality, this intervention could make society happier, since the unhappiness of the richer, from whom wealth is taken away, is more than compensated for by the additional happiness of the poor, who get the money (for the mathematical translation of this theory, see the first appendix to Chapter 2).[7] How comparisons of people's happiness can be made, and who is making them in society and why, is not made clear within this framework. However, in order to reach the preceding conclusion, an additional assumption is made: that everybody in society is the same; that is, that from equal amounts of wealth people derive equal satisfaction. Wealth, and nothing else, matters.[8]

Condemning lotteries on the basis of this theory is wrong for additional reasons. It is true, as we have seen, that mainly the poor, the frustrated, and those falling or fearing to fall behind buy lottery tickets. But then, it is this group too who get the prizes, which represent 40 to 77 percent of the total receipts (the most frequent number is 60 percent).[9] Thus wealth in this case is mainly redistributed *among the relatively poor*, some of whom thus achieve, thanks to the prizes, a standard of living that welfare payments, no matter how generous, can never provide. The usual arguments about regressivity, even if they were right (as they are not), do not apply at all to the sale of lotteries.[10]

Other critics of the states' monopoly of the sale of lotteries have argued that raising income taxes by a small percentage can generate the same revenues as the sale of lotteries, and they point to the relatively high collection costs of taxation through lotteries. But this argument for condemning lotteries is wrong too, and for a number of reasons. First, comparing collection costs is valid only if one assumes that the only role of lotteries is that of providing revenues. Once the lottery is looked upon as providing an additional *service* to the buyers (since the private sector is not allowed to offer it) – and we have seen that it does, sustaining people's hopes for a better future during harsh times – the rationale for comparing the operating costs of lotteries with the cost of generating revenues by other forms of taxation disappears.[11] Second, the implicit assumption of the critics, which is that raising some taxes when lotteries are banned would leave other things unchanged, is erroneous. Prohibition imposes a large cost on governments and society with some long-term consequences that in turn are costly to correct; some of them will be examined later in this chapter.

If brought to its logical conclusion, the view that the state's sale of lotteries is bad leads to two courses of action: allowing competition or prohibiting their sale.

If it is the first option – permitting competition – that critics of the state's monopoly of the sale of lotteries have in mind, some questions must be raised. Is the fact that the poor are spending a relatively greater percentage of their wealth on lotteries under criticism? Or is the criticism that expenditures on lotteries are taxed because of the governments' monopoly?

If it is prohibition that critics of lotteries today have in mind, then an accurate analysis justifying such a view requires raising the following questions. What will the previous buyers do if lotteries are prohibited? And what will governments do? Will they reduce their expenditures, and if so, on what items exactly? Or will they maintain expenditures and tax something else, and if so, what exactly? Without answering these questions, one cannot conclude that the present situation is better or worse than the alternatives.

Since the answers to questions concerning the option of competition are both easy and pave the way for examining the consequences of prohibition, let us look into them first.

The option of competition

One may argue that since governments had and still have today a monopoly of the sale of lotteries (since competition from both private companies and from other provinces' or states' lotteries is outlawed, and since there simply are no other financial investments that give the chance of getting rich by regularly spending a dollar),[12] the buyers may be paying a higher price for the tickets than they would if competition prevailed. It is only this difference, rather than the net revenues from lotteries, that may represent a tax – a sum redistributed from the buyers toward those who receive the money from the government. The reason for the previous statement being tentative is that there were circumstances when drawings were fraudulent in spite of competition. If the public in such cases believed that drawings could be kept honest only by restricting the sale of lotteries to governments, all of the aforementioned difference may not be perceived as a tax.[13]

Suppose, then, that because of innovations and better law enforcement, competition in the sale of lotteries is allowed, but the sale of tickets is taxed. What will happen? The public who buy the tickets would more or less stay the same as before (the poorer may even buy more tickets, since their price may be lowered), and the government would still collect regressive taxes, only in a different form. Thus the attacks on regressivity, when looked at from this angle – if the alternative to the state's monopoly is a taxed competitive sector – are hollow.[14]

There have been studies that attacked the government's sale of lotteries on the ground of regressivity from another angle, arguing that not only do the poor spend relatively more on the tickets, but the government's net revenues from lotteries are redistributed toward the relatively rich. On what premises were such conclusions reached?

Governments frequently point out the projects on which the net revenues from lotteries are spent, but make some peculiar statements. An official communication in Japan says that "gambling or lottery has never been considered as a taxable item in Japan," but then it is mentioned that 38 percent of the lottery's profits were "used for the development of educational equipment, road construction or repairs, construction of dwelling houses, expenses for public prosperity and welfare." (Is there any item in the government's budget that could not fit into one of these categories?) The famous Irish Sweepstakes, which is conducted by the Hospitals Trust, is required by acts of Parliament to pay out the net proceeds to 410 institutions that provide free medical and surgical services. The trust's communication also declares that the proceeds do not appear in the government's budget.[15] Such statements about the worthy projects on which net revenues from the sale of lotteries are spent are common in the United States and Canada too. Although in about half the states (Connecticut, Delaware, the District of Columbia, Illinois, Maine, Missouri, Ohio, Rhode Island, etc.) and one province (Quebec), the legislators had the good sense to provide that the net revenues from lotteries go to the general fund, there are other states and provinces that declare that the revenues will be used only for specific items: public education (California, Michigan, New York [at one time, but not any more], New Jersey, Ontario, etc.); conservation, parks, and recreation (Colorado, Alberta). It is on the basis of such declarations, pointing out specific uses for the net revenues from lotteries, that studies examining the regressivity of revenues from governments' sale of lotteries have been based too, and have argued that those who benefit most from these revenues are the richer.[16]

But such conclusions are also inaccurate. Can one seriously believe that, in the absence of revenues from lotteries, governments would not have decided to finance such expenditures by higher taxes, increased debt, or a reallocation of expenditures? The declarations should not be taken literally. All they imply is that less is allocated in the general fund in the directions that revenues from lotteries are being used for.[17] Steven Gold, director of fiscal studies for the National Conference of State Legislatures in Denver, confirmed this view when stating that, because of the gains from lotteries, education programs sometimes lose equal amounts from general appropriations. In New York, which has the most efficient state lottery in the United States, according to the journal *Gaming and Wagering Business*, state officials said that over the twenty years the lottery had been running, the proceeds had substituted for other funds: "The primary debate in New York has been whether lottery funding becomes a supplementary source," said Paul C. Reuss, director of budget studies for the state Senate Finance Committee. "The truth is that it is just one of the funding sources, but if we didn't have the lottery, taxes would have to be increased by $650 million."[18]

Indeed, when New York instituted its lottery in 1967, the profits were set aside for education. But when the state faced a budget crisis in 1968, the legislature shifted the net revenues from lotteries into the general fund. A similar event took place in Connecticut. Until December 1975 lottery revenues were earmarked for education. But then a special session of the legislature voted to allocate the revenues first to education, with "the balance to become part of the general fund" (whatever this "balance" means).[19]

When lotteries were prohibited, government officials in various countries during the nineteenth and first half of this century were not slow to realize that the latent demand for them enabled cheaper servicing of debt if, instead of paying interest, they promised to give a few large prizes on some bonds, with the majority of holders just getting back their initial investment. Variations on such premium bonds, as they were called, were widespread in England, Sweden, and Ireland. But it is hard to believe that the fact that governments did not call such assets lotteries could have fooled anybody. The invention of these financial assets as well as the artificial allocation of receipts from lotteries just shows that it is naive to assume that if lotteries as such were not offered, governments would change their expenditures. The change was that of vocabulary, not content.[20]

Thus, those who have examined regressivity by just looking at either the buying patterns of the poor and the rich or the government's declarations are on the wrong track. They must look at the general patterns in the government's expenditures and regulations and not at one item in isolation. One may, however, ask: If this conclusion is accurate, why do governments bother to make the aforementioned misleading declarations? There may be two possible answers. One is that it may somewhat calm those who are opposed to the sale of lotteries on religious grounds. Since for this group lotteries are bad, state monopoly of their sale must be perceived as a second best: At least the product is taxed, thus diminishing participation; and the taxes seem to be spent on items these groups approve of. Still, this answer assumes that members of this group take the government's declarations literally. A more plausible answer is that government officials and part of the public sometimes extrapolate without much thought from past evidence. As we have seen, revenues from lotteries were successfully used for building great American universities, charitable institutions, hospitals, and so forth. If such a method of financing was good for Harvard, Princeton, and Yale in the past, why shouldn't it be good for governments subsidizing education today? Students of regressivity have neglected the answer that the circumstances surrounding such financing in the past were different from today's, and that lotteries then fulfilled different roles (being either a substitute for financial institutions or an occasion for social gatherings), suggesting that their role in the past cannot be used to justify their role today. But then people do not always question the origins of customs, but often accept them unthinkingly: Since lotteries were tried out in the past and found to be good for financing education, why not try them again?

The unavoidable conclusion therefore seems to be simple. Those who criticize the states' sale of lotteries on the grounds of regressivity could logically have only one option in mind: banning their sale altogether. But justifying the viewpoint that lotteries should be banned requires much more complex consideration than just looking at people's expenditures on them. Some of these considerations are examined next.

2. Impact of prohibitions

All lotteries were abolished by the revolutionary government in France in 1793, but the government revised its decision a few years later. The reason was that, being deprived of national lotteries, people played the foreign ones illegally. As a result the French government was losing both revenues and foreign currency.[21]

Before the French Revolution, baccarat used to be played in illegal gaming halls with a great deal of cheating. It is due to the common sense of de Sartine, chief of the French Sûreté, that the government of the day was persuaded to legalize baccarat; no further mention is made of cheating.[22]

Even when lotteries were sold by governments but were prohibited for sale by private firms, the impact of prohibitions was not significantly different. Between 1760 and 1826, when the price of a state lottery ticket in England was £13 (which meant that only the rich could buy it and that such gambling was therefore prohibited to the poor), "insurance" was invented, and hundreds of illegal offices selling it to the *poor* operated in London. When this practice was stopped in 1793, the move succeeded in creating not only a black market but also protection rackets. Once lotteries were prohibited at the beginning of the nineteenth century, illegal private lotteries on a small scale multiplied, and their clients continued to be the poor.[23]

When gambling was outlawed in Sweden (until 1930), the Swedes gambled on English soccer games, thereby smuggling out substantial amounts of Swedish currency. Once gambling was legalized, the criminal elements that were involved with smuggling and gambling disappeared. China inaugurated a state lottery (not accidentally) on July 31, 1933, but lotteries were not unfamiliar to the Chinese. Hwo-Wei, a form of illegal lottery, had been very popular among the lower classes in Shanghai.[24]

In the United States until the reemergence of lotteries in the 1960s and 70s, the dominant illegal games were numbers and "insurance" (also called policy). The latter got its start in connection with the drawings of authorized lotteries, which took a long time and were expensive. The reason for the time lapse between the issuing of tickets and the drawing was that each new lottery had to get a license from the government, and there was always the possibility of not obtaining it.[25]

"Insurance" disappeared with the abolition of lotteries at the beginning of the nineteenth century, but the numbers game continued to be played in the poorer districts of large cities, and charity raffles were regularly held in the richer districts.[26] None of these seemed to attract much attention. Both in the United States and England, attention was focused on gambling linked with horse racing.

Throughout the nineteenth century, the bookmaking industry in the United States was illegal yet very popular.[27] In spite of the illegality, Western Union provided communication services to disseminate race results and odds. When in 1904 Western Union was put under increasing pressure to stop providing its services for this industry, the result was that six months later John Payne of Cincinnati had acquired an illegal monopoly to provide the desired information.[28]

During the early 1920s pari-mutuel wagering was legal only in Kentucky, Maryland, and Louisiana. Yet horse racing and gambling on the races continued to prosper in other states, since the laws prohibiting racing and bookmaking continued to be unenforced. They could not be. Whereas the entrepreneurs involved with gambling quickly used new technologies, it took years for government agencies to catch up with the innovations. Bookmakers in New York used telephones fifty years before the state authorized wiretaps.[29] Moreover, the law itself was ambiguous. Since bookmaking was illegal, track managers invented a system of oral betting, which in *People ex rel. Lichtenstein v. Langan* (1909) was held to be exempt from the bookmaking law under the unconvincing argument that successful bookmaking required "the writing out of the list of the odds laid on some paper or material so that they can be seen by those who are solicited to invest." Thus, went the decision, oral betting did not constitute bookmaking.[30] Lack of enforcement also resulted from the fact that in some southern states hostility toward gambling could be found more in judicial opinions than in legislative enactments. Blakey speculates that this phenomenon may be due to the fact that whereas many judges received their legal training in the East, where features of the frontier life were frowned upon, legislators reflected the will of the voters, who were not concerned about gambling.[31] An additional reason for lack of enforcement may be that gambling had close links with urban politics. Gamblers, police, and politicians were frequently of Irish Catholic background in many American cities, and "it was not simply that gambling syndicates influenced political organizations, but that gambling syndicates *were* the local political organization. Local bookmakers or policy writers served as precinct captains, while the leaders of syndicates became ward leaders and often won elections as aldermen or state representatives."[32]

Americans, like the Swedish and the French, also gambled on out-of-state lotteries when forbidden to play within their states. As noted earlier, this was the reason for the Louisiana lottery's spectacular success during the nineteenth century; Louisiana was the only state with surviving lotteries. Australians too gambled on out-of-state lotteries when forbidden to play within their own state, thus diminishing local tax revenues. This was the reason why New South Wales, Victoria, Queensland, and Western Australia passed laws prohibiting the Post Office from carrying lottery tickets, thus preventing Tasmania from exporting its lotteries.[33]

The fact that prohibitions in other states or nations could be used to raise revenues (thus imposing a tax on "foreigners") was and is still perceived by politicians as one of the attractions of lotteries. With only 600,000 inhabitants, New Hampshire's lottery officials knew that to succeed they must appeal to out-of-state people. They did succeed; in 1964, 80 percent of the tickets were sold to residents of Massachusetts, New York, and Connecticut, even though out-of-state residents had to travel to New Hampshire's border towns to purchase the tickets (use of the mail to move them is prohibited by federal law in the United States too). After 1964 the residents of these three states had to travel less, since New York and Massachusetts introduced very successful lotteries.[34]

Residents of other states are still traveling some distance in hopes of getting really rich. Some Delaware residents drive more than twenty miles twice a week in order to participate in the Maryland lottery. Delaware has its own game, but the prizes are small. Hoping both to prevent the outflow of funds and to keep their gamblers happy, Delaware is now making plans to offer a four-state lottery in collaboration with Maine, New Hampshire, and Vermont, with first prizes varying between $1 million and $10 million, thus competing with the glittering prizes of New York's lottery.[35]

Premium bonds, discussed in the preceding section, were not the only invention made during the nineteenth century in response to prohibitions on gambling. New sweepstakes, prize competitions, and football pools became popular in both the United States and England during this period. Although at first prize competitions and sweepstakes were prosecuted as lotteries in both countries, eventually they were dubiously distinguished – legally, but not in the public's mind – on the ground that they required the exercise of skill.[36]

But the prohibition had more serious consequences than the fact that people gambled illegally, that substitutes were invented, or that people had to travel to other states to buy tickets. The reason why the poor continued to bet in England, even after passage of the 1906 "class law," was that enforcement of the law was not always taken seriously.[37] In Scotland the law seemed to be used merely to raise revenues through penalties rather than to suppress illegal bookmaking.[38]

Lack of enforcement was due to a number of factors. Not long after the passage of the law, members of the police force criticized the law on the grounds that it was "antiquated, obscure, illogical, ineffective and falls unevenly upon different classes of the community."[39] Since the poor did not equate legality with legitimacy, the police, in attempting to enforce the law, were faced with an impossible task. The bookmakers had developed a tight organization, and the buyers sympathized with the bookmakers rather than with the police.[40] Members of the police were also bribed by the bookmakers, a corruption that led journalists to declare in the 1920s that confidence in the police was at its lowest ebb in half a century.[41]

Reactions were similar in the United States. In 1851 the New York Association for the Suppression of Gambling was established, and the Green Law of 1851 was the harshest antigambling law passed up to that time. It imposed fines on anyone found guilty of keeping a gambling establishment, exhibiting gambling devices, or assisting in any game.[42] The legislation turned out to be ineffective, and according to some estimates 30,000 people in the New York of the 1850s made their living from gambling.[43] There were several reasons for this law's lack of impact. Whereas the legislation was passed by members of the Protestant establishment, in the years between 1825 and 1855 New York State's population doubled, primarily because of the immigration of penniless non-Protestants who wanted to gamble. Too, some politicians turned out to have an interest in the gambling industry. Eventually the police commissioner, who claimed to be ignorant of the law, declined to enforce it.[44]

Surprising as it may sound today, a comprehensive law prohibiting all forms of gambling was passed in Nevada in 1909 and gambling remained a criminal offense for two decades. The result was that government revenues from licensing were lost, a large number of games were played, and corruption and "protection" became widespread, bribes coming to seem like little more than a form of license. Commentators reached the same conclusions as those reached in England:

The fact that the Nevada gambling prohibition had to be enforced along with the national liquor prohibition did not do much good in Nevada for either law enforcement program. The speakeasies had gambling tables and slot machines. The people who wanted only to gamble or only to drink felt a brotherhood. Both groups, of course, were outnumbered by that mass who wanted to both drink and gamble. One of the byproducts of all this was the creation of a lawlessness in attitude for a whole generation of Americans, and a class of dishonest law enforcement officers and public officeholders such as the nation had never known before.[45]

It was in 1930 that Nevada relegalized gambling. The change of mind can be attributed not only to the great crash of 1929 and impending crisis, but also to the recognition that people gambled anyway and that the moral reformers who were against gambling could not find any evidence of the desperation and ruin that were popularly associated with gambling.[46] The impact of the relegalization was that eventually, myths notwithstanding, the gambling industry in Nevada, which features a massive corporate structure, was characterized by honesty toward its customers.[47]

In spite of all evidence, and in contrast to the more liberal attitude adopted toward gambling in England during the 1960s, New York's legislature in 1960 passed a series of tough new *anti*gambling laws whose purpose was to facilitate convictions and, by increased penalties, to have a detrimental effect on gambling. The law was passed in spite of the fact that public opinion in New York City did not seem to condemn gambling. This is what one may infer from the fact that a public opinion survey in 1963 revealed that few New Yorkers worried about the morality of betting on races, favoring it three to one.[48]

The law does not seem to have achieved its intended impact.

Gambling and the organized crime associated with it persisted, but few convictions were obtained. If it had a significant effect, it was on the police, for whom, the Knapp Commission found, gamblers' protection money was the main source of bribes. A typical policeman on the gambling squad was able to get $300 to $1,500 per month, and his or her superiors got additional sums.[49]

These revelations led, as in England, to the decision by New York City's police commissioner, Murphy, to stop enforcing certain aspects of the gambling laws. He also argued that dismantling the gambling squads would not bring about any great increase in gambling. But it would, he argued, have the beneficial effect of diminishing corruption, enabling the police to concentrate on controlling violent crime and improving the morale of police and public.[50]

A similar sequence of events took place in Australia.[51] Legislation in Queensland in 1936 and in New South Wales in 1938, prohibiting off-course betting in newspapers or through broadcasting, led to the organization of illegal means of communication. People were employed to signal from the courses and used the telephone to handle transactions. The organizations also bribed policemen and employees of the telephone company. Because transactions were arranged by phone, a credit system was necessary; its enforcement depended on threats and the use of violence.

The lessons

A number of lessons can be drawn from this evidence and that presented in preceding chapters. Those who condemn gambling in general and recommend its prohibition must take into account the fact that the policy they have in mind does not lead to no gambling, to more progressive taxation, to less crime, or to people spending their time and money on church literature or socialist treatises. People continue to gamble, even if it is illegal, and the poor do so in particular; hence their expenditure patterns may not change. Neither is the result more progressive taxation: If the government imposes a tax on beer (as was done in England when lotteries were prohibited),[52] the situation of the poor may not improve, since they spend even more on beer than on lotteries, and more than the richer. The result of prohibition is not less crime either. Even if one does not label gamblers criminals, which would automatically increase the crime rate, the acts of the illegal organizations that take over the gambling sector and enforce illegal gambling contracts increase the crime rate. If, as a result, the government entangles itself more in this maze and spends more on enforcement (while losing the revenues of the gambling sector), it must either raise taxes or reduce its expenditures.

And all these effects are due in part to the fact that there was and still is a vocal opposition who may sincerely, but erroneously, believe in the detrimental effects of gambling. The sincerity cannot always be doubted; some people believe in ideas that have been repeated so many times that familiarity with them passes for evidence. However, one cannot discard the possibility, discussed next and raised in Chapter 3, that the opposition's words disguise selfish interests.

3. Interest groups, prohibitions, and legislation

Religious groups have been aware of the fact that if people no longer hold traditional beliefs, they will spend less time praying and more playing games of chance.[53] And recall that the English statute of 1591 that forbade the use of houses for games of chance was passed on petition of the military lobby: those involved with the production of bows, arrows, and bowstrings.[54] Later, as we have seen, the argument was that both drinking and gambling diminished the workers' productivity. Yet only gambling was prohibited, and not drinking. Although the argument was offered that gambling is more harmful than drinking, it was never documented and was probably wrong.[55] The reason for the different legislative treatment was that brewers had a strong political lobby, being linked with agricultural and industrial interests as well as with finance and retailing outlets. The alcohol industry was also a major employer of labor; sellers of drink were as numerous, for example, as sellers of food.[56] In contrast, the gambling establishment, as we saw, came from a working-class background and had no political ties. The fact that all forms of gambling were forbidden except some linked with horse racing may also be explained by the fact that racing was a traditional major pastime for the wealthy and for social elites, whereas other forms of betting were less so.

In the United States, legislative efforts to curb gambling in connection with racing were widespread during the late eighteenth and early nineteenth centuries (statutes against it were passed in 1796 in Connecticut and in 1846 in New Jersey, and by 1860 most states in the Northeast had them), but the laws were frequently not enforced. Horse racing became a favorite pastime of the wealthy in the New World too.[57] How was racing exempted in the United States in spite of the fact that it was well known that it is not commercially viable without gambling? The lawyers found a legal solution. They declared that racing was a sport, not a game, and in *Van Valkenburgh v. Torrey* (1827), for example, the court gave a liberal reading to the word "racing" and declared that trotting was not affected by the law that prohibited races for bets or stakes. (Such plays on words are just another effect of prohibition, as noted in Chapter 3 in connection with the rise of contests.)[58]

Later, in the 1920s, the New Jersey Chamber of Commerce linked the following problems with the legalization of gambling when justifying its opposition:

Department stores, clothing and shoe stores, manufacturers and wholesalers dealing in staple lines of merchandise were usually injured. Other established entertainment industries, such as motion picture theaters, suffer during the local racing season. Collections fall off, large numbers of individuals get behind on installment payments, and the incidence of defalcations and other petty crimes increases enormously during the racing season.[59]

There is no evidence to support the last statement, although, as mentioned in Chapter 2, the rate of petty crime is higher in places where there are more tourists. Transitory crowds provide an easy prey, and the criminals themselves can more easily disappear in the crowd. As for the first part of the statement, it is probably true that some traditional leisure industries will fall behind when a new one is emerging. But then the condemnation of gambling should not be taken literally; it just reflects the fact that in practice those who may fall behind will be against increased *competition*. In a society committed to the idea of competition, representatives of threatened industries cannot be expected to acknowledge that they want less of it. Instead, they can be expected to disguise their sentiments behind false accusations.

Today, in spite of the fact that there is a general trend toward legalized gambling, opposition to it is still quite evident. But the vocal opponents are no longer religious groups but, in Florida for example, business interests afraid of competition. Among the opponents are the amusement giant Disney World and, yes, pari-mutuel betting interests. In Texas, where a vote on legalizing pari-mutuel betting was held in 1986 for the fifth straight year, the opposition was still coming from religious groups and neighboring states that already allowed such betting.[60]

The evidence seems quite clear; the correlation between opposition to legalization and the opposition's private interests seems obvious. Yet there is little doubt that at times opposition to gambling has been based on ideas that some people believe in, erroneously but sincerely. The implications of these findings concern more than just future policies affecting games of chance.

Public and private interests

There is a line of thought popular today that says that laws are passed by small interest groups who expect to benefit from them, whereas the rest of society is mainly indifferent to paying a small price for them. This thought is not inaccurate, as clearly shown above, but frequently such ahistorical theorizing does not seem to lead one very far. For without a good understanding of human behavior and without attempting to enter into the minds of decision makers at a certain moment of time and understand their way of thinking and their beliefs, little can be said a priori about the type of legislation that one group or another might favor.

Could an interest-group theory predict why it was in the interest of the members of the Labor Party in England in 1906 to vote for the Betting Act, which went against the wishes, the revealed preference, of their constituents? Only if one discovers the idea that lurked behind the vote – the prospect that the opportunity to gamble, to become rich, works as an inducement for the poor to work harder in expectation of tasting the joys of capitalist society, and that the provision of such additional opportunities poses a threat to a socialist's ideology – can one understand the interest behind it. Was the vote in the *private* interest of members of the Labor Party? Or did the vote reflect a sincere belief that the whole *public* might benefit if socialism came sooner to England?

Even if one considers a narrower topic, it is not always easy to give a clear-cut answer to such questions. In 1906 senior officers of the London Metropolitan Police, whose opinions on the feasibility of enforcement of a prohibition law were sought, were not against the law. They declared that the police could enforce it.[61] One may be skeptical of such declarations and say that if the law was passed the police could reasonably expect to have more money allocated to them, an outcome that every bureaucrat favors. Thus the declaration benefited private interests. Yet one may argue that the reason for the police force's attitude in favor of prohibition reflected a genuine belief in the evils of gambling, a belief shared by many people at the time. Thus their stand might be in the public interest as some perceived it.

Twenty years later the police came out against the law, a stand taken once the press had begun to make frequent revelations of corruption. Was the new attitude in their private or in the public interest? After all, one can argue that policemen blamed the law in order to explain that their corruption was in fact legitimate, since the law was not. Also, being continually blamed for corruption is threatening, since with a diminishing reputation the resources allocated to the police (and thus the wealth of members of the force) diminish.[62] Was the change in mind due to this threat posed to the well-being of members of the police hierarchy, thus serving private interests? Or was it a sincere recognition by a majority of police that the 1906 law was illegitimate and that relegalizing gambling was in the public's interest (what some may call a social good)?

What is the public interest, anyway? And how much gambling is socially good? An answer to these questions, linked with a discussion of the elusive notion of happiness, is given in the next and final chapter.

Conclusions

Belief in a large number of erroneous ideas, along with the political power of some interest groups, has brought many countries today to a situation where the betting laws are confused. The confusions and inconsistencies are striking as many people hold onto ideas inherited from the distant past without much questioning. When opinions are so strong, as among the vocal opponents of gambling, one could reasonably expect at least a moderate knowledge of facts. But we quickly discovered that this was too optimistic an expectation on our part. So what we have tried to do is not merely to gather as much evidence as we could so that future decisions can be made on a more reliable basis, but also to understand how societies got into the maze they are presently in, and so both provide a clear path out of it and prevent – perhaps – similar mistakes being made in the future. Of course we are not under the illusion that the problem will be simple. It is never easy for people to break with their customary thinking. Facts, even when set within a framework like the one we have tried to provide in this book, are not enough to fight long-held prejudices.[63]

Many changes in gambling laws during the twentieth century seem to be isolated attempts to deal with temporary problems, rather than the outcome of an in-depth examination of gambling and speculation.[64] Thus at times the liberalization of gambling laws was an attempt to suppress the involvement of organized crime (without noticing, however, that it was the antigambling law to start with that gave the incentive for organization of criminal acts). At other times the change was made just to raise revenues from an untapped source.[65]

However, because of old prejudices against gambling, liberalization did not lead toward permitting competition but toward providing the government with monopoly power over the sale of tickets. That meant that a government bureaucracy, at first lacking both experience and the threat of competition, was involved with the introduction of lotteries. Little wonder that some of the sales programs of the first states to offer lotteries were failures. Now the situation has changed, for one state's lottery competes with those of neighboring states.[66]

Since this is the situation today, it is unclear why the private sector should not be allowed to enter the game. There is always danger in a situation where a government bureaucracy is the only one allowed to offer a service and charge the pertinent taxes. The well-being of these bureaucrats depends on this form of revenue; to ensure the continuity of their own jobs and responsibilities, they may look for ways to expand their power, advertising their services and recommending excessive reliance on gambling activities as a source of revenue. After all, bureaucrats, like anybody else, are interested in preserving their jobs rather than in examining the role of gambling in society.[67] These are typical dangers with any bureaucracy. Bureaucrats may at first simply offer a service in a nonbusinesslike manner, failing to exploit the opportunities, and later offer too much service, having no interest in exploiting new opportunities but continuing in blissful bureaucratic inertia.

The recommendation reached here is therefore simple. The rationale for decriminalizing and demonopolizing gambling is not merely that such changes will eventually diminish the power of organized crime and keep bureaucrats on their toes. Rather, these steps lead toward a situation that both provides opportunities for employment and sustains optimism and hope among those who, in the game of life, have been among the hardest hit. Since, as Leo Rosten once wrote, optimism is often a narcotic to deaden anxiety, why not let people be optimistic?[68] Isn't that better than the alternative: dealing with anxiety?

Of course nothing comes free in this world, and society must deal with the small proportion of compulsive gamblers, probably by allocating a fraction of the tax revenues obtained from the gambling sector to treatment for such players and by making the sellers of games of chance liable if they know that the buyer is an addict. Yet even passing legislation that requires setting aside funds for treatment, and the treatment itself, may be easier when gambling is legal than when it is not. For if the sector is illegal, the gamblers, compulsive or not, will by definition be criminals. So voters might be less sympathetic when asked to pay for treatment, and compulsive gamblers may be less willing to come forward and admit their addiction, since they may find themselves imprisoned instead of cured.

6. Happiness, luck, and the social good

Better be born lucky than rich.

The last few years have seen an explosion of state-sponsored lotteries, so much so that it has been said that the United States is in the throes of lottomania.[1] Massachusetts residents spent $212 per capita on lotteries in 1985. The residents of the District of Columbia followed with $180.[2] Nationwide, lotteries brought in $12.4 billion in fiscal 1986, a 32.4 percent increase over a year earlier, and five states – Florida, Idaho, Kansas, Montana, and South Dakota – were scheduled to begin lottery games in 1987 (in addition to the twenty-two states and the District of Columbia that already had them by 1985).[3] When in September 1985 the big prize in the New York State lottery reached $41 million, long lines formed at every lottery outlet.[4] When the interprovincial Canadian lottery's big prize reached $13.9 million in January 1984, the frenzy reached such proportions that in the final week 15.6 million tickets were sold in Quebec alone, and 67 million tickets were sold in the whole of Canada.[5]

In spite of the large numbers linked with gambling, they should be put in the right perspective. Outlays on all forms of commercial gambling represent about 2 percent of personal income in the United States, a figure comparable to the amount families spend on restaurant meals and beverages, or the total outlay by American women on new clothing. Moreover, if the redistributed prizes are taken into account, the net outlay on gambling is reduced to a mere 0.4 percent of personal income, comparable to what Americans spend on tobacco or on newspapers and magazines.[6]

It would be a mistake, however, to think that if gambling were prohibited, then it would disappear, the 0.4 percent of personal income would be spent on something else, and the only businesses affected would be those linked with the business of gambling. As we saw earlier, prohibitions may make matters worse. Also, gambling has had a significant impact on many industries that are perceived as respectable and legitimate. Horse racing has, of course, been strongly linked with agricultural interests, and newspaper, telegraph, and telephone companies have profited handsomely from people's willingness to gamble.[7] Today, of course, radio and television channels (some specialize in broadcasting horse racing), as well as hotel chains and government bureaucracies, depend heavily on this industry.

Thus, the arguments of the antilottery partisans, that the legalization of lotteries is a deterrent to capital investment and that gambling would be a "formidable competitor of the stock market, diverting funds necessary for the expansion of private industry to less productive channels,"[8] are inaccurate and self-serving. Legalization is not a deterrent on investment, although obviously investments are different when gambling is legalized than when it is not. It is also hard to see how lotteries can be a "formidable competitor" to the stock market. Although poorer people spent relatively more on lotteries, even in Massachusetts the average sum per capita was only $212 in 1985, and was significantly less elsewhere. Competitor? Yes. But formidable? Certainly not. And anyway, defenders of the stock market should be the last ones to say anything against increased competition, no matter from what quarter it comes. Isn't it the idea of competition itself that is embodied in this institution? As for the question of productivity, there is nothing to add to what has already been said in previous chapters.

One argument of the critics – that some enterprises will be confronted with a shrinking market for some of their products when gambling is decriminalized – is of course accurate. If people prefer to spend time and money gambling, they will necessarily spend less time, and might spend less money, on traditional activities. I say "might" for this outcome is not necessary. Giving people the opportunity to gamble increases some people's options in society and thus acts as an inducement to work harder. People may reason that with the decriminalization of gambling, it is worth working harder, earning more, and spending the additional income on gambling, which provides the opportunity either to become richer or to pass leisure time in ways not open before. Those who argue that an increase in gambling necessarily reduces spending on other things assume that wealth in society is not changed when more opportunities become available. They base their arguments on accounting principles (fitting a world of blissful stability) rather than on an understanding of how people think and act when things are far from being stable.[9]

1. Gambling and the social good

All of the aforementioned criticisms and fears seem minor next to the major indictments of gambling, which are brought out in the following questions:[10]

- Does gambling *cause* an appetite for wealth without effort that undermines the work ethic?

The answer, as we saw, was NO.

- Does gambling elevate money and the quest for material gain at the expense of concern for the "common good"?

The answer, once again, is NO. Some further clarification may be needed with this answer, clarification concerning the notion of the "social good," of the "public interest."

The evidence in previous chapters suggests that for the majority, gambling never elevated money at the expense of other concerns. On the contrary, people gambled because they did not perceive any alternative means of achieving those other concerns: better education for their children, a better family life, help for one's kin. The majority of people gambled not because they loved wealth, but because they would have liked to deal with those "higher" concerns that only the ownership of more wealth would allow.

The reason why a relationship was perceived between increased interest in gambling and diminished interest in traditional concerns was that these two reactions did indeed take place simultaneously. As we saw, when customary ways of life could no longer be maintained, people not only gambled more but also speculated more and bet more frequently on entrepreneurial ventures in many directions. These reactions threatened traditional interests, commercial, religious, and political. Thus, traditional notions of the social good were challenged.. The threatened groups reacted, among other ways by exaggerating the harmful consequences of the new pursuits, by inventing false dangers and spurious social problems, and by making it harder, even in retrospect, to properly evaluate what was going on.

So it is true that there is a positive correlation between the propensity to gamble and the disappearance of some traditionally held notions of the social good. But, there is no causal relationship between them. Both happen when sudden shocks, whose source may not be recognized at the time (like those due to significant demographic changes), disrupt people's customary ways of living and by doing so destroy the status quo and the idea of the social good that this status quo was compatible with.

The positive correlation could have been expected from observations made by Alexis de Tocqueville a long time ago.[11] In *Democracy in America* he stated that riches were well distributed in America, not concentrated, and that the American class structure was characterized by mobility rather than stratification. "Without being exactly either rich or poor," he wrote, most men in America possessed "sufficient property to design the maintenance of order, yet not enough to excite envy. Such men are the natural enemies of violent commotions; their stillness keeps all beneath them and above them still, and secures the balance of the fabric of society."[12] And, one could add, it is this balance that enables a definition of the common good, a definition to which generations may adhere – as long as things stay stable.

Once the balance is destroyed, however, and until people agree about the source of the shock and ways to adapt to it, confusion persists about the common good in particular. Groups who fall behind will advocate some policies in the name of the social good, whereas those who outdo or expect to leapfrog them will advocate others. How can one find one's way out of this maze? Which arguments should be discounted and which not?

If one suggests that finding the path is exactly what social scientists, legal scholars, and historians always have the incentive to do, the answer is inaccurate: sometimes, yes, but not always. The reason for the reservation can be inferred again from Tocqueville's observations. When he continued his reasoning on democracy, he also remarked that although reaching a balance in society has obvious advantages, it also has some disadvantages. Historical accounts, he observed, must be affected by democratic tendencies too. Historians will put the emphasis neither on chance nor on the "deeds and accomplishments of heroes and leaders, but . . . upon mass movements and general causes."[13] How is such a uniform viewpoint shaped among historians and social scientists, within or without universities, in a society that seems to celebrate individualism and originality? Well, says Tocqueville, the perfect liberty of the American mind is an illusion.[14] As Heffner, summarizing Tocqueville's views, puts it: "Once the majority has made up its mind, then all contrary thought must cease, and all controversy must be abandoned, not at the risk of death or physical punishment, but rather at the more subtle and more intolerable pain of ostracism, of being shunned by one's fellows" (1956, p. 20). Probably nothing illustrates better the accuracy of this statement than a glance at the social sciences today and at many historical works, where one can read much about happiness, welfare, the public interest, equality, capital, homogeneity, and mass movements, but much less about envy, hope, chance, entrepreneurship, innovation, and leadership.[15] Thus, among historians and social scientists too, one may find, at times, uniformity of opinion about the nature of policies that promote or contravene the somehow defined social good.

Next an attempt is made to answer two questions: Is there such a thing as an objectively defined view of the social good? And if there is, can we examine various policies in its light?

The answers to both questions are positive. In order to give them, let us turn back to where we started this book: at the origins of words. They will provide the clue to answering the first question.

2. Happiness and luck

The word "happiness," which is linked with the notion of the social good, is derived from *hap*, meaning chance, fortune, a condition due to random occurrences. Gradually, however, "happiness" acquired a different meaning, one linked with a passive state of mind that, it seems to be assumed, could be enjoyed by all (though the Oxford dictionary still defines "happy" as, among other things, "fortunate, lucky"). This linguistic relationship does not seem to be exceptional: Schoeck notes that in Middle High German *gelücke* meant an aimless, unpredictable, and uncontrollable power that shapes events either favorably or unfavorably, and that in German there is today one word (*Glück*) for both happiness and luck.[16]

If one interprets the word "happiness" in its original sense, as referring to good luck, then one can define the social good as the provision of opportunities, of hopes, for having good luck.[17] Isn't it implicit in people's thinking today, in spite of all the linguistic confusion and sterile academic invention of theories about welfare and happiness as passive states of mind, that this is indeed what people mean by happiness in their everyday life? After all, when a baby is born or one ventures into business, the universal wish is "Good luck!" Who needs more than that? Whether one wants good health, children, love, riches, or faith, good luck will bring them and make one, by definition, happy.[18] Providing opportunities to be lucky has nothing to do with, and is in fact incompatible with, Jeremy Bentham's vague, impractical, and nondemocratic criterion for the common good: "the greatest happiness of the great number." Bentham's criterion implies that somehow one can compare and add up people's happiness and base decisions on such an abstract sum.[19] His criterion can also be used to justify restrictions imposed on minorities. Neither implication holds true if the social good is identified with the provision of opportunities to have good luck: No comparisons are needed in order to make a decision about the benefits of a policy, and neither can restrictions be justified.[20] It is in the light of this criterion that the policies discussed in earlier chapters were examined.

Yet one may raise an additional question. Suppose that one accepts this definition of the social good. Now, can one say just how much gambling is socially good? The answer to this question is negative. As we have seen, when things go smoothly and according to expectations, fewer people gamble, whereas when expectations are shattered, more will do so. Although the increased expenditure on gambling may be perceived by some as being too much, the criterion defined above does not allow one to make this statement.

However, one can say that there is too much gambling when the government relies on the gambling sector to raise revenue. Then there might be too much in the sense that the government bureaucracy relies excessively on this sector and does not examine alternative sources of revenue.

In the absence of such intervention, one cannot say that there is too much gambling, and one cannot answer the question how much gambling is socially good, any more than one can answer the question how much fashion is socially good, or how much consumption of alcoholic beverages, sugar, potatoes (remember Ireland?), or books and speeches conducive to nationalist fervor are socially good. One can only give the commonsense answer that too much of anything is not good. What Pascal once said about wine: "No wine, no wisdom / Too much wine – the same," holds equally true for gambling and for speculation too. Indeed, as we saw, most people bet with their heads, not over them, and realize that gambling and speculation are good servants and bad masters. People do not need either bureaucrats or social scientists to remind them of the truth of this statement. As to the addicted minority who already consume too much, they will not heed advice in any case. The solution for this minority can be found in medical rather than legal treatment.

Let us now return to the two initial questions and see what the idea of providing opportunities means precisely in the context of the gambling sector, and thus answer the second question at the same time.

3. Luck and opportunity

Fred Smith is now known as the entrepreneur who has built Federal Express. But before he bet on the idea of providing a rapid, large-scale, and reliable method of delivering mail, he went bankrupt. As a last resort, he went to Las Vegas, was lucky, and won $50,000. He did not gamble either before his bankruptcy or after this win.[21] The $50,000 enabled him to restart his business venture, and the rest of the story is well known. What would have happened if Smith had not had the opportunity to gamble? Who knows?

Smith's experience with the role of games of chance is not novel. Cardano, controversial man-of-all-trades of the Renaissance (he was a physician, an astrologer, and also, according to some, one of the outstanding figures in mathematics), wrote that "in times of great anxiety and grief, [gambling] was considered to be not only allowable, but even beneficial. Also, it is permitted to men in prison, to those condemned to death and to the sick, and therefore the law also permits it in times of grief. For certainly, if any occasion will justify it, none is so worthy of excuse as this one."[22]

Games of chance give hope through additional channels too. Louise Meriwether, in her autobiography *Daddy Was a Number Runner* (1970), shows how the numbers game in New York's Harlem gave hope in the midst of despair and poverty. Income from a "hit" was used for family expenses, and her father's employment as a numbers runner provided an irregular but important source of income.[23]

Thus, permitting gambling gives much more than just the right to play in the hope of winning. Legal permission to play may enable a whole new sector to develop, a sector that provides opportunities for both employment and entrepreneurial venture. Since direct involvement in most segments of this sector has for a long time had a negative connotation among the more fortunate classes, legalization provides new opportunities for the relatively poor. McKibbin, whose prejudice comes to the fore in a few phrases, notes that mass betting was the most successful example of working-class self-help in the modern era in Britain:

It was at every stage a proletarian institution and bore all the characteristics of the British working class. Although illegal it was almost entirely honest.... To some working-class families ... it brought great wealth, to others some money to throw around and a certain flashy style: "they have now a bank account and enjoy the luxury of clean linen and water-tight boots.".... To the unemployed it sometimes meant a temporary job, and young boys were able to scrape a bit extra by operating on its margins. It is very difficult to say how many were employed in any capacity at all by gambling: the whole of the full- and part-time fraternity at most numbered 100,000. (1979, p. 172)

(Does such behavior really reflect a "flashy style"?) At the time, this represented about 1 percent of the total work force, which does not seem so bad in view of the fact that this 1 percent came from amongst the hardest hit. The fact that the gambling sector provides opportunities for the underclass can also be inferred from additional evidence. The leaders of Chicago's underworld in the 1930s, involved mainly with gambling and bootlegging, consisted of young, ambitious new immigrants: 30 percent of the bosses were Italian, 29 percent Irish, 20 percent Jewish, and 12 percent black, and there was not a native-born white American among them (Haller 1970, p. 620). Koeves noted that "one of the most familiar sights in the streets of South America are the street vendors offering [lottery] tickets,... more often than not consisting of old men in rags, barefoot kids, or cripples" (1952, p. 58). It does not seem a wild speculation to state that today in the United States the illegal drug market is fulfilling some of the roles that illegal gambling markets played in the not so distant past.[24]

Thus, there is no doubt that legalizing this sector provides hope and opportunities for the casualties of dynamic societies. The only objection to this conclusion that is sustained after examining the

evidence presented in this book concerns the presence of addicted
players. But gambling is a mass phenomenon, and its study must not
be confused with that of a pathological minority of compulsive
gamblers, just as the examination of a few workaholics, alcoholics,
obese people, womanizers, addicted TV watchers, and addicted ex-
ercisers is irrelevant for a social judgment on the behavior of the
billions who work, drink, eat, love and/or have sex, watch TV or
enjoy exercising with customary frequency.[25]

Yet this confusion has been made and indeed still seems to be
made. Since the nineteenth century, social disorders have frequently
been referred to as either maladies or moral problems. During the
nineteenth century it was said that a bet caused unnatural strain on
the nervous system, making people unfit to work. It was also said
that gambling involved the "suppression of reason, will ... conscience." Mental physiologists claimed that the strain resulted in
serious mischief to the brain and to the balance of people's powers.
Among members of the British Medical Association, the prevailing
view was that gambling and drinking explained the nervous tension
of fin-de-siècle England, and they worried about the hereditary
effects of the gambling mania.[26] Few pointed out that gambling is
not a disease but a symptom of a society's dynamism.

Prohibition further blurred the picture. Then buyers and sellers
involved in a gambling transaction could be associated with "illness"
or could be placed in the class of lawbreakers and become associated
with the "underworld" and its "immoral," non-middle-class elements. Gambling in general, rather than just addiction, could thus be
treated in either technical–medical or moral terms, and could be
given a negative connotation in the minds of men who never gambled
and who, without inquiring into the origins of the relationship
between gambling and the underworld, accepted the view that gambling caused crime and that the solution was either medical intervention or jail.[27]

As we have seen, it is not true that gamblers are either mentally ill
or criminals and that this is why they are or become poor. Rather,
it is the other way around: The poor and the frustrated gamble. So if
gambling is a problem, its solution has to do not with medical
treatment but with a much more general question: What should the
fortunate do with those who are not? What are a community's and
the government's obligations to people who fall behind?

This is the central question that at all times, in all societies, and in all forms of regime people have debated and not been able to agree upon. And they still cannot.[28]

Conclusion

So this is our view on where matters stand today in the history of gambling and of some forms of speculation.

It was not our goal either to present the date of every event or just to describe what happened. What we tried to do instead was to clarify the dissimilarity between past and present and explain why things changed, yet still detect patterns by keeping in mind some constants of human nature. No attempt was made to study gambling in its economic, psychological, or sociological aspects.[29] To divide people's behavior into these narrow, arbitrary, and increasingly remote disciplines, and to try to explain behavior through the tools and the vocabulary used by them, seems to us inappropriate and a method based on erroneous speculation. (Never mind that such speculation has had a long life; astrology has had a long life too.)[30] Could a narrow approach suggest that insurance companies are in part a substitute for belief in magic and witches? Or that games of chance were perceived as God's rivals?

There *are* no economic, sociological, or psychological problems and explanations. There are just problems and explanations. Complex ones, true. Yet solutions to the problems can be found without simplifying too much the frame within which they are examined.[31]

Appendix 1 to Chapter 2
Gambling, decision making, and social ranks: Theories

To devote your whole life to keeping stock, or making phone calls, or selling or buying. To suffer fifty weeks of the year for the sake of a two-week vacation, when all you desire is to be outdoors, with your shirt off. And always to have to get ahead of the next fella. And still – that's how you build a future.

Arthur Miller, Death of a Salesman (1949)

Introduction

"A new idea does not come forth in its mature scientific form. It contains logical ambiguities or errors; the evidence on which it rests is incomplete or indecisive; and its domain of application is exaggerated in certain directions and overlooked in others," wrote Stigler (1965, p. 14) in one of his essays on the history of economics.

These sentences summarize the justification for presenting in detail the model of risk taking and decision making on which the arguments in this book rely, in spite of the fact that its essential features have been presented in R. Brenner 1983, 1985, 1987. For in the previous works approximations were made, details were omitted, and some important implications were overlooked. This appendix presents corrections, puts the model on a sounder footing, and compares it with other models that try to explain decision-making and risk-taking behavior, a comparison that was only partially made in the earlier works.

The points emphasized in this appendix are only those that were judged pertinent to the subject matter covered in this book: gambling, insurance (dealt with in Chapter 4), progressive taxation (dealt with in Chapter 5), and decision making in general (dealt with in Chapters 3–5).

1. Gambling and decision making

Let W_o be one's wealth and let I_o be an interval in the distribution of wealth, defining a class with mean wealth equal to $\bar{W}_o$. This interval defines one's perception of a certain class in society, a class to which the individual expected to belong. $\alpha(\cdot)$ denotes the percentage of people who are richer than $\bar{W}_o$ in the whole society. Then the utility function can be defined as follows:

$$U(W_o, \alpha(W > \bar{W}_o) \mid W_o \in I_o) \tag{1}$$

where

$$\delta U/\delta W_o > 0; \; \delta U/\delta \alpha < 0. \tag{2}$$

The first derivative represents the usual assumption that the marginal utility of wealth is positive, whereas the second may represent sentiments of fear (of being outdone by others), envy, vanity, or ambition.[1] As is shown in R. Brenner 1983, 1985, 1987, this reformulation of the utility function makes sense only when risk or uncertainty is taken into account (words that, as shown there, can be precisely defined and distinguished within this model), and its usefulness stems from the predictions one can derive from it. Let us consider some of them, starting with the simplest.

Let W_o be one's wealth expected to be derived from all investment opportunities, excluding gambling. Let h be the price of a lottery ticket where there is a probability p of winning a large prize H that can propel people up the social ladder. On what variables does the decision to gamble depend? The mathematical translation of this question is:

$$\begin{aligned}
&(1 - p)U(W_o - h, \alpha(W > \bar{W}_o) \mid W_o \in I_o) \\
&+ p \; U(W_o - h + H, \alpha(W > \bar{W}_1) \mid W_o \in I_o) \\
&> U(W_o, \alpha(W > \bar{W}_o) \mid W_o \in I_o)
\end{aligned} \tag{3}$$

where $\bar{W}_1$ is the mean of the wealth distribution in the interval I_1, an interval representing a higher class. (We make the assumption that there is no overlapping between the two intervals I_o and I_1.) The fact that the conditional statements are unchanged suggests that the parameters of the utility function are the same as long as one does not actually win the large prize.

Note that the way the first term is written implies that when individuals spend the amount h on a lottery ticket, they do not take into account that by this expenditure the mean wealth of the class they belong to has been altered, or that the percentage of people in the various classes has changed. These assumptions do not seem strong: If there are a large number of individuals in each class, the individual's expenditure on lottery tickets changes the mean by h/N or H/N, respectively, numbers that are small relative to a group's mean wealth (even if the group is the poorest in society).

Let the utility function be linear in W_o and α, and let us see under what circumstances this inequality is fulfilled:

$$U = aW_o + b\alpha(W > \bar{W}_o) \qquad a > 0, b < 0 \tag{4}$$

$$(1 - p)a(W_o - h) + (1 - p)b\alpha(W > \bar{W}_o)$$
$$+ pa(W_o - h + H) + pb\alpha(W > \bar{W}_1)$$
$$> aW_o + b\alpha(W > \bar{W}_o). \tag{5}$$

If the gamble is fair, that is $(1 - p)h = p(H - h)$ (this is the definition of a fair gamble, since one pays h even if one wins later), condition (5) is reduced to:

$$(1 - p)b\alpha(W > \bar{W}_o) + pb\alpha(W > \bar{W}_1) > b\alpha(W > \bar{W}_o) \tag{6}$$

(since linearity implies risk neutrality, if b is equal to zero). Since $b < 0$, one obtains that the condition to buy such a ticket is:

$$\alpha(W > \bar{W}_1) < \alpha(W > \bar{W}_o). \tag{7}$$

This condition is always fulfilled, since $\alpha(\cdot)$, we recall, denotes the percentage of people who are richer than the respective means in the whole society. Since $\bar{W}_1$ is greater than $\bar{W}_o$, the inequality in (7) always holds.

If the game is unfair, that is, $(1 - p)h > p(H - h)$ (and all lotteries are), one gets:

$$a(pH - h) + (1 - p)b\alpha(W > \bar{W}_o)$$
$$+ pb\alpha(W > \bar{W}_1) > b\alpha(W > \bar{W}_o). \tag{8}$$

Dividing by b on both sides (and recalling that it is negative), one gets:

$$\frac{a}{b} (pH - h) - p\alpha(\bar{W}_1 > W > \bar{W}_o) < 0 \tag{9}$$

where $\alpha(\bar{W}_1 > W > \bar{W}_o)$ denotes the percentage of the population the winner would leapfrog if he or she won the prize (notice that the first term on the left-hand side is positive, since b is negative and the game is unfair). Briefly, the first term in (9) reflects the relative subjective cost of gambling, and the second reflects its perceived benefits.

There is a significant difference between the type of prediction that can be derived from the model presented above and the type of prediction that can be derived from others that have tried to explain gambling behavior (Kahneman and Tversky, and others).[2] One major difference is that the evidence needed to test this model cannot be reproduced in any laboratory experiment. There is no way one can become either rich or poor in a laboratory. Thus, the predictions derived from this model can be confronted with data reflecting behavior in the real world rather than with data obtained in artificial experiments.

An additional difference is that in models where gambling is viewed as a matter of taste (i.e., depending on the shape of the utility function only), one cannot explain – in a falsifiable way – why some people may suddenly start to gamble or stop.[3] Yet it is easy to explain such decisions within this model. Suppose that an individual with wealth $\bar{W}_o$ did not gamble on an unfair lottery, that is:

$$U(W_o, \alpha(W > \bar{W}_o)|W_o \in I_o)$$
$$> (1 - p)U(W_o - h, \alpha(W > \bar{W}_o)|W_o \in I_o)$$
$$+ p\, U(W_o - h + H, \alpha(W > \bar{W}_2)|W_o \in I_o), \qquad (10)$$

I_2 being the interval defined by the distribution within the higher rank, and $\bar{W}_2$ the mean.

Now suppose that one's wealth suddenly diminishes significantly. Will the individual start to gamble on the unfair lottery? Let W_1 be the lower wealth, I_1 the respective interval, and $\bar{W}_1$ the respective mean value. The question can be translated as follows:

$$U(W_1, \alpha(W > \bar{W}_1)|W_o \in I_o)$$
$$< (1 - p)U(W_1 - h, \alpha(W > \bar{W}_1)|W_o \in I_o)$$
$$+ p\, U(W_1 - h + H, \alpha(W > \bar{W}_o)|W_o \in I_o). \qquad (11)$$

The reason for not altering the conditional statements is that the parameters of the utility function were determined by the expectation of belonging to the class defined by the interval I_o. When one's wealth drops suddenly to W_1, the translation in (11) reflects the assumption that aspirations are not instantaneously lowered.[4] As is shown below in discussion of additional predictions of the model, people are expected to behave differently when their aspirations are realized than when they are not, even if they belong to the same class.

When are both inequalities, (9) and (10), fulfilled? Let us once again use the linear function defined in (4) and make the calculations. Condition (10) becomes:

$$aW_o + b\alpha(W > \bar{W}_1) > (1 - p)a(W_o - h)$$
$$+ (1 - p)b\alpha(W > \bar{W}_o) + p\,a(W_o - h + H)$$
$$+ pb\alpha(W > \bar{W}_2), \qquad (12)$$

which, when simplified, turns into the same type of expression as in (9), only with the reverse inequality sign:

$$\frac{a}{b}(pH - h) - p\alpha(\bar{W}_2 > W > \bar{W}_o) > 0, \qquad (13)$$

whereas (11) becomes (just as in (9)):

$$\frac{a}{b}(pH - h) - p\alpha(\bar{W}_o > W > \bar{W}_1) < 0. \qquad (14)$$

A necessary condition for (13) and (14) to be fulfilled is:

$$\alpha(\bar{W}_o > W > \bar{W}_1) > \alpha(\bar{W}_2 > W > \bar{W}_o). \qquad (15)$$

This condition means that the percentage of people between $\bar{W}_o$ and $\bar{W}_2$ had to be smaller than that between $\bar{W}_1$ and $\bar{W}_o$ in order for the individual to start gambling when a significant part of his or her wealth was lost. If the distribution of wealth within each interval (I_o, I_1, etc.) that defines a class is normal, condition (15) requires that there are many people at the bottom and fewer and fewer as one gets closer to the top.

Notice that for other games of chance, where winnings are small – that is, of a magnitude that keeps individuals within their class – the model presented here is not illuminating. One must deal with those games either in a model where the choice to be explained is the one about the allocation of one's time, or in models where gambling is a matter of taste and where whether or not people are involved in the act depends entirely on local properties of the utility function and, in Kahneman and Tversky's descriptive framework (1979), on deviations between realized wealth and the level of aspiration. It should also be reemphasized that the term "small" in the model presented here is defined relative to one's wealth and hence to whether or not the losses or gains will move an individual out of his or her class. A prize of $100,000 may be large for some, but a loss or a gain of $100,000 may be small for others. For people who are relatively poor, $100,000 may move them up a rank, and the model presented here may shed light on their attitudes toward gambling. However, for people whose wealth is more than, let us say, $1,000,000 and when the distribution in their class is defined over a range of, let us say, $750,000 to $1,250,000, winning or losing $100,000 causes no shift in rank. Thus, the latter group's participation in games of chance cannot be explained by the model presented here, but by another (i.e., one concerning the allocation of time).[5]

In conclusion, two predictions have now been made: a static one, that the relatively poor have a greater incentive to gamble on lotteries than the relatively rich; and a dynamic one, that people who did not gamble may start doing so when they suddenly lose a significant part of their wealth. Gambling represents one of their hopes for restoring their wealth.

2. Why do lotteries have multiple prizes?

Let us describe what factors determine the individual's choice between participating in a game of chance that gives away $1 million with a probability of one in a million, and one that gives away one prize of $500,000 with a probability of one in a million and five prizes of $100,000 with a probability of one in a million (assuming that the price of the ticket is the same and is $1).

Translating this choice in terms of the linear utility function used above, one finds that the second prize structure will be preferred to the one with one large prize if the next inequality is fulfilled (taking here, just for simplicity's sake, the actual wealth rather than the mean in the respective $\alpha(\cdot)$ terms):

$$\frac{1}{10^6} \left[a(W_o + 1,000,000) + b\alpha(W > W_o + 1,000,000) \right]$$

$$+ \left(1 - \frac{1}{10^6} \right) (a(W_o - 1) + b\alpha(W > W_o - 1))$$

$$< \frac{1}{10^6} [a(W_o + 500,000) + b\alpha(W > W_o + 500,000)]$$

$$+ \frac{5}{10^6} [a(W_o + 100,000) + b\alpha(W > W_o + 100,000)]$$

$$+ \left(1 - \frac{1}{10^6}\right) (a(W_o - 1) + b\alpha(W > W_o - 1)). \qquad (16)$$

Condition (16) translates the question: Under what conditions are multiple large prizes preferred over one large prize? By rearranging it, one obtains:

$$b\alpha(W > W_o + 1,000,000) + 5[-a + b\alpha(W > W_o - 1)]$$
$$< b\alpha(W > W_o + 500,000) + 5b\alpha(W > W_o + 100,000). \qquad (17)$$

Since a is positive, this holds if:

$$b\alpha(W > W_o + 1,000,000) + 5b\alpha(W > W_o - 1)$$
$$< b\alpha(W > W_o + 500,000)$$
$$+ 5b\alpha(W > W_o + 1,000,000) \qquad (18)$$

(for an additional number – $5a$ – would be subtracted from the left-hand side). Since b is negative, a sufficient condition for inequality (17) to be fulfilled is:

$$\alpha(W > W_o + 1,000,000) + 5\alpha(W > W_o - 1)$$
$$> \alpha(W > W_o + 500,000) + 5\alpha(W > W_o + 100,000). \qquad (19)$$

The pyramidal distribution of wealth typical of societies across countries and time where lotteries with large prizes existed easily fulfills this condition: Although there are a few millionaires, there are many more people at the bottom. If, let us say, 1% of the population have net wealth above $1,000,000, 3% have more than $500,000, 20% more than $100,000, and 50% more than W_o, then the numbers that appear in inequality (19) would be:

$$0.01 + 5(0.5) > 0.03 + 5(0.2). \qquad (20)$$

The existence of multiple large prizes thus suggests that people prefer the somewhat greater chance of belonging to the middle classes (with five prizes of $100,000 and one of $500,000) to the smaller chance of jumping higher (with just one prize of $1,000,000) and the greater chance of staying where they are – at the bottom. Recall that the sale of fractional tickets together with the provision of one large prize provides an even better choice. However, in both England and the United States the sale of fractional tickets is outlawed.[6]

But why are there a large number of small prizes? The $10, $100, or even $1,000 prize will not make people really richer, in the sense of moving them out of their class; it will not make the poor belong to the middle classes.[7] If one assumes that these small "consolation prizes" are essentially refunds that are an inducement to try again, their existence does not contradict the prediction of the model (since the motivation for playing is still the hope of winning the big prize). The issue is empirical: Do people rebet the small winnings? As noted in the text, the answer to this question is yes.

3. Why do people take out insurance?

A problem frequently mentioned by economists who want to shed light on gambling behavior is that in the usual expected utility framework, people could either gamble (in which case the second derivative of the utility function had to be positive) or insure themselves (in which case the second derivative had to be negative), but never do both (since the same utility function for the same wealth cannot have simultaneously a negative and a positive second derivative). But it is a fact that people both gamble and insure themselves.

It should be noted that this is a difficulty only if one wants to explain both phenomena – taking out insurance and gambling – by relying on a model of risk taking. If, however, one views gambling as a pastime and views only insurance as linked with risk taking, there is no contradiction in the fact that the same people are involved in both activities. Whereas this viewpoint may offer partial reconciliation of the problem that the same people gamble and insure themselves, it is hard to accept the idea that buying lotteries should be viewed in the context of the allocation of one's time.[8]

Friedman and Savage (1948) tried to solve the inconsistency differently, namely, by assuming that at relatively high and low levels of wealth the marginal utility of wealth decreases, while at middle levels it increases. This additional restriction on the shape of the utility function describes the observation that people both gamble and insure themselves, but it leads to new inconsistencies. As both Alchian (1953) and Markowitz (1952) have pointed out, if this were the shape of the utility function, the relatively rich would never insure themselves against events in which large losses with small probabilities occur, and they would never gamble. But they do both. Markowitz tried to deal with these implications by imposing further restrictions on the utility function. But he recognized that his views could not be verified. Moreover, Friedman himself recognized that his method of using the existence of multiple prizes to rationalize the upper concave section of the utility function was inaccurate.

Yet it is easy to show within the model presented here why the same individual would both gamble and insure himself. The first strategy is used for trying to get richer and the second to prevent falling significantly behind.

Let h be the insurance premium, $1 - p$ the probability that nothing will happen, and p the probability that a significant amount, H, could be lost. The condition for taking out this insurance is (for the utility function used above):

$$a(W_o - h) + b\alpha(W > \bar{W}_o) > (1 - p)aW_o$$
$$+ (1 - p)b\alpha(W > \bar{W}_o)$$
$$+ p\ a(W_o - H) + pb\alpha(W > \bar{W}_2) \tag{21}$$

where $\bar{W}_2$ is the mean of the distribution in the interval I_2 to which $W_o - H$ would belong. (21) can be rewritten as follows:

$$-ah + paH > pb[\alpha(W > \bar{W}_2) - \alpha(W > \bar{W}_o)]. \tag{22}$$

If the insurance is fair, that is $(1 - p)h = pH,$[9] one obtains:

$$-pah > pb\alpha(\bar{W}_o > W > \bar{W}_2), \tag{23}$$

or, dividing by pb (and recalling that $b < o$), one gets:

$$\frac{a}{b}h + \alpha(\bar{W}_o > W > \bar{W}_2) > 0. \tag{24}$$

Condition (24) shows that the decision to insure depends on the relative costs and benefits, h being the insurance fee, and $\alpha(\cdot)$ the percentage of the population one prevents oneself being outdone by when one takes out the insurance. Notice that there is no contradiction between conditions (24) and (7). The difference between the two is that when insurance is considered, one looks at the distribution of wealth below one's wealth, whereas when gambling is considered, one looks at the distribution above one's rank.

The same straightforward exercise as is done for gambling can be done now to show that if people did not take out insurance in the past, they might decide to do so if they suddenly become richer. The steps for the proof are the same as those in conditions (12)–(15). Thus, here too we have essentially two types of prediction, one static and the other dynamic.

4. Demand for gambling and insurance, and stopping rules

Conditions (9) and (24) can also be used to gain additional – this time familiar – insights. In condition (9), the more unfair the game is, the greater the value of the first term and, *ceteris paribus*, the less likely it becomes that the inequality is fulfilled. Thus, demand for lotteries should diminish.

However, the larger the prize H and the larger the group one may leapfrog, *ceteris paribus*, the greater the demand. Thus, demand for lotteries depends on their price, on the prizes they distribute, and on the distribution of wealth.

According to condition (24), the higher the insurance fee, h, *ceteris paribus*, the less likely that the inequality is fulfilled (since h is multiplied by $\frac{a}{b}$, and b is negative). However, if $\alpha(\cdot)$ is greater, then, *ceteris paribus*, it is more likely that the inequality is fulfilled.

One may now raise the following question: Even if it is true that losing \$5 on a lottery ticket will not change one's rank in society, what happens if one buys a hundred, a thousand, or more tickets? When does one stop buying them? There are two answers to this question within this model, one referring to the statics and the second to the dynamics of the model. In the static case, the optimal number of tickets (which determines the probability), n, is derived from the usual condition, that is, when the expected marginal utility of the cost equals the expected marginal benefit (of jumping to a higher rank). In the dynamic context, however, the answer is different: If individuals have lost a relatively large amount by playing in unfair games of chance, they may perceive that they cannot restore their position in the distribution of wealth by gambling. They may then lower their aspirations (thus changing their reference point) and gamble less (since the perceived benefits in terms of utility have diminished). Or they may change their risk-taking strategies and bet on entrepreneurial acts. The reversal of decisions provides, in the dynamic context of this model, the necessary "stopping rule," to the examination of which we now turn.

5. Decision making and uncertainty

Suppose that an individual, content with his or her rank in society, owns wealth W_o and avoids some uncertain strategies. Assume that the individual perceives that by pursuing one such strategy he or she may lose the amount P and gain the amount H. Let us make a number of different assumptions and examine the consequences.

(a) Assume that by losing P the individual would not fall to a lower rank, but by gaining H he or she might move to a higher rank (characterized by $\tilde{W}_2$ and $\bar{W}_2$). If the individual initially, when owning wealth W_o, avoided taking such a risk, the condition for the linear utility function at that time must be:

$$aW_o + b\alpha(W > \bar{W}_o) > p\, a(W_o - P)$$
$$+ pb\alpha(W > \bar{W}_o) + (1 - p)a(W_o + H)$$
$$+ (1 - p)b\alpha(W > \bar{W}_2). \tag{25}$$

Rewriting, one obtains:

$$b\alpha(W > \bar{W}_o) > -paP + (1 - p)aH$$
$$+ pb\alpha(W > \bar{W}_o) + (1 - p)b\alpha(W > \bar{W}_2). \tag{26}$$

Will the individual undertake this same strategy if his or her wealth suddenly *diminishes* to W_D (W_D still belonging to the distribution $\tilde{W}_o$)? The translation of this question is:

$$aW_D + b\alpha(W > \bar{W}_o) < pa(W_D - P)$$
$$+ pb\alpha(W > \bar{W}_o) + (1 - p)a(W_D + H)$$
$$+ (1 - p)b\alpha(W > \bar{W}_2), \tag{27}$$

assuming that even $W_D - P$ still belongs to the interval over which $\tilde{W}_o$ is distributed, and $W_D + H$ to that over which $\tilde{W}_2$ is distributed. The answer is no, since (27) can be rewritten as:

$$b\alpha(W > \bar{W}_o) < -paP + (1 - p)aH$$
$$+ pb\alpha(W > \bar{W}_o) + (1 - p)b\alpha(W > \bar{W}_2), \tag{28}$$

which contradicts condition (26).

(b) Suppose now that W_D is of such magnitude that $W_D - P$

may even put the individual into a lower class, characterized by the interval I_1, the distribution $\tilde{W}_1$, and the mean $\bar{W}_1$ (although W_D still belongs to $\tilde{W}_o$). Will the individual then bet on the previously shunned strategy? Instead of (27), we now would have:

$$aW_D + b\alpha(W > \bar{W}_o) < pa(W_D - P) \\ + pb\alpha(W > \bar{W}_1) + (1 - p)a(W_D + H) \\ + (1 - p)b\alpha(W > \bar{W}_2), \tag{29}$$

which can be rewritten as:

$$b\alpha(W > \bar{W}_o) < -paP + (1 - p)aH \\ + bp\alpha(W > \bar{W}_1) + (1 - p)b\alpha(W > \bar{W}_2). \tag{30}$$

For both (27) and (30) to be fulfilled, one must have:

$$pb\alpha(W > \bar{W}_o) + (1 - p)b\alpha(W > \bar{W}_2) \\ < pb\alpha(W > \bar{W}_1) + (1 - p)b\alpha(W > \bar{W}_2) \tag{31}$$

(since the terms on the left-hand side of the two inequalities are the same). This would imply that:

$$pb\alpha(W > \bar{W}_o) < pb\alpha(W > \bar{W}_1), \tag{32}$$

which, since b is negative, would lead to:

$$\alpha(W > \bar{W}_o) > \alpha(W > \bar{W}_1), \tag{33}$$

which can never be true, for the percentage of people above $\bar{W}_1$, the lower mean wealth, must always be greater than that above $\bar{W}_o$, the mean wealth at a higher rank.

The results in (a) and (b) suggest that if people avoided taking some risks before, they would not take them if they became *somewhat* poorer ("somewhat" being defined here as meaning that the loss did not move them to a lower rank).

(c) What will this individual's reaction be if the spread between loss and gain (P and H) is increased, but the expected value of the strategy does not change (i.e., only the variance is increased)?[10]

Here, once again, one must make a distinction among a number of possibilities:

(c_1) If the spread between P and H is increased, but in such a way that both $W_o - P$ and $W_o + H$, for all possible values of P and H still belong to the interval I_o, then if the initial strategy was avoided, so will all the rest be.

(c_2)   Suppose that the spread is increased and the values of $\alpha(\cdot)$ are such that whereas $W_o - P_1$ belongs to I_o, $W_o + H_1$ would now belong to a higher rank, defined by I_2 over which $\tilde{W}_2$ is distributed. Then for the individual to bet on this strategy, the two conditions that must be fulfilled are the following. The fact that the individual initially avoided the strategy where both $W_o - P$ and $W_o + H$ belonged to I_o only implies that the expected value of the strategy had to be negative. However, if $W_o - P_1$ belongs to I_o, but $W_o + H_1$ to I_2, one finds that, in order to undertake this strategy:

$$b\alpha(W > \bar{W}_o) < -paP_1 + (1 - p)aH_1$$
$$+ pb\alpha(W > \bar{W}_o) + (1 - p)b\alpha(W > \bar{W}_2) \qquad (34)$$

or that

$$a[-pP_1 + (1 - p)H_1] - (1 - p)b\alpha(W > \bar{W}_o)$$
$$+ (1 - p)b\alpha(W > \bar{W}_2) > 0. \qquad (35)$$

But the expected value of the strategy (the term in brackets) is left unaltered, and from the initial condition we know that it must be negative. Thus, dropping the indexes under P and H, (35) can be rewritten as:

$$a[-pP + (1 - p)H] - (1 - p)b[\alpha(W > \bar{W}_2)$$
$$-\alpha(W > \bar{W}_o)] > 0, \qquad (36)$$

and this condition may be fulfilled. For although the first term is negative, the second is positive (since both b and the difference in the second set of brackets are negative).

This result suggests that whereas people may avoid taking smaller risks, they may be willing to take bigger ones, the words "smaller" and "bigger" being defined relative to one's wealth and to the discrepancies among ranks. One implication of this conclusion is that whereas people may avoid playing some unfair games of chance (where losses and gains would maintain them within the initial class), that does not necessarily imply that they may not undertake some entrepreneurial gambles with a negative expected value.[11]

(c_3)   Let us relax the assumption that when the variability of the strategy is increased, H may move one up the ladder, whereas losing P does not move one down. Assume instead that by losing P one drops to the interval over which $\tilde{W}_1$ is distributed. Then instead of

(34) one gets (dropping for simplicity's sake the indexes under P and H):

$$b\alpha(W > \bar{W}_o) < a[-pP + (1 - p)H] \\ + pb\alpha(W > \bar{W}_1) + (1 - p)b\alpha(W > \bar{W}_2). \tag{37}$$

Rewriting, one obtains:

$$a[-pP + (1 - p)H] + pb[\alpha(W > \bar{W}_1) - \alpha(W > \bar{W}_o)] \\ + (1 - p)b[\alpha(W > \bar{W}_2) - \alpha(W > \bar{W}_o)] > 0. \tag{38}$$

Whereas the first two terms are negative, the third is positive (as in (c_2)). Thus, in principle, such behavior is possible. Inequality (38) implicitly requires conditions that may provide us with an intuition of what may be hiding behind such behavior. In order for (38) to hold, at least the last term in absolute value must be larger than the second; that is:

$$(1 - p)\,[\alpha(W > \bar{W}_o) - \alpha(W > \bar{W}_2)] \\ > p[\alpha(W > \bar{W}_1) - \alpha(W > \bar{W}_o)], \tag{39}$$

which implies that

$$\frac{1 - p}{p} > \frac{\alpha(\bar{W}_o > W > \bar{W}_1)}{\alpha(\bar{W}_2 > W > W_o)}. \tag{40}$$

Since from the initial condition (obtained by assuming that the individual avoided the game with the small variance) we know that the expected value of the game must be negative, it must also be true that:

$$\frac{1 - p}{p} < \frac{P}{H}, \tag{41}$$

implying that:

$$\frac{P}{H} > \frac{\alpha(\bar{W}_o > W > \bar{W}_1)}{\alpha(\bar{W}_2 > W > W_o)}. \tag{42}$$

For a pyramidal rank structure, the term on the right-hand side is greater than 1, which implies that the loss, P, must be greater than the gain, H, and also that the probability p must be less than 0.5. For (40) implies that:

$$\frac{1-p}{p} > 1. \tag{43}$$

Pursuing such a strategy could be labeled obsessive. It suggests an individual who is undertaking ventures with a negative expected value in order to reach the top. Yet it may happen.

(d)   Consider now another possibility when an individual is reacting to a sudden diminution in wealth. Suppose that W_D is such that it moves the individual out of his class. Then if the individual pursues the strategy one must have:

$$\begin{aligned}
a W_D + b\alpha(W > \bar{W}_1) &> pa(W_D - P) \\
&+ pb\alpha(W > \bar{W}_1) + (1 - p)a(W_D + H) \\
&+ (1 - p)b\alpha(W > \bar{W}_2),
\end{aligned} \tag{44}$$

assuming that $W_D - P$ belongs to the interval I_1 but H is large enough so that $W_D + H$ belongs to I_2, which characterizes the rank above that described by $\tilde{W}_o$. Let us see the condition under which both (25) and (44) are fulfilled. First let us rewrite (44):

$$\begin{aligned}
b\alpha(W > \bar{W}_1) &< -paP + (1 - p)aH \\
&+ pb\alpha(W > \bar{W}_1) + (1 - p)b\alpha(W > \bar{W}_2).
\end{aligned} \tag{45}$$

Let us now rewrite both (28) and (45):

$$\begin{aligned}
(1 - p)b\alpha(W > \bar{W}_o) &> -paP + (1 - p)aH \\
&+ (1 - p)b\alpha(W > \bar{W}_2);
\end{aligned} \tag{46}$$

$$\begin{aligned}
(1 - p)b\alpha(W > \bar{W}_1) &< -paP + (1 - p)aH \\
&+ (1 - p)b\alpha(W > \bar{W}_2).
\end{aligned} \tag{47}$$

Since the terms on the right-hand side are the same, it follows that:

$$b\alpha(W > \bar{W}_o) > b\alpha(W > \bar{W}_1), \tag{48}$$

an inequality that is always fulfilled (since b is negative and $\bar{W}_1$ is smaller than $\bar{W}_o$), whatever the subjective values given to P, H, and p. Once again, it should be noted that an additional implicit assumption behind this exercise is that although the individual's wealth dropped to W_D, the parameters of the utility function are not changed, implying that the conditional statement is still that the individual's aspirations (of belonging to the class characterized by $\tilde{W}_o$) have not been altered.

(e)   Let us weaken the assumptions in (d) and assume that $W_D + H$ is just expected to restore one's rank, rather than increase it to the class represented by the distribution $\tilde{W}_2$. Then instead of (45) one obtains:

$$b\alpha(W > \bar{W}_1) < -paP + (1 - p)aH$$
$$+ pb\alpha(W > \bar{W}_1) + (1 - p)b\alpha(W > \bar{W}_o). \tag{49}$$

For conditions (26) and (49) to be fulfilled, a necessary condition is that:

$$b\alpha(W > \bar{W}_o) - b\alpha(W > \bar{W}_1) > pb\alpha(W > \bar{W}_o)$$
$$+ (1 - p)b\alpha(W > \bar{W}_2) - pb\alpha(W > \bar{W}_1)$$
$$- (1 - p)ba(W > \bar{W}_o). \tag{50}$$

(This is obtained from (26) and (49) by doing the following operation: if $m > n$ and $p < q$, then $m - p > n - q$.) Reorganizing (50), one gets:

$$\alpha(W > \bar{W}_o) > \tfrac{1}{2}[\alpha(W > \bar{W}_1) + \alpha(W > \bar{W}_2)]. \tag{51}$$

(f)   Are the predictions different if, instead of assuming that one's wealth drops, one assumes that a fraction of the group to which the individual aspired to belong becomes suddenly richer?

Assume that initially an individual avoided taking a risk when $\alpha(W > \bar{W}_o) = \alpha_o$. Let $\alpha_1(W > \bar{W}_o) = \alpha_1 > \alpha_o$ (since some of the people belonging to the distribution $\tilde{W}_o$ became suddenly richer and now belong to the distribution $\tilde{W}_2'$). Assume, however, that although $\tilde{W}_o'$ and $\tilde{W}_2'$ are the new distributions, their means did *not* change; i.e., $\bar{W}_o' = \bar{W}_1$ and $\bar{W}_2' = \bar{W}_2$. Assume also that no other shifts occurred, so that $W - P$ belongs to the interval I_1, which is thus unaltered. Then in order for the inequality to be reversed, we must have:

$$aW_o + b\alpha_1(W > \bar{W}_o) < pa(W_o - P)$$
$$+ pb\alpha_1(W > \bar{W}_1) + (1 - p)a(W_o + H)$$
$$+ (1 - p)b\alpha_1(W > \bar{W}_2). \tag{52}$$

By rearranging (52), one obtains:

$$b\alpha_1(W > (\bar{W}_o) < -paP + (1 - p)aH$$
$$+ pb\alpha_1(W > \bar{W}_1) + (1 - p)b\alpha_1(W > \bar{W}_2). \tag{53}$$

Recall that the condition for avoiding this same risk was:

$$b\alpha(W > \bar{W}_o) > -paP + (1 - p)aH$$
$$+ pb\alpha(W > \bar{W}_1) + (1 - p)b\alpha(W > \bar{W}_2). \tag{54}$$

For both (53) and (54) to be fulfilled, we obtain, by making the same operation as for obtaining condition (51):

$$b\alpha(W > \bar{W}_o) - b\alpha_1(W > \bar{W}_o) > pb\alpha(W > \bar{W}_1)$$
$$+ (1 - p)b\alpha(W > \bar{W}_2) - pb\alpha_1(W > \bar{W}_1)$$
$$- (1 - p)b\alpha_1(W > \bar{W}_2). \tag{55}$$

$\alpha(W > \bar{W}_1) = \alpha_1(W > \bar{W}_1)$, since we assumed that there were changes only in ranks *above* that identified by $\tilde{W}_1$. $\alpha_1 (W > \bar{W}_o)$ equals the fraction of people who jumped from the rank previously characterized by $\tilde{W}_o$ to the one previously characterized by $\tilde{W}_2$ (and who are now characterized by $\tilde{W}'_o$ and $\tilde{W}'_2$, with the means unaltered). Let us assume that people who moved to the distribution $\tilde{W}_2$ are equally distributed around $\bar{W}_2$. Then the difference between $\alpha(W > \bar{W}_2)$ and $\alpha_1(W > \bar{W}_2)$ equals $\frac{1}{2}(\alpha_1(W > \bar{W}_o) - \alpha(W > \bar{W}_1))$. Thus (55) is reduced to (recalling that $b < o$):

$$\alpha(W > \bar{W}_o) - \alpha_1(W > \bar{W}_o)$$
$$< (1 - p)[\alpha(W > \bar{W}_2) - \alpha_1(W > \bar{W}_2)]. \tag{56}$$

Since $\alpha_1(W > \bar{W}_o) > \alpha(W > \bar{W}_o)$ and $\alpha_1(W > \bar{W}_2) > \alpha(W > \bar{W}_2)$, we obtain:

$$1 > \tfrac{1}{2}(1 - p), \tag{57}$$

which is always fulfilled. Thus, although the conditions are different, we still find that when individuals are outdone by their fellows, even if their wealth is not changed, they might now take a risk that previously they were unwilling to take. More will be said on the implications of this result when the subject of information is discussed.

(g) How can this model be linked with discussions of changes in relative prices?

A *significant* change in relative prices has two effects. First, it alters the benefits, H, and costs, P, of pursuing some ventures, since in particular the benefits of finding substitutes for the product whose relative price has increased have also increased. At the same time, such a change in relative prices may also change people's positions in the distribution of wealth. This is the mechanism through which, within this model, equilibrium may be restored when an innovation that substitutes for the product that became scarcer is found.

In Chapters 3 and 4 we shall use the various predictions derived from this section.

6. Maximization

The assumption of maximization has been implicit in the calculations up to this point, and, as shown, it is not inconsistent with the assumption that some measure of relative rank also determines one's welfare. On the contrary, it is the latter assumptions that play a central role in explaining one's attitudes toward gambling and insurance, and also one's willingness to take risks when suddenly outdone by other people. It should be emphasized that it is the assumption of maximization that is implicit behind the conditions obtained for reversing the initial inequalities.

In the concluding chapter of his book *Uncertainty in Microeconomics* (1979), Hey, for a number of reasons, criticizes the traditional approaches to the subject of risk:

Consider . . . the optimisation problems that economic agents are supposed to be solving. Most of these problems are so complicated that the economic theorist who publishes the model has probably spent several months finding the solution (and the few readers who bother to check his mathematics will probably find it equally difficult). These optimisation problems are so complicated that the "as if" methodology of economics is stretched to breaking point. Are we seriously suggesting that we are modelling economic behavior? (p. 232)

The answer to the last question seems negative, and it is linked with the next issue that Hey raises. He remarks that "the essential feature of von Neumann-Morgenstern utility theory [is] that it conceives of choice as being a once-and-for-all affair. (A sequence of choices is reduced essentially to a single choice – strategy.) Is this how we economic agents actually behave?" (pp. 232–3). The answer he gives is negative and suggests that the way we behave is that we take a decision now and, depending on how it turns out, may or may not revise it. Such a sequential decision-making process is indeed one of the characteristic features of the dynamics in this model.

It should also be noted that it is only when risk is taken into account that the model presented above makes predictions that may be falsified. Otherwise, in a model where no risks are formally introduced, the assumption of including the additional variable in the utility function ($\alpha(\cdot)$ with a negative sign) leads to no useful insights. The interpretation given to this variable is that it may reflect one's ambition; one's fear of falling behind, of being outdone by one's fellows; or one of the seven deadly sins – envy. (Some more philosophical interpretations of the utility function are given in R. Brenner 1983, 1985.)

7. Risk, uncertainty, and information

In spite of the similarity between the mathematical expression of an individual's decision to gamble and that of the decision to pursue some strategies that he or she has never tried before (or, indeed, no individual has tried), there are significant differences between them.

For lotteries, the value of the monetary prizes and prices of tickets is the same for everyone who plays the game. In contrast, when some venture is pursued, the value of the "prize," H, as well as that of the cost, P, differs among individuals. And the probability here represents a *subjective* judgment by an individual, and there is no way to prove whether he or she is right or wrong: The venture may never have been tried before. This contrasts with lotteries and insurance, in which probability is defined in terms of processes that can be repeated many times and in which comparisons can be made between the probabilities facing different people.

Let us, then, make a distinction between two situations. Suppose that in one the distribution of wealth is maintained; that is, no shift among ranks occurs. (By what mechanism such stability is maintained is explained in R. Brenner 1983, ch. 2; 1985, ch. 2.) In such a society people still take risks. They may gamble on games of chance where the outcomes are relatively insignificant, they may buy a defective product, and so forth. Yet people are insured against major losses; that is, losses that could lower their rank. The provision of such insurance – evidence about the various forms insurance takes is presented elsewhere[12] – prevents, within this model, people from undertaking new ventures in general and entrepreneurial and innovative ones in particular. An outsider looking at such a society will perceive that equilibrium or stability has been achieved and maintained; no innovations of any nature take place. Generation after generation, the same products are produced, and no additional wealth is created.

Consider now a situation in which people can move up and down the social ladder. In such a situation, innovations and ventures of all types take place (criminal as well as entrepreneurial). Wealth is both created and destroyed. An outsider may characterize such a situation as that of either disequilibrium or dynamic equilibrium. Entrepreneurial ventures represent, from the individual's viewpoint, a search for ways of adapting to the new circumstances imposed by shocks that are not under his or her control.

Another way to make a distinction between the two situations would be to call the first risky and the second uncertain. This distinction recalls Keynes 1921, but in particular Knight 1921, who also argued that only the latter situation results in "economic profits." The link between such profits and uncertainty in this model is simple. Only in the latter situation are innovations brought to life by entrepreneurs, whose rewards for discovering demands will be measured by others as economic profits.[13]

These distinctions also lead to a better understanding of the various meanings that can be given to the word "information." Suppose one examines a situation referred to above as "risky" or "stable," where no innovations or entrepreneurial acts, but only imitations, take place. In such circumstances the decision whether or not to adopt a technique has nothing to do with inclination toward taking risks, but with other variables: one's wealth or one's ability to learn and process transferred information. In contrast, suppose we are in a situation defined as uncertain, where people bet on new strategies and bring their ideas to life through an entrepreneurial venture (in particular, speculating in financial markets, as discussed in Chapter 4). In such a situation one cannot just speak about the "transfer of information." Information is created when an individual bets on a new, noncustomary idea and pursues it.

Suppose that during this process an individual strikes it lucky and outdoes his or her fellows. Success provides to the outdone members the information that some strategy that may not have crossed their minds before is now feasible. Such a revelation not only provides information about new opportunities but also, as shown in the preceding technical sections, changes the opportunity cost of staying within the initial rank: The successful person becomes a permanent reminder of the outdone people's timidity.

8. Risk and wealth

The fact that the richer avoid gambling on lotteries and insure themselves, and the fact that those who fall or fear falling behind are more likely to innovate than are those whose realized wealth provides them with a rank that exceeds their aspirations, does not imply either that the richer do not take risks or that they will not take risks that a poorer man may avoid.

On the contrary; as pointed out below, they may take risks, although the types of risk discussed here are different in their nature from those discussed when deviations from traditional behavior were examined, and fit into a framework defined in the preceding section as risky (and in Chapter 4 as investment).

Suppose that a new practice or a new technology was adopted at one point, knowledge about it spread, and both the probabilities of its being used and the monetary costs and benefits involved in adopting it are known. At such a point, the practice is no longer an innovation, and inclination to risk may not be the major element in a decision to adopt it or not. Rather, differences in wealth may explain the different attitudes toward adoption of such now-customary investment opportunities.

In order to make this point clear, consider the following examples. Suppose that there are a hundred independent investment opportunities. The monetary cost of each project is $10,000 and each has a probability of success of 0.1 and a probability of failure of 0.9. Success results in the individual's benefiting in the amount of $200,000 at present value. Then the decision to invest in *one* such project depends on whether or not the term in (58) (using the same notations as before),

$$0.9U(W_o - 10,000, \alpha(W > \bar{W}_o))$$
$$+ 0.1(W_o + 200,000, \alpha(W > \bar{W}_2)), \qquad (58)$$

is greater or smaller than $U(W_o, \alpha(W > \bar{W}_o))$, where W_o takes into account all the alternative investment opportunities.

The decision to invest in *more than one* project is, however, different, since the probability of finding oneself with more wealth than one started with is increased. For the probability of just breaking even in the preceding numerical example is 0.9763; the individual needs just five successes out of a hundred. Thus, for somebody who can find $1 million to invest in the hundred projects, instead of a 0.9 probability that he may be worse off and 0.1 that he may be better off (probability defined in terms of the individual project) there is a 0.9763 probability of success (defined in terms of the profitability of the whole portfolio), and a probability of 0.003 of losing the whole $1 million invested:

$$P(0 \text{ success}) = \frac{100!}{0!100!} (0.1)^0 (0.9)^{100} = 0.003. \qquad (59)$$

Thus, the explanation for why one individual rather than another may pursue one or more of these "risky" projects may have more to do with differences in budget constraints (including the ability to obtain credit) and the related ability to diversify the portfolio and lower risks than with differences in inclination toward taking risks. Remark, however, that neither the calculations made here nor the comparison made above can be used when innovations – that is, deviations from customary behavior – are taken into account.

9. Stability, redistribution, and progressive taxation

Remark that the mathematical conditions examined above look at the circumstances in which people may suddenly deviate from traditional behavior and bet on a risky strategy, which may be of either an entrepreneurial or a criminal nature. By just looking at the mathematical conditions one cannot make a distinction between the two. Although at first sight it seems as if it would be easy to distinguish between the two strategies if one looks at the final outcomes – criminal acts having the impact of redistributing wealth or even destroying it, and innovative, entrepreneurial ones of creating it – it is not easy to make the distinction, since the final outcome may be observed only long after the act takes place. For example, acts that may destroy some goods now may lead to expectations of greater wealth.

It is easy to illustrate this statement by examining the following question. Was Robin Hood a criminal or an innovator, a social reformer? Suppose that his actions both redistributed and destroyed stocks of goods. At the same time, his acts may have led to expectations of reforms (tax reforms in particular). Such expectations may lead a majority to expect more entrepreneurial acts in the future. Do Robin Hood's actions then increase or diminish wealth? The definitional problem in this example and the ambivalent answer arise because it is assumed, implicitly, that people do not agree with the present distribution of wealth. Where there is such disagreement, people fight not only with swords but with words too. (That is why the same person is called by one an innovator and by another a criminal.)[14]

Assume, however, that there is an agreement as to what the term "crime" means, and that the criminal acts examined are such that either a monetary reward or destroying the wealth of others is possible. Then the predictions made above concerning the bet on risky ventures in general holds true for criminal acts in particular. For, once again, the probability p and the value of the cost, P (which includes the effects of loss of reputation, loss of trust, a prison term, etc.), are subjective. Thus, within this model no predictions can be made about the propensity of the poor to commit crimes. Instead, those who suddenly fall behind are the ones whose propensity to commit crimes increases. This prediction should not be surprising. The evidence is consistent with it[15] (after all, the great majority of the poor during "normal" times do not commit crimes). And many writers have given, intuitively, the answer that "unthinking obedience" (Knight's words, which receive a literal interpretation in this model)[16] explains why the majority of poorer people do not commit crimes.

It is a straightforward exercise to link this result with the willingness to redistribute wealth. Suppose that everybody in society realizes that this is how people behave; that is, that those whose wealth is suddenly diminished are among those more likely to commit crimes or undertake revolutionary acts. Since such acts threaten the wealth of others, people may be ready to pay taxes. Such redistribution increases social stability and increases the welfare of both groups: not only those who get the money, but also those who pay the taxes.

The formal translation of this argument is the following. Let π_o and π_1 be, respectively, the probabilities of a rich person being the victim of a crime before and after the introduction of the tax, and W_o and W_1 respectively the person's expected wealth when he or she is not the victim of a crime before and after the introduction of the tax. Let H_o and H_1 be respectively the average expected costs due to crime before and after the introduction of progressive taxation, where the following relationships must hold true:

$$\pi_1 < \pi_o; \ W_1 < W_o; \ H_1 < H_o. \tag{60}$$

Then, for those who stayed relatively richer to prefer the introduction of the tax, the following condition must hold (for simplicity's sake we omit the conditional statements):

$$\pi_o \, U(W_o - H_o, \, \alpha(W > W_o - H_o)) + (1 - \pi_o)$$
$$U(W_o, \, \alpha(W > W_o)) < \pi_1 U(W_1 - H_1, \, \alpha(W > W_1 - H_1))$$
$$+ (1 - \pi_1)U(W_1, \, \alpha(W > W_1)).$$

$$\tag{61}$$

If π_1 and H_1 are sufficiently diminished by the tax scheme, this condition can be fulfilled even if W_1 is smaller than W_o. Thus *everybody's* welfare is increased. This conclusion is reached without making an interpersonal comparison of utilities, assuming diminishing marginal utility of wealth, or assuming the existence of any social-welfare function.

However, this argument, while justifying a progressive tax scheme in particular, does not say anything about just how progressive the scheme should be. This depends on the responsiveness of π (the probability of a rich person being a victim of crime) to changes in the tax rates, on the effect the redistribution of wealth has on both crime rates and on total wealth, and on how responsive the probability of detection to an increase in police expenditures is.

Traditional explanations of such redistributive taxation are based on other arguments (for an excellent critical summary, see Blum and Kalven 1966). One is that the marginal utility of wealth is diminishing; that is, that a dollar is worth less to a richer than to a poorer person. According to this argument, both the rich person and the poor person have the same utility function:

$$U = U(W), \tag{62}$$

W being the wealth. If U' denotes the marginal utility, and one assumes that it is diminishing, then:

$$U(W_R) > U(W_P) \text{ and } U'(W_R) < U'(W_P), \tag{63}$$

where W_R and W_P denote, respectively, the richer and the poorer person's wealth. These assumptions lead to the conclusion that if one redistributes wealth from the richer to the poorer people, welfare increases.

These arguments have been criticized for a number of reasons. The first is that such a justification for redistribution relies on an interpersonal comparison of utilities that, in general, is not made in economic analyses. This is a criticism leveled at all welfare economics, mitigated here by the fact that since the rich person and the poor person are assumed to have the same utility function, comparison between utilities makes some sense. The second, more important, criticism is that the behavioral hypothesis of decreasing marginal utility of wealth cannot really be inferred from the traditional models of individual behavior in which risk is not present. In these models, if one utility function with decreasing marginal utility of wealth is consistent with the preferences of the consumer, any monotonic increasing transformation of this function is also consistent with them. But the monotonic transformations that transform the marginal utility of wealth from a diminishing into an increasing function always exist. Thus, the decreasing marginal utility of wealth cannot be inferred from these models.

The second strand of justification for redistribution in general (for progressive taxation in particular) has been based on the assumption of general risk aversion: If everybody were risk-averse (that is, the marginal utility of wealth were diminishing everywhere), redistribution from the richer toward the poorer could be justified. The problems with this reasoning are the same as those raised by making the assumption that people are, in general, risk-averse. If the hypothesis is accurate, people should neither gamble nor gamble and insure themselves at the same time. Whereas Friedman and Savage's (1948) suggestion that for some ranges of wealth the marginal utility of wealth is decreasing and for others is increasing may shed light on the fact that people both gamble and insure themselves, the justification for redistribution is lost.

The differences between these explanations and the one proposed here are, therefore, that it is not assumed either that people are altruistic, that there are social-welfare functions, or that a comparison can be made between people's utilities. It is assumed, rather, that unexpected shifts in people's ranks make it more likely that they will pursue noncustomary acts of a criminal or revolutionary nature in particular. The threat diminishes the welfare of relatively rich people, who may be ready to redistribute wealth in order to restore stability. This argument points to an additional difference between this and the other approaches: Whereas the one suggested here relies on a dynamic model, the others are static in character. This difference also explains the contrast in the lines of investigation to be pursued in order to verify the accuracy of the various explanations. According to the traditional ones, it is the shape of the utility function that should be discovered: whether it is concave or convex and at what ranges of wealth it changes shape. According to the one proposed here, one should carry out a historical examination, considering the origins and first growth of a tax, a law, or an institution, and examine whether or not the innovation was introduced when symptoms of social instability were on the rise. This was the line of investigation carried out in my previous studies.[17] The arguments presented in this section will be used in Chapters 3 and 5 for various purposes.

10. Comparisons with some other approaches

A comparison between the theory of risk taking presented here and the traditional one in economics has already been made above and elsewhere.[18] But there are additional theories that have not been mentioned yet or have just been touched on. It is on these theories that we focus attention now (although at times we shall make additional references to the theory of risk aversion). Criticism of these theories sometimes relies on the theory presented here and at other times relies on additional theories. At the same time, similarities between some of the approaches and the one presented here are emphasized.

A great deal of the experimental research on risk-taking behavior carried out by psychologists is either hard to interpret or unclear as to what it implies about behavior in the real world.[19] Before examining some results, I should emphasize that the model presented here does not offer an alternative approach for carrying out any laboratory research. The model makes clear-cut predictions about gambling, insurance, and reversal of decisions, but these behaviors all stem from the fact that people are poor, unexpectedly lose wealth, or are outdone by some of their fellows. These situations cannot be replicated in laboratories. Answering a question in a laboratory about spending is not quite the same as putting your hand in your pocket.

Consider first a number of simple examples typical of laboratory experiments and the problems that arise when one tries to interpret them. Thaler (1980) found a behavioral regularity that he called the "endowment effect." This effect stipulates that an individual will demand much more money to give something up than he would be willing to pay to acquire it. This effect has been observed both in cases that involve risks and in cases that do not. Thaler mentions one of them:

Suppose you won a ticket to a sold-out concert that you would love to attend, and the ticket is priced at $15. Before the concert you are offered $50 for the ticket. Do you sell? Alternatively, suppose you won $50 in a lottery. Then, a few weeks later, you are offered a chance to buy a ticket to the same concert for $45. Do you buy? Many people say they would not sell for $50 in the first case and would not buy for $45 in the second case. Such responses are logically inconsistent. (1986a, p. 164)

But are they? No, not necessarily.

When answering the first question, people may imagine a situation where the owner of the ticket hired a baby-sitter, bought new clothes for the occasion, and fixed a rendezvous with friends. So, although he or she is offered $50, the full price of forgoing the opportunity of using the ticket at the last minute may far exceed $50 (this price also taking into account the disappointment such a decision might cause one's friends). The second scenario implies that one has $50 more that may be spent as one wishes when no other complementary expenditures have been made. If such are the situations that one imagines when answering the researcher's question, there is no inconsistency in the answers.

Thaler gives another example of laboratory experiments that, according to him, relate to the value people place on their lives. People were asked to evaluate these strategies:

Risk Situation 1: While attending the movies last week you inadvertently exposed yourself to a rare, fatal disease. If you contract the disease, you will die a quick and painless death in one week. The chance that you will contract the disease is exactly 0.001 – that is, one chance in 1,000. Once you get the disease there is no cure, but you can take an inoculation now which will prevent you from getting the disease. Unfortunately there is only a limited supply of inoculation, and it will be sold to the highest bidders. What is the most you would be willing to pay for this inoculation? (If you wish, you may borrow the money to pay at a low rate of interest.)

Risk Situation 2: This is basically the same as situation 1 with the following modifications. The chance you will get this disease is now 0.004 – that is, four in 1,000. The inoculation is only 25 percent effective – that is, it would reduce the risk to 0.003. What is the most you would pay for the inoculation in this case? (Again, you may borrow the money to pay.)

Risk Situation 3: Some professors at a medical school are doing research on the disease described above. They are recruiting volunteers who would be required to expose themselves to a 0.001 (one chance in 1,000) risk of getting the disease. No inoculations would be available, so this would entail a 0.001 chance of death. The 20 volunteers from this audience who demand the least money will be taken. What is the least amount of money you would require to participate in this experiment? (1986a, p. 163)

The typical median responses were that people would pay $800 in situation 1 and $250 in situation 2, and charge $100,000 in situation 3. Thaler states that "economists would argue that the answers should all be about the same (they would allow for a small difference between situation 3 and the other two, but nothing like the magnitude observed)" (p. 163).

It is unclear why one would expect a small difference between situations 1 and 3. Problem 1 refers to a situation that can be described by the following inequality:

$$0.001\ U(\text{death}) + 0.999\ U(W) < U(W - h) \qquad (64)$$

where h is the amount one is willing to pay for eliminating a risk that one is already subject to. In contrast, situation 3 is one where a *new* "market" is offered through which one can become *rich*. The formal description of situation 3 is:

$$U(W) < 0.001\ U(\text{death}) + 0.999\ U(W + H). \qquad (65)$$

In other words, situation 1 provides people only with the opportunity to give up part of their wealth. Situation 3 provides them with the opportunity to become significantly richer.

Thus, there seems to be no inconsistency between the two replies. But even if in another experiment one found inconsistent answers to such questions, one could question how much weight to give such "facts." Twenty-year-old students' answers to this type of question may not tell us much about how they, or older people, might behave if they really found themselves in the circumstances described by these questions. Would a young Stanford M.B.A. student really accept $100,000 for a 0.001 chance of dying within a week?

Consider now another set of experimental problems. Kahneman and Tversky (1986a, b) gave the following:

Problem 1: Choose between:

A. 25% chance to win $240 and
   75% chance to lose $760.

B. 25% chance to win $250 and
   75% chance to lose $750.

It is easy to see that B dominates A, and all respondents chose accordingly. Formally, what this choice implies is that:

$$0.25 \ U(W_o + 240) + 0.75 \ U(W_o - 760)$$
$$< 0.25 \ U(W_o + 250) + 0.75 \ U(W_o - 750). \qquad (66)$$

Then Kahneman and Tversky next set this:

Problem 2, decision (1): Choose between:

C. a sure gain of $240

D. 25% chance to gain $1,000 and
   75% chance to gain nothing.

Eighty-four percent chose C, which implies that for them:

$$U(W_o + 240) > 0.25 \ U(W_o + 1,000) + 0.75 \ U(W_o). \qquad (67)$$

Decision (2) in this same problem was:

E. a sure loss of $750

F. 75% chance to lose $1,000 and
   25% chance to lose nothing.

Eighty-seven percent chose F, which implies that for them:

$$0.75\,U(W_o - 1{,}000) + 0.25\,U(W_o) > U(W_o - 750). \qquad (68)$$

Kahneman and Tversky found that 73% of the respondents chose C and F, and only 3% chose D and E; they suggest that this choice is inconsistent with the choice in Problem 1. For, they argue, if one adds the sure gain of \$240 (option C) to option F, that yields a 25% chance to win \$240 and a 75% chance to lose \$760. This is option A in Problem 1. Similarly, they add the sure loss of \$750 (option E) to option D, which yields a 25% chance to win \$250 and a 75% chance to lose \$750. This is option B in Problem 1. They suggest this is a "violation of invariance, [and] the findings also support the general point that failures of invariance are likely to produce violations of stochastic dominance and vice versa" (1986b, p. 72).

It is unclear why this example violates either principle. The invariance principle states that different representations of the *same* choice problem should yield the same preferences. But if people interpret the two problems the way shown in the translation to conditions (66)–(68), there is no way one would be able to make a comparison between condition (66) on one side and (67)–(68) on the other (a problem that does not arise in Allais's example discussed below). Adding (C) and (F) and comparing the result to the result of adding (D) and (E) was not a choice given to respondents. Thus, Problem 2 is not a different representation of Problem 1, but a different problem. Neither does it seem related to the dominance principle, which only states that if one option is better than another in one state and at least as good in all other states, the dominant option should be chosen. It is unclear how the aforementioned experiment violates this principle.

There are other experiments, however, that pose more serious problems of interpretation and that at first sight seem to violate the invariance principle. The next example comes from a study of preferences between medical treatments (carried out by McNeil et al. 1982 and quoted in Kahneman and Tversky 1986b). Respondents were given statistical information about the outcomes of two treatments for lung cancer. The same statistics were presented to some respondents in terms of mortality rates and to others in terms of survival rates. The respondents then indicated their preferred treatment. The information was presented as follows.

Problem 1 (Survival frame)

Surgery: Of 100 people having surgery 90 live through the post-operative period, 68 are alive at the end of the first year and 34 are alive at the end of five years.

Radiation Therapy: Of 100 people having radiation therapy all live through the treatment, 77 are alive at the end of one year and 22 are alive at the end of five years.

Problem 2 (Mortality frame)

Surgery: Of 100 people having surgery 10 die during surgery or the post-operative period, 32 die by the end of the first year and 66 die by the end of five years.

Radiation Therapy: Of 100 people having radiation therapy, none die during treatment, 23 die by the end of one year and 78 die by the end of five years. (pp. 70–1)

The outcome of the experiment was that the overall percentage of respondents who favored radiation therapy rose from 18% in the survival frame to 44% in the mortality frame, and the framing effect was not smaller for experienced physicians or for statistically sophisticated business students.

Kahneman and Tversky give the experiment as an example of the failures of invariance, arguing that the "*inconsequential* difference in formulation produced a marked difference" (p. 71; italics added). But is the difference in formulation really inconsequential? It may not be.

When I read the "Mortality frame," the problem seemed abstract and easy to translate into a mathematical condition. The association the wording of the problem brought to mind was narrow: death and nothing else. In contrast, when I read the "Survival frame," the association brought to my mind by "Of 100 people having radiation therapy all *live* through the treatment" was completely different. The word "live" immediately brought up the question of what *type* of life such treatment enables. Life at the hospital? With yellow skin and loss of hair? Weakened and sitting in a wheelchair? In other words, whereas the mortality frame seemed to bring to mind an abstract problem with just one variable – death – the survival frame seemed linked with a much more complicated problem associated with the words "live through treatment," which made radiation seem a less attractive option than in the second formulation. In other words, if somebody were to ask me what I should have predicted to be the reaction to the two formulations, the answer would have been that radiation would be perceived as the less attractive option within the survival frame (as it happened to be). One can argue, of course, that the people who answered the questions could have made the translation. But why would one expect them to make the effort? Their lives were not at stake. For them, choosing between the options was just an abstract exercise.

The fact that words are important and that using different words may change a problem by bringing very different associations to mind, even if, according to some, they describe the same events, has been emphasized many times in a variety of contexts.[20] Guido Calabresi, for example, starts his book *Ideals, Beliefs, Attitudes and the Law* (1985) with the following example:

Suppose ... a deity were to appear to you, as president of this country or as controller of our legal system, and offer a gift ... which would make life more pleasant, more enjoyable than it is today.... The ... deity suggests that he can deliver this gift in exchange for one thing ... the lives of one thousand young men and women ... who will each year die horrible deaths. (p. 1)

When he asked the students "Would you accept?," they almost uniformly answered, "No."

Obviously, however, as Calabresi immediately points out to the students, they and society have accepted such gifts; one of them is known as the private automobile, one of the greatest devices for mass destruction ever invented (50,000 lives are sacrificed each year in the United States, rather than the 1,000 of the example, for the privilege of using it).

Would people react differently if Calabresi's problem were presented in the following less poetic terms:

Owing to people's creativity, their divine inspiration over centuries, our generation is offered "the car." Needless to say, it makes life more pleasant and more enjoyable, and it raises standards of living. Without it we would be poorer, and poorer also means less healthy, which, in turn, implies that we may die younger. However, accepting this gift from our ancestors means that 1,000 young people will die, on average, every year.

One can speculate that when presented with this version of the problem, the students would uniformly have answered yes to the question of accepting the car.

What this example shows is not that the invariance principle fails, but rather that the phrasing of some problems, the words one uses, are important. Kahneman and Tversky's argument that a change in words is unimportant may not necessarily be the case.

Whereas Calabresi's formulation suggests, at first sight, an abstract example (the word "deity" today immediately brings philosophical rather than concrete issues to mind), to which the students responded correspondingly (i.e., viewing it as unlinked with a concrete problem), the "modern" translation brings up a very clear-cut problem. If one really wants to test whether or not the invariance principle fails, one must be very careful to check whether or not it is indeed the *same* choice that is described by the different representations. Thus, the issue is not, as Kahneman and Tversky state, a matter of "framing" the same question differently. When one changes the words, it is not just the frame that is changed but the meaning of the question itself.

Let us now return to one of Allais's (1953) well-known examples and reexamine its possible interpretation. He argued that there is no doubt that if people were offered the choice between getting 100 million francs for sure and getting 500 million with a probability of 98 percent and nothing with a probability of 2 percent, they would prefer the 100 million in their pockets. Translated to mathematical language, this response implies that:

$$U(W_o + 100) > 0.98 \ U(W_o + 500) + 0.02 \ U(W_o). \quad (69)$$

Next Allais defined three possible outcomes:

$$P_1 \begin{cases} 0.98 & 500 \text{ million} \\ 0.02 & 0 \end{cases}$$

$$P_2 \begin{cases} \text{certitude of} \\ 100 \text{ million} \end{cases}$$

$$P_3 \begin{cases} \text{certitude of} \\ 1 \text{ franc} \end{cases} \quad (70)$$

and defined the following new games:

$$P_1' \equiv \frac{1}{100}\,(P_1) + \frac{99}{100}\,(P_3)$$

$$\equiv \begin{cases} \dfrac{0.98}{100} & 500 \text{ million} \\[6pt] \dfrac{99}{100} & 1 \text{ franc} \\[6pt] \dfrac{0.02}{100} & 0 \end{cases} \cong \begin{cases} \dfrac{0.98}{100} & 500 \text{ million} \\[6pt] \dfrac{99.02}{100} & 0 \end{cases} \tag{71}$$

and

$$P_2' \equiv \frac{1}{100}\,(P_2) + \frac{99}{100}\,(P_3) \cong \begin{cases} \dfrac{1}{100} & 100 \\[6pt] \dfrac{99}{100} & 0 \end{cases}. \tag{72}$$

($\cong$ denotes the approximation that the 1=franc outcome is put together with the one where nothing can be won.) Allais interprets the fact that people prefer P_1' to P_2' as implying that:

$$\frac{0.98}{100}\,U(W_o + 500) + 0.9902\,U(W_o)$$

$$> \frac{1}{100}\,U(W_o + 100) + 0.99\,U(W_o), \tag{73}$$

which when rearranged implies that:

$$\frac{1}{100}\,U(W_o + 100) < \frac{0.98}{100}\,U(W_o + 500) + \frac{0.02}{100}\,U(W_o), \tag{74}$$

which contradicts condition (69). He attributes the contradiction to the fact that certainty and probabilities close to 1 are evaluated differently from other ranges of probabilities.[21] This, according to him, leads to a violation of one of the postulates of rational behavior.

This conclusion may be unnecessarily drastic. The question is: Do people in a laboratory bother to make the translation to (73), or do they just make the approximation that 0.98/100 is 1%? If they do the latter approximation – and why wouldn't they? – there is no contradiction between their choice between P'_2 and P'_2 and condition (69). The main issue here, as well as in the previous discussion, is that people may not necessarily examine questions in laboratories the way they would if they faced similar problems in real life. In fact, there is nothing in Allais's example that people can relate to a real-world situation. Nobody was ever offered 100 million francs just like that, and no lottery ever offered a 1% chance of winning a large prize (the chance is closer to 1 in millions in the Canadian 6/49, for example). Thus, the answer to the question concerning the choice between P'_1 and P'_2 may, at best, only suggest that people render 0.98 as approximately 1% (Why not? What was at stake?), an approximation they may not necessarily make if faced with a real-world situation, as the case study summarized next suggests.[22]

Bob Moore, who was once an IBM financial executive, worked on the planning of the System 360, which revolutionized the computer industry in the 1960s. One of the senior engineers in charge of the team responsible for designing the integrated circuits around which the computers would be built worked with Moore in putting together the estimated cost schedule for their development. Months later, seeking to cut costs, Moore asked the engineer what would happen if his budget were reduced by $2 million. "Nothing," said the engineer. "I mean, what will it cost the project in terms of time or quality of the product?" asked Moore. "It will simply increase the probability of failure beyond its current level," answered the engineer. Moore gave an additional $1 million to the engineer. Would Bob Moore's answers in a laboratory experiment reveal that he might make such a decision? It is doubtful. What this case study illustrates is that whereas in a laboratory people may make approximations (like neglecting a 0.02% change in probability) – thus answering abstract questions by making additional abstractions – they may not do so when they have to make decisions where their wealth and reputation are at stake. The paradoxes, violations, and inconsistencies obtained in laboratory experiments do not necessarily imply that people are irrational, but rather that one must be skeptical of the way people respond in artificial environments where their money and reputation are not at stake. The fact that regularities are obtained in such laboratory experiments is not surprising; many people may make the same type of approximation.

Additional results

Although the next experimental results seem consistent with the model presented here, my reservations about experimental studies should be kept in mind. I mention these studies in order to give a more rounded picture of the types of result that have been obtained in such experiments, rather than as providing strong evidence for supporting the model. The strong evidence can only come from examining people's behavior outside the laboratory, from the types of examination made here and in my previous work.[23]

Standard risk-aversion theory, combined with the frequent assumption of either a quadratic utility function or normality in the distribution of the random variables, implies that the covariance with market returns of returns on an investment should be considered as an investment criterion in addition to the mean or expected return (an implication discussed in Fisher 1906, Allais 1953, and Markowitz 1959, among others). But does higher variance necessarily diminish the attractiveness of a venture? As shown in the preceding sections, the answer to this question within the model presented here is negative: People may avoid ventures with small variance but bet on others with large ones. The intuition is simple: Increased risk means greater spread. So, although people may become poorer through a venture, it is such a venture that provides them with the opportunity to become significantly richer too, an opportunity that ventures with small variances do not provide. Slovic emphasizes that in experiments people choose according to decision rules such as "Minimize possible loss" or "Maximize possible gain" rather than basing their preference on variance per se. "Variance appears to have correlated with the preferences only because it also correlated with these other strategies," concludes Slovic (1986, p. 190), and he remarks that "this result is in accord with comments made by Lorie (1966) who complained that it was absurd to call a stock risky because it went up much faster than the market in some years and only as fast in other years, while a security that never rises in price is not risky at all, if variance is used to define risk" (p. 190).[24]

Finally, let us return to various points in Kahneman and Tversky's (1979) approach to which the model presented bears a number of similarities. They set up their model so that gains and losses were defined by the amount of money that was obtained or paid when a prospect was played, the reference point taken being the status quo, or one's current assets. They also note that whereas such a situation may characterize some problems of choice, there are others in which gains and losses are coded relative to an expectation or aspiration level that differs from the status quo. They give as an example: "An entrepreneur who is weathering a slump with greater success than his competitors may interpret a small loss or gain [as] relative to the larger loss he had reason to expect" (p. 286). This statement, however, implies comparisons with *others* (an assumption that Kahneman and Tversky do not discuss any further), not just with one's aspirations. It is precisely on this point that the approach presented here differs significantly from theirs, and this point also implies the use of different methodology for trying to falsify it. For one cannot recreate in a laboratory the reference group relative to which one shapes one's behavior. With the minuscule terms at stake in laboratory experiments, nobody can outdo his or her fellows, or be outdone by them, and neither does the group participating in the experiment represent the individual's reference group.

But for this significant difference, the other assumptions are similar (and they also bear resemblance to Simon's 1959, p. 87, recently reemphasized in March 1988). Kahneman and Tversky (1979, pp. 286–7) note that a discrepancy between the reference point and the current asset position may also arise because of changes in wealth to which one has not yet adapted, and that such changes alter the preference order of prospects. This assumption also implies in their model that "a person who has not made peace with his losses is likely to accept gambles that would be unacceptable to him otherwise" (p. 287), and thus they emphasize that the location of the reference point emerges as a critical factor in the analysis of decisions. The difference between their approach and the one presented here is that in order to prove their point Kahneman and Tversky have to make the assumptions that the utility function is S-shaped (being steepest at the reference point), that there is a weighting function, and so on. In contrast, in the approach presented here, none of these assumptions seem necessary. The utility function may be linear in both W and $\alpha(\cdot)$: The results concerning attitudes toward gambling, insurance, and entrepreneurial ventures are obtained because of the typical shape of the social pyramid and the unexpected fluctuations among the ranks defined within this pyramid. (For the moment, there seems to be no reason to make more complicated assumptions [on nonlinearity].)

11. Conclusions

There are numerous additional aspects of the model presented here that have been explored in R. Brenner 1983, 1985, 1987. The points that have been emphasized here are only those that were judged pertinent to the subjects discussed in this book: gambling, progressive taxation, insurance, and decision making in general. As noted, the model also suggests that one should investigate the origins of institutions, laws, and opinions, a line of investigation carried out in Chapters 3 and 4 – a line that, by the way, was strongly recommended by Coase (1937) but has rarely been pursued.

Appendix 2 to Chapter 2
A statistical profile of gamblers

---

1. Quebec data

In order to test the views presented in the text, the following relationship was estimated (by a multiple regression model and a log-linear function):

$$\text{TOT}_i = \beta_o + \beta_1 \text{ SCHOL}_i + \beta_2 \text{ AGE}_i + \beta_3 \text{ WEALTH}_i$$
$$+ \beta_4 \text{ CHIL}_i + \beta_5 \text{ INC}_i + \beta_6 \text{ PER}_i + \beta_7 \text{ FAM}_i + \varepsilon_i$$

where the variables used are defined as follows:

TOT_i = annual total spending on lottery tickets of respondent i as percentage of total family income

SCHOL_i = number of years of schooling of respondent i

AGE_i = age of respondent i

WEALTH_i = an index giving the actual family wealth position of respondent i relative to what it was when he or she was young. If it did not change, the index was equal to 1; if it worsened, the index was smaller than 1; and if his or her position was improved, the index was greater than 1

CHIL_i = number of children of i

INC_i = personal income of i

PER_i = personal income of i as percentage of family income

FAM_i = family income of i

ε_i = an error term

The reasons for including these variables are the following. Recall that the views presented in the text make predictions about the relationship between one's relative position in total wealth distribution, fluctuations in this position, and expenditures on lottery tickets. The sample does not allow a straightforward testing of such relationships, since information on wealth is not available. Also, as

---

Sections 1 and 2 were coauthored by Gabrielle A. Brenner. Sections 3, 4, and 5 were done in collaboration with Claude Montmarquette and Gabrielle A. Brenner.

noted, the motivation for buying lottery tickets stems from two entirely different sources: (*a*) People who are relatively poor *plan* to spend a larger fraction of their wealth on tickets relative to richer people, and (*b*) people who have suddenly become poorer may decide to buy such tickets. But this last group may be found in any wealth bracket; misfortune may strike any category of people. If one does not separate the two groups when collecting data, one may not necessarily observe that the average income of the lottery-ticket-buying public is significantly lower than that of the public at large. Only if the fraction of people who plan to buy lottery tickets because they are poorer constitutes a large fraction of the buyers can one expect such an outcome.

Second, the data available refer to monetary income and not to wealth. But monetary income is a misleading indicator of wealth, since adjustments are not made either for age or for the number of dependents. One would expect that, holding monetary income constant, older people and people with more dependents will be disproportionately represented among ticket buyers. Another variable that may complement the information on relative wealth is the level of education. One may expect that, *ceteris paribus*, the lower the level of education, the lower one's expectations for future increases in income, and thus the lower one's wealth. If so, people with less education will plan to spend a greater fraction of their wealth on lottery tickets.

In addition to the prediction about the relationship between planning to buy lottery tickets and wealth, the other prediction that one can test concerns people whose expectations as to their place in wealth distribution have been frustrated. According to the model's predictions, they will tend to spend more on lotteries than before. If one takes one's wealth relative to the wealth one's family owned during one's childhood (and we assume that one's family's wealth shapes one's aspirations), one would expect that people who bettered their own position in the wealth distribution will tend to buy fewer lottery tickets than before and that those whose position worsened will tend to buy more.

Thus, we expect β_1, β_3, β_5, and β_7 to be negative and β_2 and β_4 to be positive. We expect β_6 to be positive, since the higher one's contribution to one's total family income, the less secure will this family's relative wealth be perceived (since its income depends more on this one person's income).

Table 1. *Regression results: Quebec survey (log-linear form)*
(N = 851) (t statistics in parentheses)

Coefficient (hypothesis)[a]	Dependent variable	(1)	(2)
	CONSTANT	−5.2*	−5.1*
		(−3.3)	(−3.3)
$\beta_1(-)$	SCHOL	0.4**	0.4**
		(2.3)	(2.4)
$\beta_2(+)$	AGE	0.5	0.45
		(2.0)	(1.97)
$\beta_3(-)$	WEALTH	−0.58	−0.57
		(−1.1)	(−1.08)
$\beta_4(+)$	CHIL	−0.07	—
		(−0.5)	—
$\beta_5(-)$	INC	−5.6*	−5.6*
		(−9.0)	(−9.0)
$\beta_6(+)$	PER	7.4*	7.4*
		(4.1)	(4.1)
$\beta_7(-)$	FAM	4.2*	4.2*
		(5.8)	(5.8)
F statistics		77	90
R^2		0.38	0.38

[a] Signs in parentheses are the expected signs.
* Statistically significant at the 1% level.
** Statistically significant at the 5% level.

The results of the estimation are given in Table 1, column (1). β_2, β_3, and β_6 are of the expected sign and are significant; β_3 is of the expected sign but insignificant. On the other hand, neither the coefficient of schooling, β_1, nor the coefficient of number of children, β_4, nor the coefficient of family income, β_7, has the expected sign. β_4 is also statistically insignificant. After having ascertained by an *F* test that β_4 is really insignificant, we reran the regression without the number of children. The results are given in column (2) of Table 1. There are no major changes in the other coefficients.

The results in Table 1 seem quite consistent with the prediction of the model: the higher one's income, the less one's spending on lottery tickets; the older one is, the more lottery tickets one buys. It also seems that the more upwardly mobile one is, the less one buys lottery tickets. The reason for the nonsignificance of the number of children may be that some may play lottery games in order to afford one more child, a hope that data on the actual number of children does not reveal.

A result that seems to contradict a prediction is the one about the influence of schooling and family income. Since several previous studies that rely on somewhat more detailed data sets (summarized in the text) have found that there seems to exist an inverse relationship between years of schooling completed and expenditures on lotteries, we did some further testing with this data set, but the results did not improve. The only explanation we can think of is the following. As noted earlier, the model makes predictions on gambling behavior for two groups of people: the relatively poor, who plan to buy tickets, and people whose expectations are frustrated. The latter may belong to any class and have any level of schooling. Only if the data set included only people from the first group would one expect to obtain a positive relationship between low levels of schooling and relative expenditures on gambling. For the other group, not only should such a relationship not be expected, but one could argue that the opposite is true. Suppose that somebody with little schooling loses his job. Transfer payments and other benefits significantly diminish fluctuations in that person's wealth, and he or she may not start gambling or may not spend more on it. However, for those with more schooling, such compensations are far from reaching the expected level of wealth and the status it defined. Thus, he or she may start gambling. This explanation is reinforced by the result we obtained in the following test. We split the data set in two; one set included people with under ten years of schooling, and the other included people who had ten or more years of schooling. We then reran the regression on each subset. For the sample with ten or more years of schooling, the relationship between years of schooling and relative expenditures on gambling is negative, whereas it is positive for the sample with under ten years of schooling. This same explanation may hold true for the positive relationship between relative expenditures on gambling and family wealth.

2. Canadian data

In spite of the strong reservation mentioned in the text, we tested our views on the data set provided by Statistics Canada's *Family Ex-*

penditures in Canada of 1982, and the following relationship was estimated:

$$\text{TOT}_i = \gamma_0 + \sum_{j=1}^{3} \gamma_1^j \text{ NAC}_i^j + \sum_{j=2}^{6} \gamma_2^j \text{ AGE}_i^j + \sum_{j=1}^{4} \gamma_3^j \text{ REG}_i$$

$$+ \sum_{j=1}^{2} \gamma_4^j \text{ STAT}_i^j + \sum_{j=1}^{4} \gamma_5^j \text{ ED}_i^j + \sum_{j=1}^{2} \gamma_6^j \text{ LANG}_i^j$$

$$+ \sum_{j=1}^{3} \gamma_7^j \text{ ENF}_i^j + \gamma_8 \text{ INC}_i + \sum_{j=1}^{2} \gamma_9^j \text{ IM}_i^j + \eta_i$$

where the variables used are defined as follows:

TOT_i = annual spending on lotteries of the family unit i as a percentage of its total after-tax income

AGE_i^j = dummy variables that characterize the age of the head of the family unit when

  $\text{AGE}^1 = 1$ if the head is between 30 and 39 years old; 0 otherwise
  $\text{AGE}^2 = 1$ if the head is between 40 and 49 years old; 0 otherwise
  $\text{AGE}^3 = 1$ if the head is between 50 and 59 years old; 0 otherwise
  $\text{AGE}^4 = 1$ if the head is between 60 and 69 years old; 0 otherwise
  $\text{AGE}^5 = 1$ if the head is 70 years old or older

  The omitted age category is 20–9. Thus all the coefficients are relative to this category.

REG_i^j = dummy variables to indicate the province or region where the family unit lives when

  $\text{REG}^1 = 1$ if the family lives in the Atlantic Provinces; 0 otherwise
  $\text{REG}^2 = 1$ if the family lives in Quebec; 0 otherwise
  $\text{REG}^3 = 1$ if the family lives in the Western Provinces except British Columbia; 0 otherwise
  $\text{REG}^4 = 1$ if the family lives in British Columbia; 0 otherwise

  The omitted category is Ontario.

STAT_i^j = dummy variables to indicate the material status of the head of the family unit, when

  $\text{STAT}^1 = 1$ if the head was never married; 0 otherwise
  $\text{STAT}^2 = 1$ if the head was neither married nor ever married; 0 otherwise

  The omitted category is a married head.

ED_i^j = dummy variables to indicate the level of education of the head of the family, when

  $\text{ED}^1 = 1$ if the head of the family has either some secondary education or completed secondary education

$ED^2 = 1$ if the head has some postsecondary education; 0 otherwise

$ED^3 = 1$ if the head has a college degree or certificate of post-secondary education; 0 otherwise

$ED^4 = 1$ if the head has a university degree; 0 otherwise

The omitted category is under 9 years of primary education.

$LANG_i^j =$ dummy variables to indicate the mother tongue of the head of the family, when

$LANG^1 = 1$ if the mother tongue is French; 0 otherwise

$LANG^2 = 1$ if the mother tongue is neither English nor French; 0 otherwise

The omitted category is English as mother tongue.

$NAC_i^j =$ dummy variables to indicate if members of a family receive un-employment insurance, when

$NAC^1 = 1$ if one member of the family receives unemployment insurance; 0 otherwise

$NAC^2 = 1$ if two members of the family receive unemployment insurance; 0 otherwise

$NAC^3 = 1$ if three or more members of the family receive unemployment insurance; 0 otherwise

$ENF_i^j =$ dummy variables indicating the number of children in the family. We defined three such variables, depending on whether there are one, two, or three or more children in the family. The category omitted is no children

$INC_i =$ income of the family unit

$IM_i^j =$ dummy variables indicating the immigration status of the family unit, when

$IM^1 = 1$ if the head of the family unit immigrated before 1960; 0 otherwise

$IM^2 = 1$ if the head of the unit immigrated between 1961 and 1970; 0 otherwise

$IM^3 = 1$ if the head of the unit immigrated after 1971; 0 otherwise

The omitted category is a native-born head.

We expect both γ_1^i and γ_2^i (corresponding to the receipt of unemployment insurance and the age variable, respectively) to be positive. The coefficients γ_3^i may be of either sign, depending on regional differences that are not captured in other variables. As noted in the preceding section, evidence exists for greater participation in the traditionally poorer regions of Canada, Quebec and the Maritimes; this would mean a positive coefficient for both γ_3^1 and γ_3^2.

We also expect that the coefficients γ_5^j will be negative, as the reference category for education is the one indicating the least education (under 9 years of primary education). γ_7^j, the coefficients of the number of family members, should be positive, and γ_8^j, the coefficient of income, negative.

The signs of γ_7^j, the number of children living with the family, γ_6^j, the language spoken in the family, and γ_9^j, the immigration status of the family unit, are not determinate. Nevertheless, the following arguments may give some idea of the expected signs of γ_6^j and γ_9^j. Several studies (see summary in Tec 1964, p. 93) have mentioned that Catholics are more likely to gamble than Protestants. As there are relatively more Catholics among French-speaking Canadians than among English-speaking ones, we expected that γ_6^1, the coefficient of Francophone families, would be positive. This argument is reinforced by the fact that, as noted in the text, French Canadians have earned less than their English-speaking brethren. As for immigration status, since immigrants are persons uprooted from their traditional way of life who have possibly not yet settled down in their new country, we would expect that new immigrants would play relatively more than native-born Canadians. We would also expect immigrants of longer standing to play more than native-born Canadians, *ceteris paribus*.

As noted in the text, a significant percentage of families answered that they did not buy lottery tickets. We are thus in the presence of a dependent variable equal to zero in a significant number of observations. The correct way to estimate the equation above is thus through probit analysis (see Theil 1971, pp. 628ff.). The results of this analysis are given in Table 2.

Quite surprisingly, the results in Table 2 mostly reflect our predictions. All age categories except the last (70 or over) gamble more than the younger group, pointing toward a positive relation between lottery spending and age. Why didn't we get the same result for the 70-and-older group? First, elderly people may be in poor health and thus less able to buy lottery tickets. Second, they may have more trouble than the average recalling how much they spent on tickets during the year. But note that if we compare these results with those in Table 3, where we estimated, by a least-squares method, the relationships described above for only the families who answered that they bought lottery tickets (thus eliminating all the families who said that they did not buy lottery tickets at all), we see that families

Table 2. *Analysis of Statistics Canada's data set* (N = 10,938; F = 33)

Coefficient	Hypothesis[a]	Independent variable	Estimate	T statistics
γ_1^1	(+)	NAC1	0.08*	6.7
γ_1^2	(+)	NAC2	0.07*	2.9
γ_1^3	(+)	NAC3	0.10	1.4
γ_2^1	(+)	AGE1	0.04*	3.2
γ_2^2	(+)	AGE2	0.05*	3.1
γ_2^3	(+)	AGE3	0.08*	5.0
γ_2^4	(+)	AGE4	0.06*	3.4
γ_2^5	(+)	AGE5	−0.04**	−2.2
γ_3^1	(+)	REG1	−0.11*	−5.9
γ_3^2	(+)	REG2	0.01	0.6
γ_3^3	(?)	REG3	−0.11*	−10.6
γ_3^4	(?)	REG4	−0.12*	−7.9
γ_4^1	(?)	STAT1	−0.11*	−7.4
γ_4^2	(?)	STAT2	−0.11*	−8.4
γ_5^1	(−)	ED1	0.03*	2.8
γ_5^2	(−)	ED2	0.06	0.2
γ_5^3	(−)	ED3	−0.05*	−3.2
γ_5^4	(−)	ED4	−0.21*	−10.3
γ_6^1	(+)	LANG1	0.03**	2.0
γ_6^2	(?)	LANG2	0.01	0.8
γ_7^1	(+)	ENF1	−0.006	−0.4
γ_7^2	(+)	ENF2	−0.008*	−2.5
γ_7^3	(+)	ENF3	−0.07	0.9
γ_8	(−)	INC	0.03*	9.4
γ_9^1	(+)	IM1	−0.02	−0.1
γ_9^2	(+)	IM2	−0.003	−0.1
γ_9^3	(+)	IM3	0.004	0.1

[a] Signs in parentheses are the expected signs.
* Statistically significant at the 1% level.
** Statistically significant at the 5% level.

whose heads were 70 or older bought more tickets than the younger groups, though fewer than the categories covering 50 to 69. Considering the bad data, there is not much reason to speculate on the reasons. It may be useful to note that in their analysis of data from Maryland, Clotfelter and Cook (1987) also found that the oldest age group (70 or more) played less.

Table 3. *Analysis of Statistics Canada's data set: families that admitted buying lottery tickets* ($N = 7,083$; $F = 17.2$; $R^2 = 0.24$)

Coefficient	Hypothesis[a]	Independent variable	Estimate	T statistics
γ_1^1	(+)	NAC1	10.3	1.7
γ_1^2	(+)	NAC2	32.9*	2.7
γ_1^3	(+)	NAC3	−36.7	−1.1
γ_2^1	(+)	AGE1	17.1**	2.2
γ_2^2	(+)	AGE2	27.6*	3.2
γ_2^3	(+)	AGE3	59.4*	6.7
γ_2^4	(+)	AGE4	51.1*	5.3
γ_2^5	(+)	AGE5	33.2*	2.9
γ_3^1	(+)	REG1	−18.1	−1.8
γ_3^2	(+)	REG2	−10.2	−1.1
γ_3^3	(?)	REG3	−48.9*	−6.5
γ_3^4	(?)	REG4	−44.6*	−5.4
γ_4^1	(?)	STAT1	1.9	0.2
γ_4^2	(?)	STAT2	−17.4*	−2.4
γ_5^1	(−)	ED1	7.3	1.1
γ_5^2	(−)	ED2	−16.3	−1.7
γ_5^3	(−)	ED3	−25.2*	−2.7
γ_5^4	(−)	ED4	−60.5*	−5.6
γ_6^1	(+)	LANG1	32.7*	3.5
γ_6^2	(?)	LANG2	26.8*	3.0
γ_7^1	(+)	ENF1	−25.1*	−3.4
γ_7^2	(+)	ENF2	−39.2**	−2.0
γ_7^3	(+)	ENF3	7.7	0.1
γ_8		INC	0.002*	10.2
γ_9^1	(+)	IM1	−4.7	−0.5
γ_9^2	(+)	IM2	32.8**	2.5
γ_9^3	(+)	IM3	52.9*	3.8

[a] Signs in parentheses are the expected signs.
* Statistically significant at the 1% level.
** Statistically significant at the 5% level.

The coefficients of the number of people receiving unemployment benefits are also positive; i.e., family units where one or more members receive unemployment benefits buy proportionally more lottery tickets than units where no member is unemployed. (But note that in Table 3 this result is inverted for families where three or more members receive unemployment benefits.) On a geographical level, residents of the West both participate less in the lottery and buy fewer lottery tickets than Ontarians; and the result is statistically significant. The result of the comparisons between Ontarians and residents of the Atlantic Provinces and Quebec is not as clear-cut. The result in Table 2 suggests that residents of the Atlantic Provinces play less than Ontarians (and the result is again statistically significant). But the result in Table 3, based on the families who did indeed buy lottery tickets, is not statistically significant. The difference may be due to the difference in acknowledged participation rates in buying tickets in the two regions. As noted in the text, 40% of families in the Atlantic Provinces and only 29% in Ontario said they did not buy lottery tickets. As for Quebeckers, the numbers in Table 2 suggest that they play more than Ontarians, although the result is not statistically significant; the numbers in Table 3 suggest that among the families who did play the lottery, Quebeckers played less than Ontarians, although again the result is not statistically significant. Thus we cannot conclude that Quebeckers buy more (or fewer) lottery tickets than Ontarians, contrary to our previous findings. On the other hand, contrary to our previous findings, the Maritime Provinces do not any longer play less than Ontario. But we have more confidence in the previous data.

As predicted, there seems to exist a negative relationship between level of education and lottery participation. People with a college or university degree buy relatively fewer lottery tickets than people who did not complete secondary education. This result is statistically significant. On the other hand, people who completed secondary education played more and people who had some postsecondary education played more, as much as, or less than people who did not complete primary education (the coefficient being statistically insignificant in all three regressions). As for mother tongue, people whose mother tongue is English buy relatively fewer lottery tickets than people whose mother tongue is not. Families whose head is married participated more in the lottery than units whose head had any other marital status, although among the families who bought tickets, families whose head was never married may have bought relatively more tickets (but the result is not statistically significant). The only results that are contrary to the predictions are the ones for families with children versus families without children, and for income. Families with children play relatively less than families without children,

Table 4. *Definition of additional variables and symbols*

AGE	Age of the head of the family
NCHD	Number of children in the family under age 16
NUB	Number of members of the family receiving unemployment insurance benefits
INC	After-tax family income

and families with higher incomes play relatively more than their poorer brethren. Possibly we can relate this last result to the significant (40%) underreporting on lotteries we found; the results are improved when one assumes that poorer people underdeclare their expenditures more than richer people. The more sophisticated statistical analysis concerning this point is presented next.

3. How to correct for underdeclared lottery expenditures

Let equation (1) define the determinants of the exact annual spending on lotteries of the ith family as a percentage of its total after-tax income:

$$\ln (E^*/\text{INC})_i = \gamma_0 + \gamma_1 \text{INC}_i + \gamma_2 \text{INC}_i^2$$
$$+ \sum_{k=3}^{p} \gamma_k x_{ik} + \zeta_i \tag{1}$$

with E_i^* = the unobserved exact lottery expenditures by the family unit;

INC_i = the after-tax income of family i;

x_{ik}, $k = 3, \ldots, p$ = the other variables of the model, defined in Table 4;

ζ_i = an error term with the usual properties.

Consider that

$$E_i^* = (1 + B_i)E_i \tag{2}$$

where E_i is the reported expenditure and B_i is an adjustment coefficient that equals the difference between the family's unobserved exact lottery expenditures and the reported expenditures divided by the reported survey expenditures.

Since, according to the arguments presented in the chapter the poorer and those who suddenly become so have greater incentives to gamble (but either their expenditure pattern is condemned or they receive the small prizes disproportionately and forget to declare them), let us assume that the adjustment coefficient varies among families according to the following relationship:[1]

$$B_i = B_o + \beta_1 \text{INC}_i + \beta_2 \text{INC}_i^2. \tag{3}$$

This relationship implies that the adjustment coefficient depends nonlinearly on the income of the family unit i. Depending on the signs and sizes of the coefficients β_1 and β_2, this equation may examine the assumption that families with lower incomes significantly underdeclare their expenditures on lotteries.

With *reported* lottery expenditures in the survey, equation (1) becomes:

$$\ln (E/\text{INC})_i = \gamma_o + \gamma_1 \text{INC}_i + \gamma_2 \text{INC}_i^2$$
$$+ \sum_{k=3}^{p} \gamma_k x_{ik} - \ln (1 + B_i) + \zeta_i. \tag{4}$$

Assume that the underdeclaration of lottery expenditures does not exceed 100% and that the overdeclaration is always less than 100% too (that is $-1 < B_i \leq 1$). With equation (3) and a series expansion of $\ln (1 + B_i)$ up to the second term, we obtain, after some manipulation, the following relationship:

$$\ln (E/\text{INC})_i = (\gamma_o + \tfrac{1}{2} \beta_o^2 - \beta_o) + (\gamma_1 - \beta_1 + \beta_o\beta_1)\text{INC}_i$$
$$+ (-\beta_2 + \beta_o\beta_2 + \beta_1^2/2)\text{INC}_i^2 + \beta_1\beta_2 \text{INC}_i^3$$
$$+ \beta_2^2/2 \text{INC}_i^4 + \sum_{k=3}^{p} \gamma_k x_{ik} + \zeta_i$$
$$= \theta_o + \theta_1 \text{INC}_i + \theta_2 \text{INC}_i^2 + \theta_3 \text{INC}_i^3 + \theta_4 \text{INC}_i^4 +$$
$$\sum_{k=3}^{p} \gamma_k x_{ik} + \zeta_i. \tag{5}$$

The coefficients of the model are identified *except* for β_o.

It is at this point that we integrate the accurate information on lottery revenues (which if the information on expenditures were not biased would not be needed). By using the sum of declared expenditures, E, and the observed revenues of lottery enterprises, E^*, we can obtain an aggregate adjustment coefficient B from the following equation:

$$E^* = (1 + B)E. \tag{6}$$

From equations (2) and (3) we obtain:

$$E_i^* = (1 + B_i)E_i$$
$$= E_i + \beta_o E_i + \beta_1 \text{INC}_i E_i + \beta_2 \text{INC}_i^2 E_i. \tag{7}$$

Summing up all the family units, assuming $\sum E_i^* = E^*$ and using equation (6) (recalling that the value of B is known), we obtain:

$$\beta_o = B - \beta_1 \sum_i \text{INC}_i E_i / E - \beta_2 \sum \text{INC}_i^2 E_i / E. \tag{8}$$

4. The results

The data set we use is the same as in the preceding section. The initial sample size is 10,938, but since it is weighted according to the ten provinces to represent the Canadian population, the adjusted sample size for each regression may vary accordingly.[2] Table 4 defines the variables and symbols that have not been defined yet.

Thirty-five percent of the respondents in the sample we took declared that they did not spend on lotteries. Thus, one has to deal with this specification bias issue in explaining lottery expenditures.[3] In order to obtain consistent estimates for the regression coefficients of equation (5), we used the two-stage estimators proposed in Heckman 1979. The results of the probit analysis of the probability of spending on lotteries reject the assumption of randomly missing observations,[4] but the inverse of the Mills' ratio introduced to correct for the sample selection bias proved statistically insignificant.

Table 5 presents the regression results both without correction for the underdeclared lottery expenditures and with correction. Most coefficient estimates are statistically significant, and the $\bar{R}^2$ are reasonable, given the large number of observations in the sample ($N = 7,083$). As expected, there are important differences between the two results for the income variables. But for most of the other variables the differences are minor. One exception is the EDUC variable; its coefficient is negative and statistically significant in the corrected regression, a change that is in the direction of supporting the predictions of the model.

Table 5. *The determinants of lottery expenditures* (N = 7,083;
T *statistics in parentheses*)

Variable	With correction for underdeclarations	Without correction for underdeclarations
REG1	0.0200	−5.610
	(0.19)	(−0.59)
REG2	−0.0087	0.0021
	(−0.15)	(0.03)
REG3	−0.2750	−0.4077
	(−1.82)	(−3.04)
REG4	−0.1960	−0.2897
	(−1.68)	(−2.76)
STAT1	0.0150	−0.0627
	(0.14)	(−0.66)
STAT2	−0.1179	−0.1831
	(−1.28)	(−2.22)
LANG1	0.2332	0.2598
	(3.620)	(4.12)
LANG2	0.1043	0.1180
	(1.83)	(2.09)
IM1	0.0024	−0.0224
	(0.04)	(−0.36)
IM2	0.1276	0.1162
	(1.57)	(1.44)
IM3	0.2921	0.2986
	(3.36)	(3.44)
AGE	0.0435	0.0574
	(2.63)	(3.87)
$(AGE)^2$	−0.0003	−0.0005
	(−2.00)	(−3.17)
NCHD	−0.0841	−0.1050
	(−2.94)	(−3.97)
NUB	−0.0099	−0.0323
	(−0.18)	(0.64)
ED1	−0.0089	0.0023
	(−2.01)	(0.05)
ED2	−0.1599	−0.1714
	(−2.69)	(−2.89)
ED3	−0.2425	−0.3084
	(−2.65)	(−3.61)
ED4	−0.4597	−0.6496
	(−2.08)	(−3.31)

Table 5 (continued)

Variable	With correction for underdeclarations	Without correction for underdeclarations
INC	−0.5078	−0.2999
	(−3.59)	(−4.63)
$(\text{INC})^2$	0.1405	0.0050
	(2.58)	(0.40)
$(\text{INC})^3$	−0.0200	—
	(−2.62)	
$(\text{INC})^4$	0.0010	—
	(2.71)	
CONSTANT	−0.589	−6.62
	(−9.45)	(−12.06)
(Mills' ratio)$^{-1}$	−0.2593	0.1244
	(−0.62)	(0.34)
$\bar{R}^2$	0.1409	0.1403

Focusing on the corrected version, we see that many results are in accord with predictions made by the model. The French-speaking Canadians (LANG1) spend more on lotteries than the English-speaking families, and it is well known that French Canadians earn less than their English-speaking brethren. (This may not be the only reason for the French Canadians' greater propensity to gamble; Catholics everywhere gamble more than Protestants, and French Canadians are mostly Catholic, but we did not have data on religious background.) Immigrants are persons uprooted from their traditional way of life whose incomes are lower than those of nonimmigrants with a similar educational background. Table 5 shows that recent immigrants (IM3) spend more than both less-recent immigrants (IM2, IM1) and native-born Canadians (the omitted category). Also, as expected, up to the age of 72.5, people gamble more with age. Strong results supporting the model occur in the education variables. The more educated spend much less on lotteries. However, the results for the number of children living with the family and the number of members in the family receiving unemployment benefits do not support the model.

Before considering the results for the income variable, let us discuss the adjustment coefficients for the underdeclared lottery expenditures.

Table 6. *Adjustment coefficients and income elasticities*

Income (in 10^4)	Adjustment equation[a]	Income elasticities[b]	
		With correction	Without correction
0.5	1.05	−0.23	−0.15
1.0	0.86	−0.53	−0.29
2.5	0.43	−1.86	−0.69
3.0	0.33	−2.45	−0.81
6.0	0.19	−7.47	−1.44

[a] Adjustment equation: $B_i = 1.271 - 0.4474 \text{ INC}_i + 0.0447 \text{ INC}_i^2$.

[b] Income elasticities: $\dfrac{\delta(E/\text{INC}) \text{ INC}}{\delta \text{INC} \ (E/\text{INC})}$: with correction: $-0.3870 \text{ INC}_i - 0.1432 \text{ INC}_i^2$; without correction: $-0.2999 \text{ INC}_i + 0.01 \text{ INC}_i^2$.

Recall that for 1982 the relationship between declared expenditures and the respective provincial lottery revenues, E/E^*, equaled 0.70 (taking into account the fact that approximately 10% of the revenues come from foreigners). Thus, from equation (6) we obtain a conservative value of 0.43 for B, the aggregate adjustment coefficient. Using B and the coefficient estimates obtained from the regression analysis (defined in (5)), we can find β_o (in (8)) and the coefficient estimates for the adjustment equation defined in (3). Table 6 presents the corresponding adjustment coefficients for different levels of family income.[5]

These results show the importance of correcting for the under-declared lottery expenditures: For a low-income family, the under-declaration reaches 100%.[6] Table 6 also shows the income elasticities of money spent on lotteries relative to the family income. There are considerable downward biases in the income elasticities when under-declared expenditures are not corrected for. As the family income rises, the uncorrected income elasticities represent between 65% and a mere 19% of the corrected income elasticities. The corrected negative income elasticities seem strongly to support the model presented here.[7]

5. Conclusions

The statistical analyses above seem useful not only because they enable the testing of the hypotheses advanced here, but also because they show a way to deal with problems of under- and overdeclarations of consumption patterns in surveys – if one has a model suggesting why such declarations are made and by whom. As mentioned, underdeclarations are typical when alcohol, tobacco, and gambling consumption is questioned. (Overdeclaration – bragging, that is – seems to be a problem when a person's sexual appetite is questioned.) But by using the relatively accurate data on the revenue side of these three industries, one can obtain better elasticity estimates. A way to obtain them was suggested in this study.

The study also points to a more general problem concerning demand curves. We found few studies (one of the exceptions being Houthakker and Taylor 1970) where attempts were made to contrast estimated total expenditures from survey data with the revenues of the respective sectors in order to check the reliability of the results. For many sectors, the lack of this step may not pose a major problem, since there is no reason to believe that people systematically under- or overdeclare spending on bread or clothing. Still, if people significantly underdeclare expenditures on gambling, alcohol, and tobacco (not to mention expenditures on drugs, prostitutes, and investment in the Bahamas), this may imply that they will consciously either declare more than they spend on legal items with a positive connotation or underdeclare income. Since expenditures on all items with a negative association, illegal or legal, are well into the tens of billions of dollars, there may be significant overdeclaration on ordinary items for which, a priori, one would have thought that only random errors existed.[8] Thus, the problems dealt with in the last section may have broader implications for both future econometric analysis and the confidence one gives to elasticity estimates derived from aggregate sectorial data for unbiased items too.

Appendix to Chapter 5
Governments' revenues from lotteries

The tables presented provide information on revenues from lotteries across countries and time. No meaningful statistical analyses can be done with these data, since regulations concerning the games have changed during the short period for which the recent numbers are available.

Canada

Table 1. *Atlantic Canada:*[a] *lottery revenues and deficit (millions of dollars)*

(1) Year[b]	(2) Net profits of lotteries	(3) Government revenues	(4) Deficit (−) or surplus (+)	(5) (2) as % of (4)
1976	—	3,009	−320.2	—
1977	5.2	3,385	−254.1	2.0
1978	14.3	3,769.1	−276.5	5.1
1979	15.7	4,317	−429.3	3.6
1980	10.9	4,851	−177.5	6.1
1981	16.3	5,312.1	−397	4.1
1982	21.8	6,002.7	−623.6	3.5
1983	20.6	6,500.6	−1,016.8	2.0
1984	32.7	7,280.8	−864.3	3.8
1985	41.4	7,984.5[c]	−707.2[c]	5.8

[a] We have amalgamated data for the four Atlantic Provinces: Newfoundland, New Brunswick, Nova Scotia, and Prince Edward Island.
[b] Fiscal years ending March 31.
[c] Preliminary figures.
Sources: Net profits of lotteries: Annual report of Atlantic Canada Lottery Corporation, 1984–5.
   Government revenues and deficits: Statistics Canada, publication no. 68–207, *Provincial Public Finances.*
Comment: Net profits from lotteries represented a maximum of 6.1% of the deficit.

Table 2. *Ontario: lottery revenues and deficit (millions of dollars)*

(1) Year[a]	(2) Net profits of lotteries	(3) Government revenues	(4) Deficit (−) or surplus (+)	(5) (2) as % of (4)
1975	—	8,925.1	−730.0	—
1976	43.3	10,021.6	−1,439.7	3.0
1977	92.8	11,715.6	−1,025.5	9.0
1978	98.4	12,521.8	−1,464.6	6.7
1979	62.6[b]	14,003.5	−1,211.7	5.1
1980	92.8[b]	15,921.0	−685.2	13.5
1981	148.8	17,335.6	−833.0	17.8
1982	157.5	19,732.6	−1,129.1	13.9
1983	163.5	21,532.5	−2,399.9	6.8
1984	216.7	23,713.3	−2,422.2	8.9
1985	249.6	26,282.1[c]	−2,074.1[c]	12.0

[a] Fiscal years ending March 31.
[b] Qualified in the report as "after extraordinary expenses."
[c] Preliminary estimate.
Sources: Net profits of lotteries: Annual report of Ontario Lottery Corporation, 1984–5.

Government revenues and deficits: Statistics Canada, publication no. 68–207, *Provincial Public Finances.*
Comment: Profits from the lottery represented a maximum of 17.8% of the deficit.

Table 3. *Quebec: lottery revenues and deficit (millions of dollars)*

(1) Year[a]	(2) Net profits of lotteries	(3) Government revenues	(4) Deficit (−) or surplus (+)	(5) (2) as % of (4)[b]
1971	24.5	—	—	—
1972	30.8	5,120.5	+86.8	35.5
1973	37.3	5,734.2	+123.3	30.2
1974	47.8	6,553.7	+209.7	22.7
1975	51.1	8,238.2	+271.5	18.8
1976	55.3	9,494	−282.6	19.5
1977	70.0	11,139	−331.5	21.1
1978	73.3	12,831.6	−59.3	—
1979	86.1	14,208.1	−445.1	19.3
1980	101.5	15,865.2	−513.1	19.7
1981	141.1	17,779.8	−1,582.1	8.9
1982	150.9	21,085.3	−1,286.8	11.7
1983	163.4	23,148.7	−2,024.2	8.0
1984	223.1	25,026.4[c]	−2,265	9.8
1985	252.9	26,968.7[c]	−1,407.7	17.9

[a] Fiscal years ending March 31.
[b] When (2) in absolute terms is less than (4). Otherwise the percentage is meaningless. When (2) in absolute terms is greater than (4), it means that the net profits were greater than either the deficits or the surplus.
[c] Preliminary estimate.
Sources: Net profits of lotteries: Annual reports of Loto-Québec, various years.

Government revenues and deficits: Statistics Canada, publication no. 68–207, *Provincial Public Finances.*

Table 4. *Western Canada:*[a] *lottery profits and government deficits (millions of dollars)*

(1) Year[b]	(2) Net profits of lotteries	(3) Government revenues	(4) Deficit (−) or surplus (+)	(5) (2) as % of (4)[c]
1975	15.4	8,698.4	+995.1	1.5
1976	11.9	10,040.8	+290.0	4.1
1977	32.4	12,227.0	+1,104.7	2.9
1978	36.0	14,573.0	+1,910.9	1.8
1979	27.2	17,044.9	+3,108.0	0.8
1980	32.9	19,661.7	+2,427.0	1.3
1981	47.8	22,489.2	+3,280.9	1.4
1982	49.9	26,125.3	+2,654.3	1.8
1983	57.1	28,716.3	−1,280.7	4.4
1984	116.2	30,995.6	−508.1	22.8
1985	166.5	32,699.2	+11.3	—
1986	132.5[d]	—	—	—

[a] The Western Canada Lottery Association includes the provinces of Alberta, British Columbia, Manitoba, and Saskatchewan plus the Northwest Territories and the Yukon.

[b] Fiscal years ending March 31.

[c] When (2) in absolute terms is less than (4).

[d] Effective April 1, 1985, British Columbia withdrew as a member of the Western Canada Lottery Corporation, receiving its share of the assets of the corporation and assuming its share of the liabilities. This withdrawal is reflected in the profits listed here.

Sources: Net profits of lotteries: Annual reports of the Western Canada Lottery Corporation.

Government revenues and deficits: Statistics Canada, publication no. 68–207, *Provincial Public Finances.*

United Kingdom

Table 5. *Lottery revenues and expenses, 1802–27 (millions of pounds)*

(1) Year	(2) Lottery income	(3) Lottery expenditures	(4) Profit (2) − (3)	(5) Income of government[a]	(6) Deficit (−) or surplus (+)	(7) (4) as % of (6)[b]
1770	0.6	0.6	0	11.3	+0.8	—
1771	0.61	0.5	0.11	10.9	+0.8	13.7
1772	0.76	0.45	0.31	11.0	+0.3	—
1773	0.04	0.6	−0.56	10.4	+0.5	—
1774	0.74	—	—	10.6	+1.1	—
1775	0.74	0.6	0.14	11.1	+0.8	17.5
1776	0.02	0.6	−0.58	10.5	−3.5	—
1777	0.49	—	—	11.1	−4.1	—
1778	0.4	0.5	−0.1	11.4	−6.5	—
1779	0.54	0.48	0.06	11.8	−7.9	0.7
1780	0.44	0.49	−0.05	12.5	−10.1	—
1781	0.48	0.48	0	13.2	−12.6	—
1782	0.42	0.48	−0.06	13.7	−15.5	—
1783	0.52	0.40	0.12	12.6	−10.9	1.1
1784	0.28	0.48	−0.20	13.2	−11	—
1785	0.39	0.36	0.03	15.5	−10.3	0.2
1786	0.57	0.5	0.07	15.2	−1.7	4.1
1787	0.73	0.5	0.23	16.4	+1	23.0
1788	0.78	0.5	0.28	16.7	+0.4	70.0
1789	0.74	0.48	0.26	16.6	+0.6	43.4
1790	0.86	0.5	0.36	17.0	+0.3	—
1791	0.78	0.5	0.28	18.5	+0.6	46.6
1792	0.81	0.5	0.31	18.6	+1.7	18.2

Year						
1793	0.75	0.5	0.25	18.1	−1.5	16.6
1794	0.67	0.5	0.17	18.7	−10	1.7
1795	0.81	0.5	0.31	19.0	−15.1	2.0
1796	0.91	0.5	0.41	19.3	−23	1.7
1797	0.49	0.5	−0.01	21.3	−36.3	—
1798	0.64	0.5	0.14	26.9	−20.5	0.6
1799	0.69	0.5	0.19	31.7	−15.7	1.2
1801[c]	0.79	0.5	0.29	31.5	—	—
1802	1.1	0.8	0.3	39.1	−26.4	1.1
1803	1.1	1.0	0.1	41.2	−13.6	0.7
1804	1.3	0.9	0.4	42.4	−10.6	3.7
1805	1.1	0.8	0.3	50.2	−12.6	2.3
1806	1.3	0.8	0.5	55.0	−16.4	3.0
1807	1.2	0.5	0.7	60.1	−12.8	5.4
1808	1.3	1.1	0.2	64.8	−8.5	2.3
1809	1.1	0.5	0.6	68.2	−9.8	6.1
1810	0.8	0.6	0.2	69.2	−12.3	1.6
1811	1.1	0.6	0.5	73.0	−8.6	5.8
1812	0.9	0.6	0.3	71.0	−16.3	1.8
1813	1.0	0.6	0.4	70.3	−24.5	1.6
1814	0.9	0.5	0.4	74.7	−36.4	1.6
1815	1.1	0.7	0.4	77.9	−35	1.1
1816	1.1	0.8	0.3	79.1	−20.4	1.1
1817	1.0	0.6	0.4	69.2	−2.1	1.4
1818	0.8	0.5	0.3	57.6	−1.1	19.0
1819	0.8	0.6	0.2	59.5	+1.9	27.2
1820	0.8	0.6	0.2	58.1	+0.6	10.5
1821	0.8	0.6	0.2	59.9	+1.5	33.3
1822	0.9	0.7	0.2	61.6	+3.2	13.3

Table 5 (cont.)

(1) Year	(2) Lottery income	(3) Lottery expenditures	(4) Profit (2) − (3)	(5) Income of government[a]	(6) Deficit (−) or surplus (+)	(7) (4) as % of (6)
1823	0.8	0.6	0.2	59.9	+3.4	5.9
1824	0.6	0.6	0	58.5	+4.2	—
1825	0.6	0.4	0.2	59.7	+4.2	4.8
1826	1.0	0.7	0.3	57.7	+3.6	8.3
1827	0.3	0.4	−0.1	55.2	−0.9	—
1828				54.7	−1.2	
1829				56.5	+3	
1830				55.3	+1.6	
1831				54.5	+2.6	
1832				50.6	−0.9	
1833				51.1	+0.5	
1834				50.2	+1.4	
1835				50.4	+1.5	
1836				50	−15.2	
1837				52.6	−1.4	
1838				50.4	−0.7	
1839				51.3	−0.4	
1840				51.8	−1.6	
1841				51.6	−1.6	
1842				52.2	−2.1	

[a] Up to 1801, net income; from 1801, gross income.

[b] When (4) in absolute terms is less than (6).

[c] Data for 1800 are missing.

Source: Mitchell and Deane 1962, Table 3, pp. 392–5; Table 4, p. 399.

Comments: The data on lottery income and expenditures show that the English lotteries had losses in some years. As the lottery was persistently defended by the Chancellor of the Exchequer, this throws some doubt on the data. Still, when the lottery had a loss, we did not compute its "contribution" to the government's finances.

France

Table 6. *Lottery revenues and expenses, 1797–1828*
(millions of francs)

(1) Year	(2) Gross revenues	(3) Expenditures (administrative and prizes)	(4) Net profit	(5) Total government receipts[a]	(6) Deficit (−) or surplus (+)[a]
1798	21.9	16.5	5.4		
1799	36.7	28.4	8.3		
1800	31.0	23.5	7.5		
1801	53.3	44.4	8.9		
1802	74.9	61.9	13		
1803	75.7	60.2	15.5		
1804	70.1	54.9	15.2		
1805	69.3	56.3	13		
1806	77.8	65.5	12.3		
1807	74.3	62.1	12.2		
1808	71.4	58.6	12.8		
1809	72.6	59.5	13.1		
1810	88.2	64	24.2		
1811	63.5	46.8	16.7		
1812	70.4	57.5	12.9		
1813	76.7	65.9	10.8		
1814	33.2	33.6	−0.4		
1815	32	24.5	7.5	876	−55.1
1816	42.4	33.2	9.2	1,037	−19.1
1817	48	42.3	5.7	1,270	+81.1
1818	58.8	48.5	10.3	1,414	−19.7
1819	53.6	47.9	5.7	937	+40.7
1820	57.6	40	17.6	939	+32.5
1821	51.4	42.1	9.3	935	+26.4
1822	52.3	39.7	12.6	950	+0.8
1823	49.4	37.5	11.9	1,042	−75.3
1824	50.9	42.7	8.2	990	+3.5
1825	57.2	46.3	10.9	979	−3.2
1826	51.3	43.6	7.7	982	+5.8
1827	51.7	44.5	7.2	948	−38.2
1828	53.2	42.5	10.7	1,029	+4.8

[a] Available only from 1815 on.
Sources: (2) and (3): *Moniteur Universel*, May 14, 1830, as quoted in Leonnet 1963; (5) and (6): *Annuaire Statistique de la France*, 1966, Table 1A, p. 484.
Comments: This table shows that although the lottery's profits represented only a small part of the total receipts of the French government (a maximum of 1.8% in 1820 and a more standard 1% in the other years), they made a significant contribution to the reduction of the deficit when there was one.

United States

Table 7. *New Jersey: Annual revenues and expenditures and lottery contribution (millions of dollars)*

(1) Year[a]	(2) Total revenues	(3) Lottery profits	(4) Surplus (+) or deficit (−)	(5) (3) as % of (4)[b]
1976	5,739	66.1	−114	58.0
1977	7,038	78.1	+210	37.1
1978	7,438	96.0	+501	19.1
1979	7,881	122.0	+163	74.8
1980	8,822	145.8	+285	51.1
1981	10,269	175.9	−11	—
1982	11,341	220.0	+189	—
1983	12,604	295.0	+840	35.1
1984	14,677	358.3	+2,042	17.5
1985	—	390.8	—	—

[a] Fiscal years ending June 30.
[b] When (3) in absolute terms is less than (4).
Sources: Lottery profits: Annual reports of the New Jersey Lottery, various years. State public finance data: *Annual Abstract of the United States*, various years, and *State Government Finance* publications of the Bureau of the Census.
Comments: Profits from the lottery have contributed significantly to New Jersey's income.

Table 8. *New York: Annual revenues and expenditures and lottery contribution (millions of dollars)*

(1) Year[a]	(2) Total revenues	(3) Lottery profits	(4) Surplus (+) or deficit (−)	(5) (3) as % of (4)
1977	22,667	94.8[b]	+1,414	6.7
1978	23,426	91.2	+2,030	4.5
1979	25,181	90.9	+2,473	3.6
1980	27,199	85.6	+2,221	3.8
1981	30,003	103.0	+2,223	4.6
1982	33,396	179.8	+3,236	5.5
1983	35,851	275.2	+3,930	7.0
1984	42,412	390.5	+6,495	6.0
1985	—	600.0	—	—
1986	—	607.8	—	—

[a] Fiscal years ending March 31.
[b] Estimate for September 8, 1976, to March 31, 1977.
Sources: Lottery profits: Public Notice of the New York Lottery Corporation based on annual reports.

State finances: *Annual Abstract of the United States*, various years, and *State Government Finances* publications of the Bureau of the Census.

Notes

Chapter 1. The uneasy history of lotteries

1 See Ezell 1960, p. 2; *Encyclopaedia Judaica* 1971, "Lots," pp. 510–12; Bolen 1976, pp. 7–9.
2 Huizinga (1955, p. 79) mentions that the word *urim* has affinities with a root that means casting lots and shooting as well as justice, law: *yore*, meaning "shoot," and *thorah*, referring to law.
3 Kassuto 1963, p. 105.
4 This has been interpreted to mean that, unlike Moses, who could consult God directly, Joshua had to go through the priest and the lot-casting procedure to know what God's wishes were (ibid., p. 109).
5 These examples are also quoted in Lorenz 1985, but the analysis is different. Apparently the garments of Christ were also divided by casting lots (Matt. 27:35).
6 Even in our day, the selection of soldiers for the Vietnam War was made with the help of a government lottery (Blakey 1977, p. 656). By this means superiors could avoid feeling responsible for the death of a soldier.
7 Drawing lots remained the practice of the Jews, as can be seen from two cases reported by Josephus Flavius in *The Jewish Wars*. First, when Josephus, a general of the Jews who rebelled against Rome, was defeated by the Romans, he took refuge in the city of Jotapata. The town was besieged by Vespasian, and the defenders, despairing of their fate if they were captured, decided to commit mass suicide against Josephus's earnest wish. Failing to convince them, he decided to "stake his life on one last throw," and he convinced the others to "draw lots and kill each other in turn." As suicide is abhorrent to God, the last two men had to kill each other. But by either luck or trickery, Josephus was one of the last two, and he convinced the other that he should surrender (pp. 202–3). The second case reported by Josephus, who by now had become a renegade, is the case of the mass suicide by the defenders of Massada. The rebellion having been brutally quelled in all of Judea, and Jerusalem having been destroyed, the last rebellious Jews made a stand in the formidable fortress of Massada on the Dead Sea. Being besieged by the Romans and foreseeing their eventual defeat, they decided to kill themselves instead of falling into the hands of their enemies. Each man killed his family. Then they drew lots among the men to choose ten, who killed the other defenders. The ten remaining drew lots among themselves to choose one who would kill the other nine and then kill himself (ch. 23). These two examples show that casting lots was still used by the Jews of the first century C.E. to choose people for an important task or mission. See also *Encyclopaedia Judaica* 1971, pp. 510–12.

8 Sumner and Keller 1927, vol. 3, pp. 2069–70; Caillois 1958, p. 231; Pryor 1977. Some writers (Lea, Tarpy, and Webley 1987, for example) interpret this evidence as implying that people played games of chance. But the discussion in this section suggests that initially both the use of the dice and the perception of acts we now view as games of chance were not viewed as such, but were part of a ritual where chance was not perceived as playing a role. Only later, much later, was the secular notion of chance linked with these practices, and then the nature of the acts changed. Other authors have noticed that the casting of dice and use of cards were instruments of religion and magic, yet they have still written that these acts were perceived as games of chance. See, for example, Martinez 1983, p. 14, and Feinman, Blashek, and McCabe 1986, p. 3. Devereux (1980, App. A, pp. 1016–21) at times presents an argument similar to the one advanced here, but his discussion is confused; he says that "to appeal a matter to chance is to appeal it directly to God, for he decides the outcome of chance events" (p. 1021). This argument is inappropriate for the simple reason that the notion of chance had no place in those systems of belief (see *Encyclopaedia Judaica* 1971, pp. 501–12). Notice that this view is in contrast with the Mesopotamian idea that the gods, as well as men, are subject to the fall of the lots (ibid., "Lots").

9 See Rosenthal 1975, p. 33.

10 Ibid., ch. 3.

11 At-Tabari, as quoted in ibid., p. 83.

12 Ibid., p. 33.

13 Ibid., p. 159.

14 This legend is reported in Rouse 1957, p. 16.

15 Not only are we unaware of what the Urim and Thummim were, but we are also unable to make out exactly what all these stories, biblical or Greek, tell us. Vico, for example, in his *New Science* (1982) argues that these stories are all metaphors and use a language that we no longer understand and that we therefore misinterpret. See discussion of Vico's views in Berlin 1976.

16 Huizinga 1955, p. 94, and note 2 above.

17 Rubner 1966, p. 15. It should be noted that the word "luck" is only a rough equivalent of the Greek word *tyche*, since *tyche* does not necessarily refer to random or uncaused events, but means what just happens to a person as opposed to what he or she does or makes. See extensive discussion on this point in Nussbaum 1986, ch. 11.

18 Suetonius mentions that Augustus created categories of magistrates who were chosen by lots (Life of Augustus XXIX). Moreover, the vestal virgins were chosen by lots among patrician girls.

19 See discussion of these issues in a different context, and references, in Brenner 1985, pp. 29–37.

20 Huizinga 1955, p. 39.

21 Ibid.

22 Ibid., p. 57.

23 Mackay 1980, pp. 281–303; Eade 1984; Tester 1987, pp. 176–201.

24 Mackay 1980, pp. 281–90; Eade 1984.

25 Wesley 1958–9, vol. 8, p. 451; Thomas 1971, p. 119. It should be noted that some social scientists view the substitution of astrology for religious

belief as a sign of decline in culture, an impoverishment of personality, and a diminishment of people's moral and spiritual nature rather than mere substitution of one form of decision making for another. For, they argue, "Man had previously been understood in terms of what the poets, historians and philosophers had made of him – a being not exempt from weakness and villainy, but yet versatile, adventurous, resourceful, enterprising, adaptable, aspiring and in great measure his own master. Now he had shrunk to being the puppet of the stars, whose relation to the powers that rule his destiny could be presented in a mathematical diagram" (Cohen 1964, p. 189). This complaint should sound familiar, for it is precisely on the grounds of their pseudo-scientific aspects and the fascination exercised by the exactness of their procedures that some social sciences (economics in particular) are criticized today. The problem is not in using geometry or other branches of the mathematical language to check the consistency of one's arguments, but in using the mathematics that approximate the movements of planets, falling bodies, and chromosomes to describe people's behavior. Cohen (p. 173) noted that astrology has left its mark on the language we use: Apparently "consider" initially meant "contrasting the influence of the various stars" (*sidera*) on the "contemplated" decision, "con-templation" meaning the construction of a diagram quartering the sky (called *templum*). More than that: The astrologer's column is known to every reader in Western countries; 2,000 American periodicals publish horoscopes. In the United States there are 30,000 professional establishments for astrology and 20 specialized magazines for half a million readers; $200 million is spent annually on "information" derived from the stars. In Britain, 20 million persons are estimated to read the daily horoscopes, and in France *Elle* claims to have the best such column (Cohen 1964, pp. 172–4). Nancy Reagan's use of astrology became a *cause célèbre* during her husband's presidency.

26 In other words, although lots and dice were used in antiquity, their use was unrelated to games of chance. The mistake of calling their use gambling may have been due to a fact that some historians have noted: People fail to change vocabularies every time they change customs (see Bloch 1953; Berlin 1976; Vico 1982). Hence some writers failed to examine what was happening and just looked at the fact that dice and lots existed. Most writers mentioned in the bibliography seem to miss this point and include the summarized evidence, from whatever period, in their history of gambling.

27 See Thomas 1971, pp. 360–82; Tester 1987, pp. 176–201.

28 See Bolen 1976. Fleming (1978, p. 2) notes that Plato suggested that a demon named Theuth created dice. Those who gave the credit to Palamedes also attributed to him the invention of weights, measures, and the alphabet. Bolen also notes that Palamedes had "the questionable distinction of being the first gambler cheater to be put to death for deceptive gambling practices" (1976, p. 9).

29 Ashton 1898, p. 6; Rubner 1966, p. 15. Ezell (1960, p. 2) mentions an even weirder lottery conceived by the emperor Heliogabalus: In the drawing of his lottery at the Circus he gave equal odds on winning a gold vase or six flies!

30 Ashton 1898, pp. 6–8. The emperors also gambled. Suetonius mentions that Augustus was a great gambler all his life, even quoting Augustus's letters on the subject. He also mentions that Nero lost great sums of money gambling.

31 Blanche 1950.

32 Tacitus's *Germania* reports of the ancient Germans that they "are so reckless in their anxiety to win, however often they lose, that when everything else is gone they will stake their personal liberty on a last decisive throw. A loser willingly discharges his debt by becoming a slave" (p. 121). The same love of gambling is noted by Caesar in describing the people of Gaul.

33 Blanche 1950; Rubner 1966, p. 14. In Flanders in 1579, for example, Antoine Fererist was given the right to sell lotteries where the prizes were pieces of furniture.

34 In 1466 Madame Jan van Eyck, widow of the Flemish painter, organized a lottery to raise money for the poor in the city of Bruges (Fleming 1978, p. 57).

35 Kinsey 1959, p. 13; Labrosse 1985, ch. 1, pp. 12–16.

36 Handelsman 1933, pp. 45–7.

37 Blanche 1950; Ezell 1960, p. 2; Rubner 1966, p. 14.

38 Coste 1933, p. 83; Desperts 1982. Betting on the outcome of elections was already known: It occurred in 1520 during elections for the Great Council of Genoa. The form this betting took is at the source of the modern numbers games: Five senatorial candidates were chosen at random from a predetermined list of aspirants. People bet on who would be selected. From this developed the game of lotto where numbers from 1 to 90 were substituted for names. This is still the standard system (Smith 1952; Labrosse 1985, p. 15).

39 Coste 1933, p. 21; Leonnet 1963, p. 13.

40 Leonnet 1963, p. 15. The revenues also provided funds for a hospital.

41 Cohen 1964, p. 44. The restoration of more than half of the Parisian churches between 1714 and 1729 was financed by revenues from lotteries (Leonnet 1963, p. 15).

42 See Labrosse 1985 for a review of French lotteries. Coste gives a list of the public projects that were financed by lotteries in France: the Parisian general hospital in 1660; fire pumps for Paris in 1701; the relief of Lyons's poor in 1699; a hospital in Amiens and a school in Angers (1933, p. 23).

43 The Lottery of the Roman States began in 1732. The pope's involvement with a lottery may have convinced the very Catholic Louis XVI that lotteries were a legitimate means of raising money (Leonnet 1963, pp. 17–18).

44 Ibid., p. 18.

45 Coste quotes Chaumette, the public prosecutor for the department of Seine, who called the state lottery "a scourge invented by despotism to quiet the people by giving them a false hope" (1933, p. 28). During the debate in the National Assembly, Mirabeau sent an open letter to his fellow members accusing the ones who were in favor of a lottery of supporting a "tax whose proceeds stem from folly or despair" (Leonnet 1963, p. 37).

46 The argument presented at the Council of the Five Hundred (as the parliament was then called) sounds almost modern: "Of all kinds of contribution, no other has fewer detractors and more supporters than the lottery.... All other taxes must be paid whether one wants them or not. One is free not to contribute to the lottery" (Handelsman 1933, p. 18). The partisans of its continued suppression also used modern arguments: "Ask this desolated mother whose children die of hunger; she will tell you: My husband was addicted to the lottery and we are left without resources. Ask this firm why it is bankrupt; the lottery is the cause" (Leonnet 1963, p. 42). It should be noted that similar reactions did not lead later governments to such a rapid change; see Chapter 5.

47 Leonnet 1963, pp. 49ff.

48 Henriquet 1921, p. 23.

49 Ezell 1960, p. 4.

50 Woodhall 1964; Ashton 1969, pp. 20ff.

51 Ezell 1960, p. 8.

52 Ashton 1969, p. 40.

53 Ezell 1960, p. 9.

54 The details of this lottery are given in Woodhall 1964.

55 To give an idea of how widely lotteries were used, Ashton (1898, p. 229) states that in a randomly picked issue of *The Tatler* of 1710 no fewer than six lotteries are mentioned, some with money prizes and some with prizes of merchandise.

56 Ibid., p. 230.

57 Ashton 1969, pp. 231–2.

58 These details are taken from Woodhall 1964.

59 For instance, in 1818 a member said that on the tomb of the Chancellor of the Exchequer of this time should be written: "Here lies..., once Chancellor of the Exchequer; patron of Bible Societies,... an encourager of Saving's banks – a supporter of lotteries!" (Ashton 1898, p. 238).

60 Ibid., p. 161.

61 Quoted in ibid., pp. 239–40.

62 See a discussion of gambling during and after the Industrial Revolution in Brenner 1985, ch. 3.

63 These details on English lotteries are taken from Blanche 1950 and Ezell 1960.

64 Similar characteristics can be detected in the history of lotteries in Poland. Introduced by an Italian around 1748, the lotto game soon attracted the attention of the Polish Diet, which in 1768 established a system of state concessions to the private lotteries' promoters in order to increase the state's revenues. To this first lottery another – the class lottery – was added in 1808, with much more expensive tickets. As in other European countries, calls were heard during the nineteenth century to abolish the main lottery on the ground that it exploited the poor. This opinion indeed led to its abolition in 1840 because of (the law states) "its bad influence on the moral character of the poor." But the class lottery, with tickets too expensive for the poor, continued undeterred until 1915 when war ended it. At the end of the war, the new Polish Republic resurrected the state lottery. See Handelsman 1933.

65 Details of the history of lotteries in early America can be found in Smith

1952, Ezell 1960, Devereux 1980, and the other sources referred to here.
66 Quoted in Ezell 1960, p. 13.
67 Ibid., p. 28.
68 Quoted in ibid., p. 49.
69 Blanche 1950, p. 78.
70 An investigation of the lottery in New York in 1818 also damned "insurance" because it "entices women, children, apprentices, Negroes, and the poorest" (Ezell 1960, pp. 189–90).
71 The most famous of these was the Baldwin libel case. Baldwin, the editor of the *Republican Chronicle* in New York, in September 1818 published a series of articles in which he accused the lottery of rigging the results, so that insurers (who bet against a number being drawn) lost heavily. The directors of the lottery sued Baldwin for libel, and the resulting trial (in which Baldwin was acquitted) unveiled all the means that were used to rig the lottery (ibid., pp. 188ff.).
72 It is noteworthy that the spur under which the Massachusetts legislature acted was the suicide of a 35-year-old bookkeeper and treasurer of a large Boston mercantile house who had gambled away all his property and embezzled $18,000 of his employer's money (ibid., p. 211).
73 Details of the history of Canadian lotteries are taken from Labrosse 1985.
74 Ibid., pp. 55ff.
75 Ibid., p. 69.
76 Ibid., p. 64.
77 Ibid., pp. 76–9.
78 The church first had an amendment passed that permitted raffles of unsold objects with a value of no more than $50. But with the passage of the British North American Act in 1867, Quebec obtained its own assembly, which passed the new law (ibid., p. 83).
79 Kinsey 1959, p. 20.
80 For the story of the Spanish lottery, see Altabella 1962.
81 Labrosse 1985, p. 63.
82 Landau 1968, p. 3.
83 Handelsman 1933, pp. 22ff.
84 Kinsey 1959, p. 28.
85 Rubner 1966, p. 38.
86 Landau 1968, p. 19.
87 Kinsey 1959, p. 29.
88 Dixon 1984.
89 Weinstein and Deitch 1974, p. 14.
90 Abt, Smith, and Christiansen 1985; Mikesell and Zorn 1985, p. 1; Clotfelter and Cook 1987a, b.
91 This history of Canadian lotteries relies on Labrosse 1985.
92 The system worked as follows: People were urged to pay a voluntary tax to the city of Montreal in units of $2; each month there was a drawing from the list of those who had paid the tax, and the winners were awarded bars of silver. The biggest prize had a value of $150,000. In order to keep up the fiction that this was not a lottery, each winner was asked to answer a "skill question." The origins of such questions are examined in Chapter 3.

Chapter 2. Why do people gamble?

1 See R. Brenner 1983, ch. 1, and 1985, ch. 2, for examinations of this answer.
2 These questions were raised, and evidence presented, in R. Brenner 1983, 1985; G. A. Brenner 1985, 1986; and G. A. Brenner and Tremblay 1986. Here much more evidence is gathered and the subjects are treated in more depth.
3 See Friedman and Savage 1948; Markowitz 1952; Alchian 1953; Arrow 1970; Schoemaker 1982. In correspondence with us, Friedman admits that whereas in his 1948 article with Savage they used the existence of multiple prizes to rationalize the upper concave section of the utility function, they subsequently came to the conclusion that that was not a valid rationalization. More will be said on this point later. Most recent articles about risk taking either make slight mathematical variations on the traditional approach or carry out laboratory experiments. See the collections of articles in Kahneman, Slovic, and Tversky 1982; Arkes and Hammond 1986; Hogarth and Reder 1986. The value of laboratory experiments to explain behavior in circumstances where large sums are at stake seems, in the light of the model and evidence presented in this chapter, questionable. See also Cohen 1964, p. 61, making this point. Zeckhauser (1986, p. 260) also notices that economists have not succeeded in shedding light on gambling. See also Eadington 1987. More is said on these issues in Appendix 1.
4 Freud 1929.
5 For a summary of psychological interpretations, still relying on Freud's initial insights, see Kusyszyn 1984; Lea, Tarpy, and Webley 1987. On compulsive gamblers, see Bergler 1957; Herman 1967b; Lea et al. 1987; and, for a very different view, Dixon 1980.
6 Friedman and Savage 1948, however, suggest that the poorer may have greater incentives to gamble.
7 Other sociologists' viewpoints are reviewed in Chapter 3, where Devereux's viewpoint is also discussed in further detail.
8 See R. Brenner 1983, chs. 1, 2. Frey notes what Downes et al. (1976) remarked too; namely, "the absence of any hypotheses, much less any interrelated propositions about gambling behavior that could be designated a theory. Thus, several quasi-theories or propositions about anomie, alienation, working-class culture, functionalism, decision-making, risk-taking, work-centered leisure, and home centeredness were tested by Downes and his associates" (1984, p. 118). Frey suggests that although a strictly Marxist interpretation of gambling behavior does not exist, gambling can take its place alongside religion and sport as an opiate of the masses (pp. 112–13). But, as is shown in the next two chapters, this interpretation is contradicted by the facts. The richer have frequently condemned gambling and some other pastimes of the poor. For various approaches, see also Newman 1972; Lester 1979.
9 See the formal translation of this prediction in Appendix 1.
10 See Appendix 1.

11 Such examinations have already been made in R. Brenner 1983, 1985, 1987.

12 See references in R. Brenner 1985, ch. 2.

13 Weinstein and Deitch 1974, p. 36. See also Desperts 1982, emphasizing that in France it was always the large draw that provided the attraction.

14 Sullivan 1972, p. 111. See also Cohen 1964, p. 48, on the preference for fewer but larger prizes.

15 *Gambling in America* (1976), p. 157; Landau 1968, p. 34. Such findings are also reported in Kallick et al. 1979. Koeves also notes that "the real love of the South American masses remains the lottery. The prizes are often very high. In Mexico, special drawings reward the winner with $250,000 and Argentina's Christmas Special dishes out the grand total of $1,500,000. One of the most familiar sights in the streets of South America are the street vendors offering tickets, a persistent lot, more often than not consisting of old men in rags, barefoot kids, or cripples. Some of the vendors make the rounds and shout out their numbers at the crack of dawn, hoping that a prospective purchaser has dreamed about that particular number" (1952, pp. 57–8).

16 Rubner 1966, pp. 17, 45. He also notes that the pronounced preference of the public for big prizes can best be studied by comparing the "investment" in football fixed-odds and treble-chance pools; the former type, with relatively small prizes, is more akin to betting, whereas the latter is but a modified lottery with high prizes. More than four out of five "investors" in 1965–6 preferred the treble chance, and the football-pool promoters are so convinced of the relative attractiveness of the large prizes that they enhance them at the expense of lower "dividends" (pp. 45–6).

17 Sprowls 1954, p. 354.

18 See discussion and references in section 1 of Chapter 6.

19 We must nevertheless remark that bingo games with very high stakes have recently been introduced by some Native American tribes on their lands in order to increase the tribe's wealth. These games are completely different from the traditional ones and are similar to lotteries.

20 We could not find evidence on this point for other countries.

21 See Appendix 1 for the mathematical translation of this argument.

22 Such substitutes provide only a second-best. Disputes in the family may prevent one from easily finding a buying pool. Also, because of the negative attitude toward gambling, the unfortunate unemployed person (the one who may be most willing to spend a few dollars on the ticket) may have the greatest difficulty in joining a pool. See G. A. Brenner and Brenner 1987.

23 Sprowls 1970, p. 82. The "consolation prizes" are perhaps like coupons attached to goods one has bought. See also note 16.

24 See also Lea et al. 1987.

25 A similar picture emerges from Spiro's study (1974).

26 Newman takes into account the varying retention rates in the different gambling activities and, from the £1,497 million ($3,548 million) turnover in 1964, arrives at net expenditures of £269 million ($637 million), the average annual net expenditure for each Briton turning out to be a mere £4.85 ($11.50), less than the cost of one packet of cigarettes a week.

Kinsey (1963) draws a similar picture. He estimates that in 1950 even those who played at least once a week spent an annual average of $140 on dog-race totalization wagers, $14 on football pools, and $28 on off-track betting on horse races. The percentages of adults who gambled frequently on these three games were, respectively, 1, 28, and 11.

27 This reversal should be expected. It is probably the richer who play in casinos, which they use as a form of entertainment. Unlike a lottery, a casino takes up the gambler's time. Unsurprisingly, Newman also found that betting shops were concentrated in districts inhabited mostly by people belonging to the lower-level manual classes (1972, p. 99). Grussi mentions that in *ancien régime* France, jealous husbands fostered their wives' gambling in hopes of preventing dalliance (1985, p. 115) – once again a matter of choosing one's leisure activity . . .

28 Rubner notes that frequently one hears the idea that lotteries and sweepstakes are wicked because they depend entirely on chance, whereas betting ought to be permitted because it depends, to some extent, on knowledge (1966, pp. 3–5). These arguments are misguided, as Rubner points out, and he presents the following evidence to support his view: During a cold spell at the beginning of 1963, football matches could not be played for several consecutive weeks. But national football was played in play-acting sessions on television, with prominent figures guessing what the results would have been had the matches been played. He concludes that "national football as an instrument permitting gambling to take place during ice and snow is commendable, but it also exposes the hollowness of the claim that filling in a football coupon calls for substantially more skill than picking a lottery ticket out of a hat" (p. 4). See also Cohen and Hansel 1956, p. 142.

29 Tec 1964.

30 Ibid., p. 47.

31 Sources can be found in R. Brenner 1983. It should be noted that for the sample to be unbiased, the number of tickets bought should be taken into account. We did not have this information.

32 This survey was undertaken by Kaplan et al. (1979) for Loto-Canada.

33 The hypothesis that, but for statistical error, the proportions among the younger and the older are the same may be rejected at the 5 percent and 10 percent significance level respectively. This test is based on a comparison of the percentage of people among the winners' sample and in the general population. A draw of a young winner in the general population is a random variable with binomial distribution. As the sample is large for statistical purposes (more than 40), we assume that this variable has a normal distribution and test the hypothesis that the two proportions are the same.

34 The sample included winners of Cdn. $1 million and more in Ontario, Cdn. $100,000 or more in Quebec, and Cdn. $50,000 or more in the other provinces. Thus it is not exactly a random sample of lottery winners and so of the lottery-ticket-buying population. However, if there is a bias, its direction is not clear. We will make the assumption that the sample is random.

35 It may be useful to note that in a 1984 survey of lottery winners in the United States, including 576 winners in twelve states, Kaplan found that

"prior to winning, [the] respondents' incomes were clustered in the *lower* range with 69 percent of the winners and 75 percent of their spouses earning less than $20,000 a year" (1985a, p. 10). In a later study of this same data set, he also found that the average age of winners was slightly over 54 (1985b). A 1984 Loto-Québec survey also found that people in the 35–64 age group were much more likely to be regular lottery-ticket buyers. Also see Table 2.5, which shows the distribution of buyers according to age.

36 Robert Sylvestre 1977, vol. 4, tables 1–5, series 9.
37 Devereux 1980, p. 807.
38 In an article in the *Wall Street Journal*, Ronald Alsop gives some examples of unemployed workers who in the midst of recession saw the lottery as their last hope. One of them said of his weekly bet: "The way things are now, I've got to try something" (Feb. 24, 1983, p. 31). Li and Smith also found in their study (1976) of a 1971 Gallup survey of attitudes toward gambling that there was a weak statistical link between frustrated expectations and the propensity to gamble.
39 A. Campbell and Converse 1972, pp. 172–3.
40 See Royal Commission on Bilingualism and Biculturalism 1967, vol. 3, p. 21; Kuch and Haessel 1979; Vaillancourt 1979; Lacroix and Vaillancourt 1981.
41 See Tec 1964, p. 93, and Chapter 3 below for a detailed discussion.
42 Tomes (1983, p. 129) found that male Catholics earn 7 percent less than the mean income of his sample, and Protestants 6 percent more.
43 These numbers are based on the 1976 Canadian census.
44 These estimates are calculated by using the weights given by Statistics Canada, weights reflecting the different rates of response among regions, the kinds of family unit interviewed, and so forth.
45 In 1985 the revenues of the various lotteries in Canada exceeded $2 billion (American billion) dollars, and it has been estimated that Americans spend $200 million on Canadian lotteries. This estimate was given in "Canadian Lotteries Attract U.S. Dollars, As Well As a Lot of American Complaints", *Wall Street Journal*, April 8, 1986.
46 Although this explanation may be plausible for some countries, for others where lottery winnings are not taxed (Canada, for instance), it might not be. But underdeclarations on lottery expenditures seem to be a quite universal phenomenon (see Rubner 1966, p. 123). In fact, another notable property of the data set comes to the fore when one looks at the answers to the question whether or not people spent any money on lotteries. Forty percent in the Atlantic provinces and 26.5 percent in Western Canada answered that they never bought lottery tickets in 1982. But penetration studies of Loto-Québec have found that in 1984, 84 percent of Quebeckers bought such tickets and 92 percent admitted that they had bought them at least once in their lifetime. (These numbers were given to the authors privately by Loto-Québec.) These facts together with those mentioned in the text suggest that either on purpose or inadvertently people answered the Statistics Canada survey misleadingly.
47 Another explanation may be that one of a couple may not reveal to the other that he or she is spending a few dollars a week on lotteries.
48 McKibbin 1979.

49 Ibid.
50 Rubner 1966, p. 123, and see comments on studies based on surveys in Glock 1967, p. 249, and Moser and Kalton 1972, pp. 379, 389–90. Neither of the last two suggests solutions for correcting the errors.
51 There seem to be no more data available than those summarized in this chapter. Dixon noted that "the lack of officially collected information on gambling seriously hampered constructive discussions about gambling in Britain down to the Rothschild Commission which concluded, in 1978, that 'there is a serious shortage of reliable and accessible information about gambling in the United Kingdom. Routine information about participation in the various forms of gambling, how the gambling industry works, how much is staked and spent, and how much excessive gambling there is, is markedly lacking'" (1981, p. 26). As suggested in the text, Dixon may have too much confidence that officially collected data may help. When collected thoughtlessly, without knowing what questions to ask or how to ask them, they may turn out to be of limited use.
52 See section 3 in Appendix 2.
53 Gallup 1972; Cornish 1978, p. 39.
54 Smith and Razzell 1975; Downes et al. 1976.
55 Devereux 1980, p. 827.
56 Downes et al. 1976.
57 Newman 1975, p. 543.
58 Newman, like Tec (1964), also found that gamblers show a greater awareness of public affairs than nongamblers, and that "a possible change in life situation was conceived only in terms of higher income.... Within this context, a noticeably more aspiring attitude seemed to prevail amongst 'the gamblers,' expressed in greater preoccupation with pay issues, with acquisition of consumer goods and furthermore a budget awareness, a determination to make optimal use of one's financial resources" (1972, p. 223). Herman (1967a) is also struck by the evidence of careful deliberation and disciplined composure on the part of racecourse attenders.
59 Tec 1964.
60 See summary of this work in Skolnick 1982.
61 See also Lea et al. 1987 for a summary of similar evidence.
62 Royal Commission on Betting, Lotteries and Gaming 1951, pp. 49–50.
63 Ibid., p. 53.
64 Ibid., p. 45.
65 Ibid., p. 40.
66 Ibid., p. 52. The report also adds that although the authors do not doubt that there is some connection between dishonesty and excessive gambling among persons of a generally dissolute character, they cannot regard this as evidence that gambling is, in itself, a cause of crime. The authors also conclude that they could not find evidence to support the view that gambling is a cause of juvenile delinquency. Parts of the report referring to these issues are reprinted in Herbert L. Marx Jr. (ed.), *Gambling in America* (New York: Wilson, 1952), pp. 195–207.
67 Rowntree 1901, p. 144, quoted in Dixon 1981, p. 10.
68 Allen 1952; Tec 1964.
69 Cornish 1978, p. 68.

70 See a formal proof of this statement in R. Brenner 1983, ch. 1 and its appendix, and 1985, ch. 2 and appendix to ch. 1.

71 F. Campbell (1976) quotes Schragg's conclusion here. Newman also concludes that "gambling constitutes for the overwhelming majority of participants, a pastime rather than an addiction. Both frequency of participation, as well as volume of expenditure appear to be moderate, and subject to personal self-direction and control. For no more than a small and numerically insignificant minority can gambling...be regarded as unmanageable and obsessive" (1972, p. 226). Of course this is not a very exciting image, and some of the critics of gambling noted that, but they reached an erroneous conclusion. Perkins, for example, wrote that "[gambling] is the easy but mistaken reaction to risk, and is retrogressive rather than progressive in its effects. It has seldom been put better than by Maurice Maeterlinck: 'Gambling is the stay-at-home, squalid, imaginary, mechanical, anaemic, and unlovely adventure of those who have never been able to encounter or create the real, necessary, and salutary adventure of life'" (1958, pp. 34–5). But can one imagine how the world would look if everybody abandoned customary behavior? For an example of what happens in such a situation, see Lewis Thomas's (1974, pp. 107–11) description of a small African tribe, the Ik.

72 Kaplan 1985a, p. 6.

73 Ibid., p. 8; italics supplied.

74 Ibid., p. 16.

75 Ibid., pp. 16–17.

76 Among the winners of relatively big prizes (above $250,000) in Kaplan 1978, the quarterly average expenditure on lottery tickets prior to winning was $67. After winning, this amount increased to $100. This increase implies a decrease in the percentage of wealth dedicated to the purchase of lottery tickets when $\frac{67}{W} \geq \frac{100}{W + 250,000}$, W being the individual's initial wealth. For this condition to be fulfilled, the initial wealth had to be less than half a million dollars. Given the characteristics of the winners, this condition seems to be fulfilled.

77 Rubner 1966, p. 25.

78 In a different context, Guttman (1986) remarks that Andrew Carnegie was in favor of taxing inheritances. He believed that a parent who leaves enormous wealth to children generally deadens their talents and energies and tempts them to lead less useful lives than they otherwise would.

79 A similar conclusion is reached in Lea et al. 1987.

80 Bolen (1976, p. 10) quotes P. C. Squires's study "Fyodor Dostoyevsky: A Psychological Sketch," *Psychoanalysis Review*, 24 (1935), which made a similar point. Squires wrote that Dostoyevsky's intemperate gambling was an artistic necessity and that it was during the period after he lost everything that the creative spirit moved him with renewed force.

81 In some developing countries, state lottery officials admit that they consciously appeal to the poorer strata of the population. In Mexico, for instance, a state lottery in which the top prize is $2 million has existed for 203 years, and when a wealthy man wins – a rare occurrence – lottery players and officials alike are dismayed. Foster notes that in traditional peasant societies "modern lotteries are very much functional equivalents

of buried treasure tales..., and at least in Tzin tzun tzan the correlation is clearly understood. One elderly informant, when asked why no one had found buried treasure in recent years, remarked that this was indeed true but 'Today we Mexicans have lotteries instead...' This, I think, explains the interest in lotteries in underdeveloped countries....The man who goes without lunch, and fails to buy shoes for his children in order to buy a weekly ticket, is not a ne'er-do-well; he is the Horatio Alger of his society who is doing what he feels is most likely to advance his position....The odds are against him, but it is the *only* way he knows in which to work toward success" (1967, p. 318; italics in original). Recent almost daily evidence continues to confirm the picture drawn in the text. In December of 1984 a humble home for the elderly and a Spanish emigrant to Australia received the big prizes in Spain's Christmas lottery. Lottery officials were quoted as saying that the big prize ("El Gordo" – the Fat One) breeds a spirit of generosity and that Spaniards are happiest when the prize is shared or goes to the poor. The same month Claude Carpentier, a forty-eight-year-old electrician unemployed for the last four years, won Cdn. $4 million in the Lotto 6/49 draw (*Montreal Gazette*, Dec. 23, 1984). Canada's largest lottery prize, Cdn. $13.9 million, was won in January 1984 by a retired truck driver who died of cancer six months later. A prize of $11 million was won by immigrants from East Africa. The reason why these events were announced in the newspapers' headlines is that the prizes were unusually large; no one had won for a number of weeks.

Chapter 3. Why is gambling condemned?

1 See *Encyclopaedia Judaica*, 1971, "Gambling."
2 See Cohen 1964, ch. 10, esp. pp. 186–9. For a lengthy discussion of chance and fate in Greek religion, see Murray 1955. See a brief discussion in a different context in R. Brenner 1985, appendix to ch. 1.
3 Quoted in Cohen 1964, p. 188.
4 Perkins 1962, p. 8, quoting W. Warde Fowler. Cohen (1966, p. 199) remarks that of all the Roman deities, Fortuna seems to have been the most popular. Every marketplace had an altar in her honor, and in the Forum a splendid temple was dedicated to her. It was apparently the favored spot for women seeking to maintain their husbands' attentions.
5 Rosenthal 1975, p. 159.
6 McNeill 1963, pp. 421–6.
7 Rosenthal 1975, p. 149. For other ancient societies our information is limited, although it seems to confirm the picture drawn here. According to Rubner (1966), Buddha condemned gambling. But Hinduism has few rules that apply to all its adherents. What is a sin for a high-caste Brahmin may not be for the low-caste Kshatriya. Hindu priests regard gambling with disdain but do not view it as a serious moral lapse for low-caste Hindus, among whom gambling is said to be widespread. Shintoism seems to be the only religion that has no pronounced views on gambling and neither regards the absence of material goods as admirable nor striving for them as evil. Lotteries in Japan go back to 1624, and there seems to be no opposition. According to Wagner (1972,

p. 13), gambling predates China's 4,000-year written history. But until Confucius (551?–479 B.C.E.) nobody bothered to condemn it.

8 Starkey 1964, p. 35.

9 See Thomas 1971; Cohen 1964, pp. 150–1, who gives as an illustration the poem "Fortuna Imperatrix Mundi" ("Luck Rules the World"), written during the twelfth century (best known today from Carl Orff's use of it in *Carmina Burana*). He also notes from the sixteenth century that when Montaigne, traveling in Italy, reached Rome, his books were returned with the warning "not to be too lavish of the word Fortuna where Providence would be more in place" (p. 151, quoting *The Diary of Montaigne's Journey to Italy*).

10 See additional quotes from the *Institutes* in Cochrane and Kirshner 1986, pp. 366–86. See also Thomas 1971, pp. 78–85. Thomas remarks that Calvin pointed out that the perils of daily existence would have made life intolerable for men who believed that everything happened by chance and that they were subject to every caprice of arbitrary fortune (p. 81).

11 Thomas (1971), p. 78.

12 Ibid., p. 84.

13 Thorner 1955, pp. 161–2.

14 See discussion in Thomas 1971, p. 122.

15 Stone 1965; 1972, p. 110; Goldstone 1986.

16 Plumb 1967, p. 5.

17 See Stone 1965, 1972; Plumb 1967; R. Brenner 1985, ch. 3; Goldstone 1986. Stone emphasizes that the 100 years between 1540 and 1640 were also characterized by the fact that families and individuals were moving at an unprecedented pace both geographically and socially. The statistical information on which Stone's conclusions are based concerns the transfer of manors during these years.

18 Thomas 1971, p. 4.

19 See G. A. Brenner 1985 on changes in life expectancy during this period and the possible impact on inheritance laws.

20 Thomas 1971, p. 5.

21 According to Malcolmson 1981, pp. 14–16, typical comments of social analysts during this period emphasized that social order was not a human construct but divinely ordained: God, not man, had created social inequality. "There is nothing more plain nor certain, than that God Almighty hath ordained and appointed degrees of Authority and Subjection; allowing Authority to the Master, and commanding obedience from the servant unto him," said one text in 1681. Social inequality "is not by chance," said another text, published in 1693, "but by the Sovereign Disposer of the Lord of all." "It is God's own Appointment, that some should be Rich and some Poor, some High and some Low" and "It has pleased the almighty Governor of the world to make a difference in the outward condition of his subjects here below; and though high and low, rich and poor . . . are all his Servants, yet in the course of his providence he has thought good to appoint various orders and degrees of men here upon earth" were statements written, in 1708 and 1746, respectively, that repeated the same ideas, and their acceptance was viewed as a condition for achieving happiness. Such state-

ments were written by the clergy and the relatively well-to-do and, as Thomas points out (1971, pp. 127–8, 198–206), do not reflect the poorer people's attitudes. But one must pay attention to them in order to understand perceptions of gambling in such views of the world, their impact on legislation, and their emergence in the confusion and prejudice of more recent times. This was also the period when the new entrepreneurial class, linked to industry, expanded and established itself. Of course, before the 1760s "industrialists" could be found in Europe. But, as Bergier points out, "some of them, wholesale dealers often called manufacturing merchants, merely organized commercially the output of a host of wage-earning artisans, without ever attempting to modify ... the methods and techniques involved. . . . The other 'industrialists,' small independent artisans, mostly lacked sufficient means and (especially) sufficient imagination and breadth of mind to make significant innovations – from which they would constantly have been precluded in any case by the strict rules of the guilds" (1973, p. 408). Later, when guilds broke down and some industrialists became rich, they still did not merge with the traditional upper classes linked to Parliament, administration, and finance. The latter distrusted the parvenu industrialists, whom they perceived as challenging the status quo. Although this new, richer industrial class shared the characteristic features of the entrepreneur, it had at first no unity, no solidarity. But gradually cohesion was achieved, an ethos was articulated, fitting the entrepreneurial features of the new class (both in its emphasis on effort and as an insurance against the animosity of some other classes, whose positions they threatened). As Bergier (1975, p. 417) notes, in 1784 Boulton was not merely speaking for himself but for the whole group when he protested against the government's bill for a duty on raw materials; and afterwards the English industrialists, led by Boulton and Wedgwood, formed a "General Chamber of Manufacturers" that had a significant influence on the trade treaties with Ireland (1785) and France (1786).

22 See also Malcolmson 1981, ch. 4; Walvin 1978, p. 48.

23 It is precisely this idea that some groups may reject. Max Weber noted long ago that religion has psychologically met a very general need: "The fortunate is seldom satisfied with the fact of being fortunate. Beyond this, he needs to know that he has a *right* to his good fortune. He wants to be convinced that he 'deserves' it, and above all that he deserves it in comparison with others. He wishes to be allowed the belief that the less fortunate also merely experiences his due. Good fortune thus wants to be legitimate fortune" (1946, p. 271; italics in original). Schoeck gives an alternative explanation, closer to the implication of the model presented in Chapter 2, in his book about envy and the institutions invented throughout history to mitigate it, when he concludes that the ability to provide hope and happiness for believers, be they rich or poor, may be no more than the provision of ideas that both free the envious person from envy and the person envied from his sense of guilt and his fear of the envious. Belief in such ideas may be particularly important because people can begin to make something useful for their lives only when they cease to focus their attention on the good fortune of others.

Without mentioning envy, Devereux too argues that "frustration is inherent in a system in which economic aspirations are unbounded by conventionally defined standards and wants" (1980, p. 758), everyone being under pressure to succeed. Since not all can succeed, some beliefs, religious in particular, will help the individual to accept frustrating outcomes. "The less successful ... blame themselves, and ... stand in awe of their economic and moral superiors" (p. 758), and a new order is ensured. Thus institutions based on religious beliefs and around selling games of chance compete one with the other; by ritualizing people's hopes, both provide escape and a symbolic "play" with status, one by a game and the social interactions around it, the other by a set of beliefs and institutions organized around it. Both provide solutions to the problem of how to get acquainted with strangers too: one by practicing the same religion, going regularly to the same church; and the other by social interaction through games of chance. Geertz (1973, pp. 433–47) and Olmsted (1967, ch. 4) make some similar points.

24 Thomas 1971, ch. 1, esp. pp. 17–19, who also concludes that one of the central features of the beliefs and actions of the sixteenth and seventeenth centuries was a preoccupation with an explanation for and relief of human misfortune.

25 Blakey 1977, pp. 4–5.

26 Ibid., pp. 5–7; Sasuly 1982, ch. 1.

27 Malcolmson 1973, p. 5; Blakey 1977, p. 6; Sasuly 1982, p. 37.

28 See R. Brenner 1987, esp. ch. 7.

29 The information in this paragraph is based on Blakey 1977, pp. 13–15.

30 See Stone 1965, 1972 and n. 17 above. One may, however, still ask: If these and the views presented in the preceding chapters are accurate, that is that the poorer and those who fall behind have a greater incentive to gamble on lotteries, why was legislation that at times clearly protected the richer sometimes perceived as necessary? The answer may be that the richer could lose much property in a game of chance, even if for them it was mere "entertainment" (see Appendix 1 to Chapter 2), and still stay relatively rich after losing. Other players who might not have belonged to the richer classes before the game could thus become significantly richer – by chance. But in France, Grussi notes, Louis XIV *encouraged* excessive gambling among the nobility at court in order to ruin them and thus diminish their ability to revolt (1985, p. 61). One may also speculate and suggest that one impact of the 1710 statute may have been the development of a code of honor among aristocrats requiring them to pay their gambling debts.

31 Tom Brown, *Amusements Serious and Comical*, ed. A. L. Hayward (New York: Dodd, Mead, 1927; first published in 1700 as *London Amusements*), pp. 52–3, as quoted in Devereux 1980, p. 243. See also Malcolmson 1973, ch. 1.

32 R. Hey, *A Dissertation on the Pernicious Effects of Gaming* (1784), as quoted in Blakey 1977, pp. 31–2. See also Devereux 1980, pp. 112–13.

33 Andrew Steinmetz, *The Gambling Table: Its Votaries and Victims* (London: Tinsley, 1870), as quoted in Devereux 1980, p. 242; and see lengthy descriptions of such resentments in many of the chapters in Devereux's book when he discusses horse racing. Miers and Dixon (1984, p. 380)

also remark that it was precisely the mixing of the classes in the surviving traditional recreations that so exercised the indignation of the middle-class moralists. See also Sasuly 1982, pp. 44–5, who remarks that by the 1840s the English society was one with shifts in class lines. He also notes that "adventurers, sharpers, and even highwaymen" could get access even to private clubs where the nobility gambled. "It was inconvenient," he writes, quoting Algernon Bourke, "that one of these gentlemen should rub shoulders with the judge who might afterwards have to sentence him for highway robbery" (p. 9). On similar points in the New World, see Fabian 1982, pp. 52 and 315, who says that "proper social barriers [fell] away" when games of chance were played and lawyers, doctors, and bankers found themselves in bad company.

34 By the middle of the eighteenth century, certain games came to be regarded as undesirable because they were believed to lead to excessive gaming, to be too favorable to the promoters, or to open the way to fraud. In order to control the situation, George II signed three statutes that forbade some games of chance. In 1739 ace of hearts, pharaoh, basset, and hasard were outlawed. In 1740 all games involving dice (except backgammon) were prohibited, and in 1745 roulette was abolished (the first two statutes, however, did not apply to the royal palace). In 1752 a statute was passed regulating gaming houses, and was made perpetual in 1755. See Blakey 1977, ch. 1. The exception was horse racing. By the middle of the eighteenth century, thoroughbred racing had set itself apart as a mixture of caste ritual, sport, animal husbandry, and gambling on a large scale. Sasuly remarks that the "rise of Thoroughbred racing over the course of the 18th century coincided with severe dislocation in British agriculture. The rapid increase in enclosures (some 3,500 enclosure bills during the reign of George III affecting more than five million acres, where previously the whole number was only in the hundreds) was 'merely the most dramatic...aspect of a general process by which farms grew larger, farmers relatively fewer, and the villagers more landless,' according to E. J. Hobsbawm. Christopher Hill noted another aspect of the extreme pressures on marginal landowners, even quite large holders: '...the victory of the gentry in 1688 led to increasing disgruntlement of the Tory squires as the land tax which paid for the French wars eliminated the economically unfit,' and in the same context he referred to the 'desperate poverty of the northern Catholic gentry.' It was scarcely an accident that a disproportionate number of the new race courses were established in the northern counties of England. And it seems highly probable that some of the genuinely great sums staked on Thoroughbred races represented a last hope of paying off debts and preserving a land hold" (1982, pp. 10–11).

35 See the sources quoted on English lotteries in Chapter 1, and also Blakey 1977, ch. 1; Miers and Dixon 1979. Findlay remarks that "critics of the lotteries accelerated their attack in 1620 and 1621. In the midst of a nationwide economic slump, townspeople complained about interruptions to trade and industry and worried about agitating 'the Common sort'" (1986, p. 14).

36 See Blakey 1977, p. 894, and Miers and Dixon 1979, p. 375, on the high prices. The revenues provided were seen as a substitute for taxation.

They were perceived as a viable alternative for an administration incapable of raising money quickly through taxation and, probably more important, a short-term solution to the substantial uncertainty that still existed about the allocation of the power to tax between the crown and Parliament.

37 As quoted in Blakey 1977, p. 33.

38 Blakey 1977, p. 28, and see sources quoted in n. 35 above.

39 Blakey 1977, p. 30. He quotes R. and J. Dodsley's work, *A Modest Defense of Gaming*, published in 1754. In this book it is argued that, in contrast to the viewpoint expressed in earlier centuries, gaming *developed* the nation's officer corps. Officers who had seen their fortunes change were viewed as more suited for command than nongamblers: "Men in easy circumstances are not the fittest to go upon desperate Adventures.... Those who have charged through a Troop of Creditors, are most likely to have the same success when they face an enemy" (quoted in Blakey 1977, p. 30).

40 R. Hey, *A Dissertation on the Pernicious Effects of Gaming* 1784, as quoted in Blakey 1977, p. 31.

41 Ashton 1898, pp. 239–40; italics added. Rubner remarks that the Select Committee on the Laws Relating to Lotteries in 1808, when lotteries were still legal, maintained that the poor rates were going up because large numbers were being made destitute through playing state lotteries. "These sagacious gentlemen," writes Rubner, "were convinced that by the effects of lotteries, 'idleness, dissipation, and poverty are increased, the most sacred and confidential trusts are betrayed, domestic comfort is destroyed, madness often created, crimes...are committed, and even suicide itself is produced.... Such have been the constant and fatal attendants upon state lotteries'" (1966, pp. 1–2.)

42 Walvin 1978, p. 60, quoting Peter Mathias.

43 Miers and Dixon 1979, p. 377.

44 On "crime" rates when customs break down, and on social instability both in general and during the Industrial Revolution, see R. Brenner 1985, ch. 3. On gambling and leisure in this context, see also Bloch 1951. He remarks that gamblers are condemned for their failure to perform the normal productive functions ordinarily expected of them rather than because of the nature of gambling itself, and that leisure may be respectably enjoyed only when work is put first (p. 215). But Bloch does not put the discussion in a historical context.

45 See Malcolmson 1973, 1981; Bailey 1978; Walvin 1978; and 1980, who give detailed accounts of popular recreations during the eighteenth and nineteenth centuries and contrast them with recreations of earlier times. Sources concentrating on specific recreations will be quoted below. On rites related to gambling in other societies, see Geertz 1973, the chapter on Balinese cockfights, pp. 412–53. This last point will be discussed in detail in Chapter 4.

46 This point is elaborated ·in R. Brenner 1983, ch. 2; and its various implications are discussed in R. Brenner 1983, 1985.

47 Quoted in Read 1979, pp. 107–8. See also Walvin 1978, p. 6; Cunningham 1980, pp. 58–62.

48 See Harrison 1971 on the rise and fall of the temperance movement.

Walvin remarks that "visitors to England in the 1830s and 1840s were often struck by the paucity of recreational facilities for the common people; the country seemed to offer a sharp contrast to the more abundant leisure pursuits of Europe and North America" (1978, p. 2).

49 Josiah Tucker, *Six Sermons on Important Subjects* (Bristol, 1772), quoted in Malcolmson 1973, pp. 92–3 (with the italics).

50 Quoted in Malcolmson 1973, p. 161.

51 Quoted in Cunningham 1980, p. 46. See also Walvin 1978, ch. 1.

52 Cunningham 1980, p. 17; Harrison 1964. Harrison quotes W. Howitt's claim in 1838 that the decline in brutal sports represented a "mighty revolution" in popular pastimes and summarizes the process underlying the decline. Urbanization deprived working people of space, and mechanization deprived them of physical exercise during working hours. The substitutes, by codifying sporting rules and regulating games of uncertain duration, saved time. See also Harrison 1971, pp. 330–1.

53 Cunningham 1980, p. 19.

54 The information on drinking is mainly drawn from Harrison 1971 and Walvin 1978.

55 A selection of these articles is reprinted in Razzell and Wainwright 1973.

56 Ibid., pp. 9–10.

57 Malcolmson 1973, p. 104. See also Harrison 1971, pp. 321–6.

58 Harrison 1971, p. 50.

59 Ibid., p. 21. Harrison goes on to say, "The Victorians often failed to distinguish between alcoholism, drinking and drunkenness.... Not till the 1860s and 1870s did American experiments convince the Englishmen that habitual drunkards required voluntary or compulsory asylum treatment, and that alcoholism was ... more a disease than a crime."

60 Harrison notes that voluntary organizations (the temperance societies) were not the only ones trying to provide alternatives to the drinking places. Railway promoters, coffeehouse keepers, dancing halls, promoters of new sporting events, and promoters of tea and soft drinks (the Schweppes; see Harrison 1971, p. 300) offered some of the slowly emerging alternatives.

61 Malcolmson 1973; Lee 1976; Bailey 1978; Walvin 1978; Read 1979; Cunningham 1980.

62 Cunningham 1980, p. 180. After 1885 church attendance as a proportion of the population was still declining (Read 1979, p. 265).

63 Cunningham 1980, p. 181; Harrison 1971, p. 325.

64 See Malcolmson 1973, ch. 6; Cunningham 1980. The attacks, as noted, always had their class undertones. Harrison remarks that "eyes accustomed to the very different class relations of the mid-twentieth century may seem in organizations like the temperance movements' mere attempts to impose middle-class manners on the working class" (1971, p. 24). But he shows that this is not accurate. The temperance movement was helped by an elite of working men: "In the temperance movement, the respectable members of both middle and working classes united against the aristocrat who encouraged the worst recreational tastes of the poor" (p. 27), and the movement was a source of reliable men for key posts in the factory (p. 96). Harrison also suggests that the temperance movement was one of several transitional secular move-

ments channeling energies previously devoted to religion into party politics: "Throughout the nineteenth century, the movement tried to substitute a united moral reform crusade for the traditional concentration on liturgical, doctrinal and organizational questions.... In the early Victorian period, the teetotalers and prohibitionists directed attention away from an other-worldly paradise towards an earthly utopia" (p. 31). But above all the temperance movement tried to change people's attitudes toward diet, perceiving poverty as being due, in part, not to inadequate income but to mistaken ways of spending it. In times of increased poverty, people bought drink instead of food, since drink provided relaxation and sociability. Promotion of dietary change was also linked with industrialization: Dietary patterns that impeded punctuality and careful workmanship had to be discouraged (pp. 32–40). Persuasion was also needed to convince working-class families that they should change their patterns of saving. McKibbin remarks that "the whole edifice of working-class thrift was, in fact, built up on burial insurance..., a...saving that consumed up to 10 percent of a household budget" (1979, p. 161). Part of that amount was spent on drinking in connection with the rituals of death, a custom the temperance movement attacked (Harrison 1971, p. 93).

65 Quoted in Malcolmson 1973, p. 97.
66 See discussion in ibid., ch. 5, esp. p. 87.
67 McKibbin 1979.
68 Cunningham 1980.
69 Dixon 1980a, pp. 109–10.
70 Bailey 1978; Walvin 1978.
71 Hood 1976, p. 170; Blakey 1977, pp. 904–5; Cunningham 1980, p. 186; Dixon 1980a, b.
72 Harrison too concludes that "most drunkenness in nineteenth century England resulted from a social situation; teetotalers, by treating it as though it were compulsive or addictive, were usually on the wrong track" (1971, p. 355). This was not the only misunderstanding. Whereas legislation concerning drinking was, in part, based on inaccurate information about people's social requirements (as Harrison notes on p. 380), so were other laws. Housing laws, for example, arose not only because some houses were bad but also from a desire to prevent sexual promiscuity. Public supervision of the water supply sprang largely from the desire to curb drunkenness (Harrison 1971, p. 207). Read too asks, "Did drinking cause poverty, or was poverty a cause of drinking?" (1979, p. 112), and concludes, "Many middle-class commentators too readily accepted that drunkenness was the main, even the sole, cause of poverty. But more perceptive observers recognized that working people mostly turned to drink to escape from their miserable circumstances, 'the shortest way out of Manchester.' Booth's London survey at last offered some firm statistics to deflate the exaggerated claims of causal links between drink and poverty. He found that only 13 percent of the poor and 14 percent of the very poor owed their misfortune directly to drink. Illness, unemployment, and family size, concluded Booth, were the main causes of working-class poverty. But heavy drinking was likely to persist until poverty came under control, and until the mental hori-

zons of the poor had been widened. 'You or I take a book, and so get into a new world and change of thought; the poor have very little of this, therefore they drink' " (p. 112). And one should add: And therefore they gamble.

73 Dixon 1980a, pp. 111–12.

74 Quoted in ibid., p. 112.

75 This was N. D. Mackenzie's *The Ethics of Gambling* (1902), taken, according to Dixon (1980a, p. 113), as the definitive statement on the matter.

76 Walvin 1978, ch. 5; Read 1979, pp. 228–32. The slump in the 1880s was not linked with the significant fall in birth rates in the 1860s; see Read 1979, p. 383, on the demographic changes.

77 Read 1979, pp. 228–32, 300–2; Dixon 1980a, pp. 111–17.

78 Read 1979, p. 300.

79 Ibid.

80 Ibid., p. 301. Read remarks that this view was behind the term "unearned increment" that Henry George made popular in his *Progress and Poverty* (1879) and that was adopted by politicians who advocated taxing the rich and helping the poor. It is not accidental that even today the U.S. Internal Revenue Service calls interest unearned income.

81 See Read 1979, pp. 228–32, on issues related to this point, in particular the appearance of the term "technical education."

82 Dixon 1980a, pp. 112–13.

83 Ibid., p. 112.

84 They did pay attention to the tariffs imposed in other countries. See Read 1979, pp. 228–35.

85 Dixon remarks that "anti-gambling writers came to regard their attack on working class betting as a crusade to save England from economic and social disaster, to maintain political stability, to preserve the Empire, even to halt the degeneration of the English race and so to defend civilization" (1980a, p. 117).

86 Dixon 1980a; 1981a, b. On the Labor Party's reaction in Australia, see O'Hara 1987.

87 See discussion and references in R. Brenner 1985, ch. 2.

88 Lee 1976; Cunningham 1980, p. 177. Dixon (1981a, p. 52) notes that by 1910 radical papers too started to publish betting news, arguing that a radical paper with betting news was better than no radical paper. Only the *Daily News*, managed by a Quaker family, chose not to publish betting news; it survived only on the subsidies this family provided.

89 But the thought is not more peculiar than another one related to gambling. After World War II, the National Anti-Gambling League organized a series of classical music concerts at Methodist Central Hall to divert London's youth from gambling. Of course the affair turned out to be a financial disaster; afterwards the League lost its major support and disappeared (Dixon 1980b, p. 159).

90 Robert Slaney, as quoted in Cunningham 1980, p. 184.

91 Cunningham 1980, p. 184.

92 Dixon concludes that "in political terms, the 1906 Act can be seen as a restatement of who (and whose values) ruled the country" (1980, p. 109) and that "the moral change, the respectability which it had been

thought democracy would produce had not emerged: rather than modelling themselves on their social superiors, the 'new masters' threatened
to turn to socialism.... Gambling was corrupting and disturbing the
lower orders out of the relative passivity of the third quarter of the
century, and was explicitly linked to the rise of socialism in Seton
Churchill's influential *Betting and Gambling*, 1894.... Just as a century
before, the reformation of manners and the prevention of revolution
were regarded as coincident" (p. 110).

93 See discussion and references in R. Brenner 1985, ch. 2.

94 At this point one may raise two questions. The first is: Why was
prohibitive legislation passed against gambling but not against drinking
or horse racing? The answer seems simple. Whereas all three activities
were attacked on similar grounds, the bookmakers, coming from the
working classes, did not have a powerful political lobby of their own, in
contrast to the drinking and racing interests, which had. See Dixon
1981a, p. 29, and Harrison 1971, who remarks that "the drink interest
in the 1820s was allied with the powerful agricultural interest: this helps
to explain the temperance reformer's political impotence in the 1830s;
and the regional variations in the support for this movement" (p. 57),
and Read 1979, p. 111, who notes that the 1871 licensing bill provoked
vociferous opposition from the drink interest and was withdrawn, and
another was defeated in 1872. On the events surrounding the lack of
success in prohibiting horse racing, see Blakey 1977; Dixon 1981a.

The second question is: Why prohibit gambling rather than regulate
it? According to Dixon, the British were unfamiliar with administrative
law. The influential writer on the topic was A. V. Dicey. He wrote, "'In
many continental countries, and notably in France, there exists a scheme
of administrative law ... which rests on ideas foreign to the fundamental assumptions of our English common law, and especially
to ... the rule of law.' ... Dicey was xenophobic, misinformed and out
of date, but his work was enormously influential and blighted legal
thought about State administration for decades.... The lack of discussion of administrative methods of control meant that regulation of
betting by the use of licensing and registration was not regarded as a
viable option by a tradition-bound Home Office, despite the inevitable
comparison to the growing administrative regulation of drink. Their
tool was the criminal law" (1981a, p. 27).

95 Dixon 1981a, pp. 61–2. On additional legal angles, see Street 1937.

96 Quoted in Dixon 1980a, p. 124. It may be surprising in the face of
Dixon's numerous insightful studies devoted to gambling, that he
admits (in 1981, p. 22) that he is not at all interested in the question why
people gamble.

97 Blakey 1977, ch. 2. But Blakey also remarks that the origins of some
opposition may have been in "economic envy": "During their struggle
for spiritual reform in England, the Puritans developed a deep scorn for
the lifestyles of those who opposed them. Economic envy was probably
intertwined with this contempt, for the Puritans were originally drawn
from the lower and middle classes" (p. 43).

98 Ch. 17, Massachusetts Province Laws 1736–7, as quoted in Blakey
1977, p. 48.

99 Hughes 1983, chs. 4, 11.

100 See S. P. Lee and Passell 1979, p. 20, on incomes in the New World during these times.

101 A. Spofford, "Lotteries in American History," *American Historical Association Annual Report*, 1892, as quoted in Blakey 1977, p. 75.

102 This information is given in Blakey 1979, p. 65.

103 Blakey 1979; 1977, p. 163. Blakey also remarks that by this time "the idea that property could be acquired by chance was fundamentally in opposition to the notion that it should only be acquired by honest labor.... Judge Parker remarked in *Amory vs. Gilman* (2 Mass. 1, 5–6 [1806]): 'It would seem a disgraceful occupation of the courts of any country, to sit in judgement between two gamblers, in order to determine which was the best calculator of chances.... There could be but one step of degradation below this – which is, that judges should be the stakeholders of the parties' " (1977, p. 63).

104 Blakey 1977, p. 167. Blakey gives a detailed description of events surrounding gambling in New York. He remarks that "during the 1830's and 40's, New York was gripped by the evangelical Christian reform movement experienced in differing forms in many parts of the country.... Liquor, slavery, the lack of institutions for the poor, and women's status as second-class citizens all came under attack" (p. 152) in addition to gambling. At the same time, just as in England, horse racing was viewed differently: "In *Van Valkengurgh vs. Torrey* [1828], the court relied on a literal reading of the word 'racing' and declared that trotting was not affected by the law" (p. 175).

105 By 1832 eight states in the East were raising a total of $66.4 million per year by lottery, when the entire federal government spent only a quarter of that amount. But by 1833 Pennsylvania had banned all lotteries, and by 1839 New York, New Jersey, Massachusetts, Connecticut, New Hampshire, Maine, Vermont, Ohio, and Illinois had all joined. In 1842 Congress enacted a ban on federal lotteries. Texas and California banned the games in their first state constitutions. In 1930 forty-five states banned lotteries, thirty-five of them in their constitutions (Blakey 1977, pp. 669–78; Devereux 1980, pp. 118–19). Blakey (1977, p. 164) also remarks that by 1817 a strong movement against lotteries had commenced with the founding of the Society for the Prevention of Pauperism.

106 See Blakey 1977, p. 311, who also enters into details about legislation in the Midwest.

107 See details in ibid., ch. 5. But one must be skeptical about the image of the new western towns being crippled by gamblers who also drank and committed crimes. According to R. Dykstra's *The Cattle Town* (quoted in Blakey 1977, p. 383), the myth that the frontier townsfolk were besieged by armed desperadoes flocking to casinos, brothels, and saloons and finishing their visit with a violent shoot-out is just a myth, an invention. The record suggests that this was not the case, and the origins of the attacks on drinking and gambling are associated with the settlement of the West by farmers who came from the East and reflected "politicized anger," gambling being viewed as a speculative enterprise taking advantage of the hard-working farmer. Blakey also concludes

that antigambling provisions were carried "unthinkingly" into the constitutions of the western states.

108 Blum 1973, p. 220; Blakey 1977, pp. 81–88, 385–7.

109 Hughes 1983, p. 439. The population of New York nearly tripled from 1790 to 1810, and Pennsylvania's doubled to almost a million (Blakey 1977, p. 668). In Massachusetts during the nineteenth century, population increased 10 percent or more each decade. The immigrants came from Canada, Italy, and Ireland. Many of them were Catholics who did not view gambling in as severe terms as Protestants. But, as Blakey remarks, "the newcomers had not yet transformed their numbers into political power, either legislatively or judicially; the rule of the Protestant establishment thus continued" (1977, p. 72).

110 Hughes 1983, p. 439. See also North 1978, making general points on the sequence of events.

111 In 1800, 90 percent of Pennsylvania's population, for example, lived and worked on farms. "By 1860, only 69 percent worked in agriculture. Irish Catholic immigrants and displaced farmers formed the laboring class in the emerging coal and iron industries." See Blakey 1977, p. 73, who also concludes that "the story of immigration, urbanization, and industrialization in New York, New Jersey, Connecticut, and Rhode Island followed a similar pattern. Even New Hampshire and Vermont experienced similar, if less dramatic change." Recall that population growth in the United States in these years was dramatic: In 1790 the population was only 4 million; by 1850 it was 23 million, by 1930, 123 million. Sasuly states: "In the afterglow of nostalgia, the United States in 1900 seems a place of industrial vigor and opportunity for all, in a time of fun and simple pleasure. For some, it was all those things. But for many others it was none of them.... The Populist platform of 1892 asserted that the country had been 'brought to the verge of moral, political and material ruin.'... Behind the Populist platform could be heard the muted voice of a rural majority. During a third of a century of poor farm prices and high rail rates... 'farmers had found little sympathy in the federal government and had won no great measures of legislative policy designed to give them relief.' Hundreds of thousands of newly employed industrial workers fared, if anything, worse. They organized greater and lesser strikes (in 1877, 1892 and 1894, for example). All the strikes were broken, forcibly" (1982, pp. 83–4). The Populists became a force in the Democratic Party in 1896, and the Interstate Commerce Commission took steps toward railroad regulation from 1887 on; other regulations and antitrust legislation followed. See Sasuly 1982, ch. 7; Hughes 1983, ch. 22.

112 Cowing 1965, p. 5.

113 Duster makes some similar points in other contexts, talking about the temperance movement and legislation concerning drugs. He remarks that "in its earliest development, Temperance was one way in which a declining social elite tried to retain some of its social power and leadership. The New England Federalist 'aristocracy' was alarmed by the political defeats of the early nineteenth century and by the decreased deference shown their clergy" (1970, p. 5). In Australia, O'Hara notes, "the growth of sweepstakes matched the rapid spread of illegal totalisa-

tion betting shops. They were not the only gambling initiatives . . . in the late nineteenth century, but they were among the most prominent. This very feature made them the focus of attack from the element of the Australian community which opposed gambling. The urban middle-class element which had been an almost insignificant component of Australian society . . . began to find a stronger voice" (1987, p. 5). There were also fears that Australia was in danger of becoming a non-Christian country. Fabian also notes that gambling was condemned because it "appeared to preserve both a remnant of upper class manners and a glimmer of hope for the very poor. It was not the vice, passion or problem of the American bourgeoisie" (1982, p. 11).

114 One should recall that from the beginning of the twentieth century to the late 1950s, the population in the Northeast increased dramatically and its religious background changed. See nn. 109, 111. At the same time, industrialization and urbanization continued.

115 Quoted in Devereux 1980, p. 175. For other opinions expressed during the Depression, see ibid., pp. 170–212.

116 There might be several reasons, the most plausible being that Protestant spokesmen by custom unthinkingly repeated what their leaders in the past had said and written. Recall the discussion at the beginning of this chapter on Calvin's views in particular, and recall that Luther also wrote that "money won by gambling . . . is not won without self-seeking and love of self, and not without sin" (*Works of Martin Luther*, vol. 4 [Philadelphia: Muhlenberg, 1931], p. 58). Additional explanations might be that whereas Protestants tend to identify law with morality, and to view illegal acts as immoral, the Catholic Church does not seem to share this outlook: The state has the right to forbid gambling, a temporal matter, but the legal prohibition does not make it immoral. The view of the Catholic Church seems to be that gambling is immoral only if one cheats or gambles excessively, depriving one's family. But the rationale most frequently put forward during the discussion was the one empha-sized in Chapter 2, namely the Protestant rejection of the idea of getting something for nothing. When fighting liberalization of the gambling laws in New Jersey, the Protestant churches, which led the fight, de-clared that lotteries are morally wrong because they appear to offer the individual something for practically nothing, or at least hold out hope of a return utterly disproportionate to any effort or investment on his or her part. An additional explanation might be linked with the point Duster made when he remarked that "Ranulf and Weber are among the many observers who have noted that Roman Catholicism has a more wholistic integrated view of 'good and evil' in human action. . . . Per-haps the essence of the problem is demonstrated in the manner in which the Southern Catholic countries view forgiveness of sins. Quite the opposite, the Lutheran and Calvinistic strains make no allowances for sin and are thus 'religious doctrines without forgiveness'" (1970, p. 90).

117 Blakey 1977, pp. 111–27.

118 Rubner also remarks that the socially prominent Mrs. Oliver Harriman deliberately violated postal regulations in connection with a drawing sponsored by her group in order to be brought into court and so arouse public interest (1966, p. 99). See also Devereux 1980, pp. 165–212, on

the debates surrounding games of chance during the Great Depression.

119 Devereux 1980, pp. 170–212. In 1931 Nevada legalized gambling statewide (Sasuly 1982, p. 233).

120 Devereux 1980, p. 204.

121 Ibid., pp. 209–10.

122 See quotations from various judgments on the legality of contests in Blakey 1977, ch. 6. Bender remarks that "25 million Americans . . . try at least two contests a year. Over 12 million are definitely contest conscious and try as many as they have time and ideas for" (1938, p. 3).

123 Devereux 1980, pp. 121–2.

124 Devereux suggests that the reason may be that the resale value of such items was much lower than the value quoted by the sponsors (1980, p. 184).

125 Rubner 1966, p. 15.

126 S. S. Smith 1952, p. 63; Blakey 1977, p. 103. It is against this background, as in England, that the legislation movement of the 1930s began taking place. Bender remarks that "prizes in the form of amenities are becoming increasingly popular. Sometimes they offer . . . credit slips to be used at the local grocery store or are orders for dental work" (1938, p. 10).

127 Bender 1938, p. 3. It may not be surprising to find that these groups were against the legislation of gambling. See Blakey 1977, p. 104.

128 Devereux 1980, pp. 98, 181; Blakey 1977, p. 100.

129 See Blakey reference in n. 122.

130 Perkins 1958, p. 30.

131 Ibid., p. 37. Miers and Dixon note that "for the 1932 Royal Commission, the objection of principle, that they entailed socially harmful consequences, itself resolved into two lines of argument, which have been standard weapons of the objectors' armoury. The first is that lotteries, involving no element of skill, foster a belief in the value of chance, which conflicts with the general dictates of the protestant work ethic, which places value on thrift and industry as the route to material (and spiritual) reward. . . . Although a common argument, that lotteries foster a belief in luck, it is one which is double-edged, for the capitalist system itself which relies upon acceptance of the work ethic, is to a degree a risk-based enterprise" (1979, p. 394). A discussion of the issues raised by this last remark appears in Chapter 5.

132 Leonard 1952; Newman 1972, p. 28. It is not accidental that it was on July 31, 1933, that for the first time in its history China introduced a state lottery. Whang 1933 notes, however, that How-Wei, a form of lottery, was very popular among the lower classes of Shanghai, though it was publicly prohibited.

133 Blakey 1977, p. 913, quoting the royal commission.

134 Dixon 1981a, pp. 73–4. In the 1930s the invention of the totalizer (which diminished the possibility of fraud) helped in bringing about the legalization of pari-mutuel betting in most eastern states (New Hampshire was the first in 1933). See Blakey 1977, p. 113.

135 Quoted in Devereux 1980, pp. 779–80.

136 The numerical information that follows is taken from Levy 1988, who summarizes his study of changing income distribution in the United States. Notice that what matters in the model used in our book to

explain gambling behavior is not just the distribution of wealth but whether or not fluctuations in wealth have increased or diminished. Thus information on Gini coefficients, or even data of the type given in Duncan 1984, are not sufficient. Duncan provides information of the following type: Since the 1960s only 40 percent of families in the United States stay in the same fifth of earners from one generation to the next. Fifty-two percent of the children from the top 20 percent have moved down at least one rung, whereas 45 percent of the children from the bottom fifth have moved up at least one rung. A survey of 5,000 American families reveals that among those who were poor in 1978, only 7 percent were in poverty in each of the ten years between 1969 and 1978, but 20 percent of the sample were in poverty in at least one of the ten years. It may also be useful to point out – more in the context of a relationship with entrepreneurship, discussed in Brenner 1987, ch. 2 – that a survey taken in 1912–13 in Northampton, Warrington, and Reading, Massachusetts, of 665 working-class households with children out at work counted 472 families where the job status of all children remained the same as their fathers' and 128 where some children had lost job status (Read 1979, p. 401).

137 See Koten 1987. Let us reemphasize that the fact that there has been no significant change in the concentration of income for the past twenty-five years (although the middle class became somewhat smaller) is irrelevant and cannot explain any change. It is the movement within the distribution that matters. The fact that since the 1960s the top 20 percent of earners have 40.2–42.9 percent of all income; the top 5 percent, 15.2–16.6 percent; and the bottom 20 percent, 4.7–5.5 percent provides little help in predicting attitudes toward gambling, speculation, and entrepreneurship. It is the turbulence *within* the distribution that provides us with useful clues for explaining both the increased willingness to gamble and altered attitudes toward games of chance. Church 1988, p. 27, cites the Congressional Budget Office for some 1988 figures reflecting the trends mentioned in the text. The richest 5 percent earned $94,476 in 1977 and $129,762 in 1988, whereas the poorest 10 percent earned $3,673 in 1977 and $3,286 in 1988 (all figures in 1988 dollars).

138 See Feinman, Blashek, and McCabe 1986, ch. 1. The Taiwan government makes ingenious use of lotteries. Everybody has a tax number that must be recorded on all invoices and receipts. To encourage the use of receipts, the government holds lotteries with prizes of the equivalent of $67,000 using receipts as tickets. See "The Shadow Economy," *Economist*, Sept. 19, 1978.

139 "Cash for Trash," *Wall Street Journal*, Feb. 17, 1987; "New State Lottery! No Cash Prizes!" *New York Times*, Sept. 6, 1987.

140 Brand 1987.

141 "What a Deal!" *Newsweek*, Feb. 9, 1987. The word puzzle involved is so elementary that the skill required to win is symbolic.

Chapter 4. Gambling, speculation, insurance

1 By definition, the speculator goes against established opinion. When one buys, one hopes that "the market" is wrong and prices are too low. When one sells, one hopes that "the market" is wrong and prices are too

high. In science too, the "speculator–entrepreneur" goes against established, customary opinion. See Hieronymus 1971, ch. 1. Perkins (1962, p.
4 and ch. 4) suggests that one can distinguish between "constructive
speculation" and "gambling speculation," but I cannot understand how.

2 Hawley, for example, remarks that "the essential point . . . is that the
enterpriser performs a service for which he expects to receive a reward,"
whereas "the speculator . . . does not render, or does not mean to render,
any service to anybody" (1924, p. 78). First, the speculator does render a
service: provides insurance against fluctuating prices. Second, neither the
speculator's nor the entrepreneur's goal is to provide the service; their
goal is to become richer. Their means are different. In speaking about
speculation in stock and futures markets, I cannot avoid making a critical
reference to standard economic analysis. Whereas these markets are
frequently given as examples of competitive ones, they illustrate the flaw
in drawing supply-and-demand curves. The word "supply" in "grain
market language" (which speculators use) must refer to the buyers' and
sellers' (speculators' and hedgers') estimates and *opinions of supply*
rather than some impersonal factor that an economist can find. See Boyle
1921, p. 8, and Brenner 1987, chs. 1 and 3, for discussion of the implications of this viewpoint for the theory of the firm, competition, and so
forth.

3 The Board of Trade won the legal battle on the dubious ground that
price quotations were its property and bucket shops could not use them.
But if this argument was correct (and it might not have been: A strong
claim could have been made that information about prices on exchanges
was public property and could not be restricted [Hieronymus 1971, pp.
87–91]), all the Board of Trade had to ask for was a fee from the bucket
shops for using the information. The Board of Trade, however, did not
seem to be interested in a solution that would still allow competition.
First the board severed its ties with Western Union Telegraph and set up
its own phone company – the Cleveland Telegraph Company – to prevent quotations from reaching the bucket shops. When this step turned
out to be insufficient, the board turned to the Supreme Court, which
decided in its favor in 1905. The bucket shops were also accused of many
fraudulent acts, but no evidence exists to support these claims. (Boyle
1921, pp. 89–96; Hieronymus 1971, pp. 87–91. Hieronymus also notes
that the surviving documents on futures markets give us contemporary
impressions and do not analyze, and that the words "manipulation" and
"corner" should not be put in a modern context [p. 82]). MacDougall
remarks that "members of stock and commodity exchanges have always
coveted the business which went to the bucketshops" (1936, p. 70). See
also Cowing 1965, ch. 1.

4 Miers and Dixon 1979, p. 379. See also Downes et al. 1976, ch. 6, and
Sasuly 1982, pp. 38–43, making similar points, and Hawke 1905a, b. The
last notes that "there is . . . great difficulty of drawing a line between
commerce and gambling" (1905b, p. 147).

5 Hieronymus quotes a sarcastic definition: "An investment is a speculation gone sour" (1971, p. 244).

6 Kolb (1985, p. 286) summarizes the performance of some commodity
funds in recent years. For 1981, thirty-six funds had an average increase

in wealth of 5.43 percent with a standard deviation of 24.49 percent. In 1982, the average wealth changed by −1.72 percent, with a standard deviation of 23 percent. Since the funds hold over 50 percent of their assets in money-market funds, they may carry less risk than if all the money were invested in futures trading. Keynes seems to make a similar distinction (1970, ch. 12). With his typical elitist view, he also suggests that, just like casinos, the stock exchanges too should be "inaccessible and expensive" (p. 159). For more on Keynes's views, see Brenner 1985, ch. 5. And see n. 8 below.

7 Even Boyle (1921, p. 116), who is in favor of speculation, gives a confused definition referring to motivation.

8 Blakey 1977, pp. 96–7. Also note that in most economic models, investment is dealt with in a deterministic framework. It may not be surprising that relatively few wealthy Americans invest in high-risk ventures. Although the survey does not distinguish between the old and the new rich, *Success in America: The CIGNA study of the Upper Affluent* (i.e., those worth $500,000 or more) reveals that in 1986, 21 percent of the members of this group invested in precious metals, 12 percent in commodities, and 8 percent in junk bonds. But 79 percent invested in real estate, 76 percent in stocks, 71 percent in money-market funds, between 54 and 58 percent in passbook accounts, life insurance, mutual funds, bank money-market accounts, and bank certificates of deposit, and 46 percent in tax-free bonds (*Newsweek*, May 25, 1987, p. 5). Keynes's distinction between speculation and investment is different. Speculation, according to him, describes a situation where, instead of trying to make a forecast about the probable yield of an investment over its whole life, people try to guess how the market, under the influence of mass psychology, will value it three months or a year hence (1970, pp. 154–5).

9 The hard work of some speculators is not always visible: Being informed about price changes and appraising their effects, and collecting information about the possible impact of political changes, domestic and international, and about changes in statutes, regulations, and taxes, are not easy. It is easy to ignore such things when all is going well. "Bull-market geniuses" in commodity markets (and in science too) appear during such times. Hieronymus also notes that a personality trait that seems necessary for speculation is a "combination of bravery and cowardice, of egotism and humility. When he takes a position, the speculator is challenging the wisdom of the market. He is saying: 'I know more than the market does about the price that will equate supplies and requirements.... This requires a strength of ego that borders on arrogance. Backing this challenge with money is not a game for the faint of heart'" (1971, p. 260).

10 Sasuly remarks that "both gambling and making loans at interest serve to increase the velocity of a circulating medium of exchange. In their simplest forms − even among children and in primitive societies − both gambling and debt support attempts to acquire goods which otherwise do not come readily to hand" (1982, p. 41). A similar point is made with respect to futures markets by Hieronymus 1971; Telser and Higinbotham 1977; Kolb 1985. On another role of futures, Hieronymus wrote: "There is something ridiculous about explaining to a chemist or a private detective that he, fine and noble entrepreneur, is furnishing the equity capital

to feed cattle or produce plywood. Told, he is apt to reply, 'Who, me? I'm just trying to make a fast buck in a market where I can get high leverage on money that I am willing to lose (heaven forbid)'" (p. 135). Telser 1958; Friedman 1969; Owen 1982; Williams 1982; Carlton 1983, 1984; Kolb 1985; and collections of studies in Hardy 1924 and Marx 1952 explain what roles speculators and futures markets play. Hieronymus, for example, thus summarizes the view: "Futures markets are devices for shifting price risks from people who are unwilling and unable to carry them to speculators, and through this process markets become devices for generating equity capital" (1971, p. 285). "The general goal here is to maximize the economic efficiency of the commodity production and marketing processes. Specifically, the objective is to get the risks of price variability assumed and the equity capital for the financing of commodity value variations provided at a minimum cost. To achieve this objective, the job should be turned over to speculators, for they do it free" (p. 283). The end result is also that the forecasts of future prices drawn from the futures market are more accurate than other forecasts. See also Dorfman 1987.

11 The list of critics, well into the 1930s, is numerous. Among them are MacDougall 1936 and Rowntree 1905, where references to the critics, who essentially repeat the same argument – that speculation in futures is gambling, and both destabilize – can be found. It should also be re-marked that when writers condemn speculation in general, and specula-tion in futures in particular, it is not always clear what alternatives they have in mind. For John Maynard Keynes, worrying about speculation due to excessive liquidity, the alternative meant proposing a substantial government transfer tax with a view to mitigating the dominance of speculation in enterprise in the United States. Frequently it is just not made clear what the alternative is. To prohibit speculation by law? To educate people that speculation is "bad"?

12 See, for example, Hawley 1924 and discussion in Friedman 1969.

13 Bunce 1952, p. 139.

14 In recent memory, large fortunes were made by the Reichmans in Canada and the Trumps in New York buying up real estate in New York when that city was bankrupt and few, apparently, had confidence in its future. See also wrong accusations made in Lahey 1952.

15 Hieronymus 1971, p. 286. He also remarks that the seasonal variation in cash onion prices during the period of active futures trading was approx-imately equal to the cost of storing onions from harvest to spring, and that "from these things it follows that the more of the risks that are assumed and financed by speculators, the lower will be the cost associ-ated with the commodity processes" (p. 287). See also Teweles, Harlow, and Stone 1969.

16 Boyle 1921, pp. 123–7.

17 Ibid., pp. 182–96.

18 See, for example, Cowing 1965, ch. 1.

19 Fisher 1924, p. 348; italics added. He shares Mackay's views in the classic *Extraordinary Popular Delusions and the Madness of Crowds.* Not in vain does the title refer to *"popular* delusions" and *"crowds"*; the book neither condemns the speculators nor suggests that speculation in general is bad. In the "money mania" episode linked with the 1719–20 Mississip-

pi scheme, Mackay emphasizes that the speculator John Law was in fact an outstanding financial entrepreneur who "was more deceived than deceiving, more sinned against than sinning" (p. 1). However, he made one grave mistake in not anticipating that, in the midst of the severe financial confusion following the extravagant spending of Louis XIV, "confidence, like mistrust, could be increased *ad infinitum*, and . . . hope was as extravagant as fear . . . just as it was with Law and the French people. He was the boatman, and they were the waters" (pp. 1–2). But the source of the fluctuating prices was a belief in mistaken ideas. This outcome, however, is unavoidable, emphasizes Mackay. For, he explains, dissatisfaction with one's lot, far from leading to evil as at first might be supposed, has been "the great civiliser of our race." This characteristic, writes Mackay, has tended more than anything else to raise the human race above the condition of the brutes. It is true, however, that the same discontent that has been the source of all improvement has also been the source of follies, speculations, absurdities, and the seeking for remedies that have "bewildered us in a wave of madness and error. These are death, toil, and ignorance of the future. . . . From the third [sprang] the false science of astrology, divination and their divisions . . ." (pp. 98–9). This view of human nature seems to be similar to the one assumed in this book.

20 Mackay 1980, pp. 89–97. See also Schama 1988, ch. 5, esp. sect. 3.

21 See Fisher 1924. In 1983 Granville thought that another Great Depression was coming and recommended selling stocks. Paul David Herrlinger created false rumors of a takeover for the Dayton Hudson Company in 1987. He was later hospitalized and his mental health questioned. See Dorfman 1987; Fromson 1987. See also Mackay 1980; Train 1985. The analyses of these and other cases are similar.

22 In her book *The March of Folly*, Barbara Tuchman too commits this error. First she defines wisdom as the exercise of judgment acting on experience, on available information. The question is how such wisdom can be used when people find themselves in circumstances that have never taken place before. Following Tuchman's definition, one cannot use wisdom and common sense, since there is no experience to rely upon. People will *bet* on new ideas, and, as with all bets, some may turn out to be lucky (and historians will praise the originator of the idea to the skies), and others will not (in which case the originator of the idea is blamed for destabilizing speculation and folly). But when can one be sure that an idea is wrong? You can be stubborn, consistent, and stick to your ideas (and maybe be burned as a heretic). If you turn out to be right, your strong will will be admired by later generations. If you fail, you will be called a blockhead, wooden-headed. Again, this is an ex-post judgment. In the Preface to her first book, Tuchman admits that year after year editors turned down her manuscript. Finally, New York University Press published it. Today Mrs. Tuchman is viewed as a courageous historian, among the very few who worked outside the security of academia. But how was she viewed during the years when every editor refused her and yet she persisted?

23 See n. 21 and the sources quoted there. An episode on the futures market is sometimes given as an example of destabilizing speculation. But is it? In 1979–80 Bunker Hunt and his brothers bought up so much silver that

the price rose from $10 an ounce in August 1979 to $50 an ounce in January 1980. It was estimated that the Hunts held about one-sixth of the Western world's stock of silver. Yet in January the price dropped to $10 and the Hunts lost an estimated $1 billion. When accused of trying to corner the market, Herbert Hunt argued that they had not tried that but had expected – erroneously – that the metal would become more valuable (see *Washington Post*, March 5, 1980). Thus, once again, it is in the sense explained in the text that one can say that their speculation was destabilizing; indeed, in 1988 the Hunt brothers declared bankruptcy.

24 Ashton 1898, p. 275.

25 Also see Brenner 1983, 1985 for further detailed discussion of this point. Perkins tries to distinguish between insurance and gambling, but his distinction seems false. He remarks that the differences between the two are that "insurance implies unavoidable risk, while gambling is based upon an unnecessary or artificial risk" (1962, p. 57). Why is gambling "unnecessary," and according to whom, if indeed, as argued here, the opportunity of gambling sustains people's hope for a better future? And why are driving a car and car insurance "unavoidable"? One doesn't have to drive. Perkins further argues that "insurance involves no loss so far as the insurable risk is concerned, while in gambling the gain of the winners is provided by the loss of the losers" (p. 57). This statement is inaccurate. The feasibility of insurance increases production, giving people some peace of mind and the ability to concentrate on other matters. But so does gambling. It is true that by gambling one redistributes wealth, but one also gains hope. The opportunity to gamble is an inducement for some, sustaining their hopes, and for others it prevents more drinking. In this sense gambling too does not involve a loss. Perkins finally notes that "insurance introduces the law of averages to eliminate chance, while gambling puts the uncertainty of unnecessary risk in the place of control" (p. 57). As pointed out above and in the text, if we take into consideration the alternatives, to permit gambling does not imply the existence of unnecessary risk. This point will become even clearer in Chapter 5.

26 That is, whether an individual is one or the other is viewed in standard neoclassical economic theory as depending on the shape of the utility function. See discussion in Brenner 1983, 1985 as well as in the mathematical appendix to Chapter 2.

27 Friedman 1969, p. 286. An alternative explanation for the dislike can be inferred from Brenner 1987, ch. 5.

28 Friedman 1969, p. 286. Several writers have criticized gambling on the ground that it is an illegitimate way of making money. Perkins, for example, wrote: "There are only three ways of obtaining or raising money. We can leave out the saving of money, which is really only postponed use. The first is on the basis of service rendered.... The second is on the basis of exchange of values.... The third is by an act of benevolence or a free gift" (1962, p. 48). Why don't games of chance fit into the category of service rendered or of exchange of values? Perkins's implicit answer seems to be that this market leads to a reallocation of property by chance. Elsewhere in his book Perkins remarks that "gambling increased ... during the period of economic and industrial depression

between the two wars, where the fascination of possibly winning something by luck did undoubtedly make its appeal to men and women who
were living under conditions of financial stringency" (p. 37).

29 Fisher 1924, p. 347. Similar points are made in Teweles et al. 1969, pp.
4–6.

30 See Cohen 1964 ch. 10, on how widespread the use of astrology still is,
and on divination in general. Also see the *Wall Street Journal* piece by
Hughes (1986), as well as Leiren 1987 and Gardner 1987 on some recent
religious revivals. Also see discussion about the role of magic in Thomas
1971; Malcolmson 1981, pp. 83–93.

31 The word "inevitably" in Fisher's text is somewhat problematic.
Attempts can be made to prevent or diminish both kinds of risk by
freezing the status quo in one case and by prohibiting adjustment to
changed circumstances in another. China and India have made such
attempts; so did European societies during the Middle Ages.

32 Jacoby 1952, p. 19; Perkins 1962, p. 56; Sasuly 1982, p. 41.

33 See Noonan 1957 and Brenner 1983, ch. 3, on usury, the origins of the
word "interest," and changing attitudes toward lending money. It is not
accidental that at times lotteries and usury have been compared. Many
have pointed out that forbidding banking and the medieval principle of
the just price froze "the orders of society in proportions they assumed in
the Middle Ages. What was interdicted was neither commerce, nor
wealth but the increase of commerce at the expense of feudal powers"
(Ayres 1944, p. 28).

34 Daston 1987, p. 256 n. 9.

35 Ibid.

36 See extensive discussion on this point in Daston 1987.

37 Thomas 1971, pp. 651–4.

38 See Brenner 1985, ch. 3 and sources quoted there.

39 Thomas 1971, pp. 651–4; Daston 1987.

40 Daston 1987, p. 249.

41 See extensive discussion and references on these points in Brenner 1983,
chs. 2, 3, and Thomas 1971, esp. pp. 662–80.

42 Daston 1987, p. 253. The point made in this paragraph is worth emphasizing, for it is linked with a major point made by Coase (1937). He
argued that the basic issue concerning firms is that it worth investigating is
their origin. As argued in Appendix 1 to Chapter 2, one implication
of the model was that its testing should be linked with an investigation of
the origins of some institutions. Such analysis has been done here.
Another point worth repeating is one made in Brenner 1983, 1985, 1987,
namely, that one cannot separate economic issues from others. The fact
that insurance companies were a substitute for roles played by witches
and belief in magic makes this point quite clear.

43 Daston 1987, p. 253.

44 Blakey 1977, p. 98; Labys and Granger 1970, pp. 2–6. MacDougall
(1936), himself confused, quotes a large number of confused legal decisions. See also Street 1937 for discussion of legal problems in the United
Kingdom.

45 Blakey 1977, p. 342.

46 Teweles et al. 1969, p. 6.

47 Blakey 1977, p. 343.
48 Ibid., pp. 393–4.
49 John T. Flynn's *Security Speculation*, as quoted in MacDougall 1936, p. 69.
50 MacDougall 1936, p. 69.
51 See discussion at the end of Section 1 above.
52 See Teweles et al. 1969, pp. 6–7.
53 Quoted in ibid., p. 6.
54 Quoted in ibid., p. 7.
55 For a long time, transactions not only in futures markets but in stock markets too were viewed with suspicion. Hawke, for example, wrote that "a very large proportion of the business done upon the Stock Exchange is nothing else than gambling. No stock passes. It is merely gambling in the rise or fall for differences" (1905a, p. 41).
56 Wilson 1905, pp. 45–69.
57 Ibid., p. 46. Nor can one exclude the possibility that Telser mentioned, namely, that if gambling is illegal, some will gamble on futures markets: "In a society that imposes many obstacles to gambling, it may well be that commodity futures exchanges serve the function of the gambling casino. Although people . . . gamble in the hope of winning, they are not dissuaded by the knowledge that there is a 'house take'" (quoted in Eadington 1973, p. 13).
58 See Hieronymus 1971. Mackay made a somewhat similar point when he noted that during the progress of the South Sea Bubble "England presented a singular spectacle. The public mind was in a state of unwholesome fermentation. Men were no longer satisfied with the slow but sure profits of cautious industry. The hope of boundless wealth . . . made them heedless and extravagant for today. A luxury, till then unheard of, was introduced, bringing in its train a corresponding laxity of morals. The overbearing insolence of ignorant men, who had arisen to sudden wealth by successful gambling, made men of true gentility of mind and manners blush that gold should have power to raise the unworthy in the scale of society" (1980, p. 71). Notice the similarity to arguments described in Chapter 3.
59 See discussion of this term in Brenner 1987, appendix to ch. 1, where both Adam Smith's and Marx's view of "necessities" is briefly discussed.
60 Bauer 1981, esp. pp. 156–63; Owen 1982.
61 Bauer 1981, esp. pp. 156–63.
62 Whitaker, Clifton, and Foote 1987, p. 29.
63 See Gilder 1989; Niederhoffer 1989; James Gibney. The latter, who is acting managing editor of the *New Republic*, commented on the civil case against Michael Milken, the financial entrepreneur who created the junk-bond market and became very, very rich. He is quoted as saying, "Mind you, part of me wants to see Milken suffer not out of any highfalutin sense of moral outrage over securities law violations. No, like the millions of Americans who gloated over the fall of plutocrats Adnan Khashoggi and Harry and Leona Helmsley, I want Milken to suffer because he is filthy rich. What better way to close an eight-year era of officially sponsored greed than to go after one of its prime movers? I only hope that Donald Trump is next. As far as ritual sacrifices of the rich and

powerful go, that would be 'quality'" (*Wall Street Journal*, "Notable and Quotable," Oct. 20, 1988).

64 See Brenner 1987 for detailed discussion, esp. chs. 1, 3, 5.

Chapter 5. Governments, taxation, and the impact of prohibitions

1 See discussion and references in Chapter 3, section 6. A priori, one could think of another possible reason for banning lotteries: Since there is no doubt that compulsive playing is costly for society and the benefits of lotteries are diminished for the government when it has surpluses in its budget, one could imagine that the ban was associated with the appearance of such surpluses in the 1830s in Europe as well as on the American continent. But no such correlation can be found. In the United States, for example, there were periods of major expansion with federal government surpluses during 1825–6, 1844–6, and 1850–7, but deficits were run during the downswings of 1820–1, 1837–43, 1847–9, and 1858–60. Nor was there a trend toward diminishing government expenditures during the nineteenth century; expenditures continued to grow at least at the rate the economy was growing.

There is one change that could account for the diminished importance of lotteries at the state level in the United States (though nothing similar happened in Europe). Between 1790 and 1795 the states' wartime debts were taken over by the federal government, putting them on a sound financial basis. This could have diminished the states' incentive to offer lotteries (but not the federal government's). But there was another change during these years that, in principle, may have worked in the opposite direction to encourage the states' sale of lotteries. Under the new U.S. Constitution, the states lost their right to issue money (although the banks they created by acts of incorporation could do so, and did). Still, the loss of this right might have limited the local governments' options in generating revenues and redistributing wealth through inflation. In any case, in spite of the paper currency issues of "wildcat banks," there was no sustained inflation until the 1860s.

It should be noted, however, that frequently legalization of games of chance has followed one form or another of crisis: sudden decline in government revenues or sudden increase in expenditures. In Louisiana the introduction of lotteries followed the Civil War, and in Florida it was a response to the abrupt decline in tourism in the late 1920s and Florida's being hit by two of the worst hurricanes of modern times. Horse racing, on the other hand, was decriminalized with the Depression (Blakey 1977, pp. 282, 289, 290, 303, 398, 399). But Blakey remarks that in those states that traditionally took a firm position against gambling, people often chose to pay higher taxes rather than to legalize gambling (p. 399). Sometimes lotteries were introduced because they were preferred to alternative forms of taxation. For example, New Jersey had no income tax, and for years refused to introduce one. The lottery was established to provide required revenues (Blakey 1977, p. 109). In communist countries too, ideology notwithstanding, similar circumstances have led to the introduction of lotteries and casinos (recently in Hungary). See "The Jackpot: Gambling in the Soviet Bloc," in Herman 1967.

2 For detailed information and sources, see tables in the appendix to this chapter.

3 For detailed information and sources, as well as information on other states and countries, see the appendix to this chapter. It should be noted that these revenues underestimate the impact of gambling. The advertising of gambling generates revenues for newspapers and other channels of information. Horse racing generates revenues for agriculture, and both this and other types of gambling attract tourists. And one must take into account the fact that if gambling is banned, people will gamble illegally, the revenues from such gambling will be untaxed, and those now working in the underground gambling industry may even declare themselves to be unemployed and receive welfare. Thus it would be wrong to assume that if gambling were prohibited only the declared current revenues would be lost.

4 A simple correlation between unemployment rates and revenues from lotteries for the last ten years may not, however, be negative, for more and more games have been legalized during this period. Thus, whereas relatively few lotteries were available (or the number of locations where tickets were sold was small) in the early 1970s when unemployment rates were high, the number of lotteries and locations at which tickets are sold have both increased since the late 1970s, even though unemployment rates have been falling. We could not find sufficient evidence about locations to examine statistically the impact on lottery revenues of the relationship between locations and changing unemployment rates.

5 George Bernard Shaw (1926, p. 52) once made the accurate observation that "creating employment" does not have an unambiguous positive meaning. Criminals create a lot of employment; they provide jobs not only to policemen but also to the producers of alarms and security locks, to doormen, and so forth. See Chapter 6 on the criterion of the "social good" implicit behind this statement.

6 For a lengthy criticism, consult Blum and Kalven 1966; for a nontraditional explanation, see Appendix 1.

7 See Brenner 1987a, ch. 5, for a discussion about the persistence of wrong ideas among "scientists." Rubner (1966, p. 3) notes that he examined 186 books on public finance and found that only 4 made reference to gambling. Recent books on public finance make no reference either, the reason being (as noted in Chapter 2) that traditional economic theory has nothing useful to say about either gambling or risk taking.

8 It should be noted that good arguments can be made to justify taxing the richer and redistributing the sums to those falling behind. One is that such redistribution prevents increased social instability. See Brenner 1985, ch. 2. This argument, however, does not imply that selling lotteries is bad. Note also that Mishan (1960, p. 247) is among the few who mention that envy is absent from discussions of "welfare economics." But he does not have a clear view on the subject.

9 See Rubner 1966, ch. 11, pp. 118–19.

10 Some may still argue that one must also examine what the government is doing with the money that is not redistributed through prizes. This issue is addressed later.

11 See Hood 1976, ch. 10, too for this argument.

12 Sweepstakes are substitutes, but they cannot always be found regularly, and the prizes are in general smaller than in lotteries.

13 We saw in Chapter 4 that such seemed at times to be the perception in the United States.

14 Suits (1979, p. 50) too points out that state-sanctioned gambling can raise revenues in two different ways: either by imposing a tax or by maintaining monopoly power. The burden – if there is one – is in both cases the same. When people say that lotteries provide a "voluntary tax," they confuse form and substance, for the tax on a ticket is no less a tax because the buyer is free not to buy it. Indeed, one reason for taxation is to diminish the quantity demanded.

15 See Rubner 1966, ch. 3.

16 Kaplan 1984; Livernois 1985; Mikesell and Zorn 1985. Mikesell and Zorn conclude, erroneously, that "lotteries are substantially less efficient vehicles of revenue generation than more traditional sources" (p. 12), whereas Livernois erroneously infers redistributive effects by looking at what net revenues from state lotteries are spent on. Kaplan (p. 99), however, concludes that the odds are that programs viewed as essential would have been funded if lotteries were not available. In general, he notes, politicians look on earmarked lottery revenues – for example, for education, the most commonly earmarked category – as an exchange item in their budgets. Monies realized by a lottery are allocated to education, but total education funds may not be increased, because a like amount may be withheld from other sources. Students and institutions do not receive a $50 million bonanza; they get what the legislature and governor thought they should have to start with.

17 See Blakey 1977, p. 399; Kaplan 1984.

18 Eichenwald 1987.

19 Blakey 1979, p. 76.

20 Rubner 1966, pp. 14–17, for details about premium bonds. Such bonds are extremely popular now in China (Dunnan 1987). Rubner also notes that when lotteries were suppressed in 1826, the abolition was attacked on the grounds of "depriving labourers of the privilege of drinking low-taxed beer.... Public opinion accepted as a foregone conclusion the raising of the beer tax to compensate the Chancellor for the revenue lost through the abolition of lotteries" (p. 20). On July 19, 1826, a London newspaper wrote that "a deficiency in the public revenue ... will, however, be the consequence of the annihilation of Lotteries and it must remain for those who have ... supported the putting a stop to Lotteries, to provide for the deficiency" (quoted in Rubner 1966, p. 21). Rubner also remarks that "while Gentiles spend more than twice the amount of money on alcohol than on gambling, the average British Jew's consumption pattern shows the opposite trend: gambling plays a much larger role than drinking. This presents a classical confirmation for the thesis put forward in this book that social evils are largely interchangeable. The compliment paid to the Jewish community for having to its credit a low rate of drunkenness ought to be seen in the perspective of the substitution effect, namely its proportionately larger participation in gambling" (p. 104). Also see pp. 32–7 on the sometimes wildly imaginative vocabulary used by government officials to justify one form or another of gambling.

Blakey makes a similar observation when he notes that betting linked with horse racing was exempted from antigambling legislation in the United States when "in *Van Valkenburgh v. Torrey*, the court relied on a literal reading of the word 'racing' and declared that trotting was not affected by the law" (1977, p. 175). Back to premium bonds: Their gradual disappearance during the second half of this century is, unsurprisingly, correlated with the legalization of lotteries and other games of chance.

21 See Chapter 1, n. 46.

22 Rubner 1966, p. 12.

23 See discussion in Chapters 1 and 3; Miers and Dixon 1979, pp. 376–9. Rubner (1966, p. 19) remarks that the amount of money wagered on "insurance" was said to have equaled the sales volume of the actual lottery tickets, and that there were on average 200 insurance offices operating during this period. Ashton (1969, p. 298) notes that at their peak there were 400 such offices. See also Blakey 1977, p. 897.

24 See Chapter 2, n. 68, for the sources on Sweden; Whang 1933 on China.

25 Clotfelter and Cook 1987, p. 11, and discussion in Chapter 4, section 5.

26 Blakey 1977, p. 913. Miers and Dixon (1979, pp. 379–82) remark that with the enactment of the Lotteries Act in 1823, illegal private lotteries on a small scale multiplied, and apparently newspaper prize competitions became widespread.

27 See Blakey 1977, pp. 142–203; Devereux 1980, pt. III. But it should be noted that even racetracks were of questionable legality, since they derived their revenues from gambling.

28 Blakey 1977, pp. 121–3; Reuter 1985, p. 15.

29 Blakey 1977, pp. 123–5.

30 Ibid., pp. 201–2. Judge Van, in his dissent, showed more common sense when he argued that "engaging in the business of public gambling by quoting and laying insidious odds to a multitude of people was the evil aimed at, not the making of record of the business which is comparatively innocent" (p. 202). Blakey also remarks that much legal discussion concerned the question whether horse racing was a game or a sport.

31 Blakey (1977, p. 384) remarks that in Nebraska agrarian interests, reflecting their eastern origins, dictated an absolute ban on gambling as soon as they gained control of the legislature.

32 Ibid., p. 350, quoting an unpublished paper by Haller, "Bootleggers and American Gambling 1920–1945: An Overview," and also relying on Haller's "Urban Crime and Criminal Justice: The Chicago Case," *Journal of American History* (1970).

33 Blakey 1977, p. 674. Drawings from the Louisiana lotteries took place daily in Boston, Cincinnati, Denver, and San Francisco. And legislators were bribed. New York, in order to protect the success of its own lotteries, passed a law in 1759 that imposed a fine on anyone who sold foreign lotteries inside the state (ibid., p. 137). On Australia, see Rubner 1966, p. 148.

34 Blakey 1979, p. 73; 1977, pp. 682, 701–2. Blakey, quoting Senator Eastland, also remarks that the impact of the mail prohibition was that the lottery statutes in their present form did not cover many forms of betting "transported daily across State lines, for they do not meet the traditional

definition of a lottery.... Even out-and-out lottery tickets may be shipped across state lines with impunity if they are printed in blank, shipped, and then locally overprinted with the paying numbers" (1977, p. 583). But it was already during the Great Depression of the 1930s that the great success of the Irish Sweepstakes opened some government officials' eyes to the fact that government revenues could be obtained even during recessions without raising a public outcry, and that prohibitions made other governments richer. In fact, the Irish game was used in arguments during the 1960s to justify the legalization of lotteries.

35 See Gruson 1987, from whose article one can infer that 50 percent of the buyers in Maryland's small communities near the border come from Delaware. She notes that Delaware's problem is faced by many of the twenty-two states that were operating lotteries: "It is getting more difficult to attract people to play lottery games that offer anything less than million-dollar jackpots." This is, of course, one of the results of competition among the state-owned lotteries. Gruson also remarks that the attraction of big prizes "has led eight states, including New York, to consider banding together to offer regular multistate lottery drawings. Officials estimate that it could often produce jackpots of $80 million, nearly double the current record of $41 million, set two years ago in New York." But it should be noted that federal law still prevents the resurgence of nationwide private lotteries (Blakey 1979, p. 71). In Prussia, a solution to competition among the states was found when the other German states gave up their lottery privileges and accepted a budget subvention in return for permitting the sale of Prussian tickets (Rubner 1966, p. 148). In Nevada too, where by the 1960s gambling was the largest industry, similar aspects of the industry were not lost on the politicians, who realized that the state depended heavily on outsiders for its tax dollars (Blakey 1977, p. 467). According to Blair 1986, sixteen of the twenty-two states with lotteries and the District of Columbia were talking about banding together to offer a regular multistate lottery drawing that officials said would increase state revenues and produce jackpots of more than $50 million.

36 Blakey 1977, p. 381.

37 Hood 1976, p. 170.

38 Ibid. Hood notes that this does not imply that the law was "ineffective." It prevented the development of large-scale bookmaking businesses, which could be visible, thus making betting more expensive for the poor and diminishing government revenues. The reason why the growth of large-scale businesses was hampered was that the system depended on bettors being personally known to the bookmakers' agents, both to ensure that casual bettors were not plainclothes policemen and because no written receipts were given.

39 Dixon 1984, p. 2, quoting the assistant commissioner of the Metropolitan Police in 1923.

40 McKibbin (1979, p. 159) notes that bookmakers would arrange for an arrest to be made if new officers were known to be on duty, so that the police who gave evidence in court could be identified and later avoided. See also Dixon 1984, pp. 37, 63.

41 Dixon 1984, p. 35. According to him, the evidence from England, based

on autobiographies and memories of men who had contact with book-makers after the passage of the 1906 law, is unanimous. Payoffs to the police were an inevitable part of the street bookmaker's expenses, taking the form of either a bribe or "betting with the bookmaker on the simple system of receiving on winners but not paying on losers" (p. 66), and he concludes that whereas "before the war, the police had greeted the Street Betting Act as an addition to their power, they now began to perceive it as a threat to their authority" (p. 67).

42 Blakey 1977, p. 154.
43 Chafetz 1960, p. 228; Blakey 1977, pp. 156–7.
44 Blakey 1977, pp. 154–8.
45 W. Turner, *Gambler's Money* (1965), quoted in ibid., p. 432.
46 Blakey 1977, p. 465.
47 Ibid., p. 466. Notice that this outcome is not unlike the situation in England, where the honesty of bookmakers is noteworthy.
48 Weinstein and Deitch 1974; Blakey 1977, pp. 208–9.
49 Blakey 1977, pp. 195–8. He remarks that the 1971 Joint Legislative Committee on Crime discovered that an arrested gambler faced only a 2 percent chance of going to jail, and even then his sentence would be light. In one heavy gambling district, of 1,225 arrested bookies, only 10 were fined over $500, only 19 were imprisoned, and only 3 of these 19 received sentences in excess of ninety days. It was also estimated that each arrest cost the public forty times the fine recovered.
50 Ibid., pp. 197–8. In testimony before the legislature, it was revealed that the typical person involved in off-track betting earned $12,300 a year, was a high school graduate forty-two years of age on average, male, white, often of Italian or Irish extraction, very often Catholic, and a blue-collar worker who was not a compulsive gambler. Forty-three per-cent had prior experience with some form of illegal gambling. See ibid., pp. 211–12.
51 See O'Hara 1987 and Dixon 1987, and extensive evidence and sources quoted there.
52 See Rubner 1966; Williams 1956, p. 561; and discussion in Chapter 3, section 3.
53 See discussion in Chapter 3.
54 See discussion in Chapter 3, section 2.
55 Harrison 1971, p. 65; Walvin 1978, p. 37; Read 1979, p. 111. Joyce remarks that "the closest parallel to the treatment of gambling is the prohibition of alcohol, and many obvious comparisons are frequently drawn in the modern press. The . . . antilottery movement was part of a more general reform movement occurring in the latter part of the 19th century, which was antialcohol as well . . . although antilottery amend-ments were more common than antialcohol amendments" (1979, p. 149).
56 Blakey 1977, pp. 88–90, 174–8.
57 Ibid., p. 175. Pari-mutuel wagering, available in Europe from 1865, was not widely adopted in the United States until 1920, in part as a result of the political influence of the bookmaking lobby, notes Reuter (1985, p. 14).
58 For example, when usury was still prohibited, the word "interest" was invented, and paying it was legal.

59 Quoted in Blakey 1977, p. 104.
60 "Odds Improve for Legalized Gambling in Several States," *Wall Street Journal*, Mar. 6, 1986, p. 1.
61 Dixon 1984, sect. 1.
62 Dixon remarks that "police corruption must be taken into account as a likely social cost of the legislative creation of 'victimless' crimes: this is a widely accepted conclusion of extensive academic and official investigations in the United States" (ibid., p. 8), and he discusses facets of the corruption in England (pp. 8–22). He also writes that by the 1920s "attempts to enforce [the 1906 law] were stirring up open resentment against the police which was threatening the toe-hold of public consent upon which they depended" (p. 44) and that "consent to policing in liberal democracies relies heavily on the presentation and perception of the police as the enforcers of apolitically neutral law" (p. 45). Dixon also quotes E. P. Thompson's opinion in *The Making of the English Working Class* (1963) that a law that is partial and perceived to be unjust will prevent the law from performing its vital ideological work: It "will mask nothing, legitimize nothing, contribute nothing to any class's hegemony" (p. 45). Dixon concludes that "herein lies the significance of anti-gambling legislation of this type: it threatened not merely the 'moral standing' of the police which attempted to enforce it, but by necessary implication the legal system as a whole and the law itself as a legitimizing ideology" (p. 69).
63 See Brenner 1987a, ch. 5, on resistance to innovations in business and science.
64 Blakey 1977, pp. 364–5, 681–713.
65 Ibid., pp. 700–34, 873–5.
66 Ibid., pp. 681–713, "The Economic Case against State-Run Lotteries," and *Business Week*, Aug. 4, 1975, where the critics failed to understand the reasons for the failure of the first lotteries. On bureaucracy in general, see Brenner 1987b.
67 See Brenner 1987b.
68 See Rosten 1941, p. 39.

Chapter 6. Happiness, luck, and the social good

1 Kaplan 1985a, b.
2 "Lotteries: A Big Payoff for the States," *Business Week*, Sept. 8, 1986. Passell 1989 provides recent figures: In 1988 Massachusetts residents spent $235.
3 Blair 1986; "Aging State Lotteries," *Wall Street Journal*, Sept. 3, 1987, p. 1. The growth was due primarily to new lotteries. Passell (1989) cites the 1988 figure for lottery revenues, $16 billion.
4 *Newsweek*, Sept. 2, 1985.
5 *Montreal Gazette*, Jan. 9, 1984; Wayne 1984. The number indicates an average of more than two tickets per Canadian.
6 Kallick-Kaufman 1979, p. 19. Rubner (1966, ch. 12) makes similar calculations for the United Kingdom and shows that whereas the gross outlays on gambling are of the same order of magnitude as expenditures on alcoholic and tobacco products, the net outlays equal about half of

this amount because of the redistributed prizes (pp. 119–23). See also n. 31 below explaining why for this same reason (i.e., that newspaper articles do not, in general, distinguish between gross and net outlays on gambling) the numbers newspapers publish are very misleading.

7 Discussed in Chapters 3, 5. Dixon (1981, pp. 51–2) emphasizes that betting has provided significant revenues for newspapers as well as for the post and telegraph and telephone companies. In 1923, 7 percent of all telegrams in England were linked with betting or racing.

8 See Baker 1958, p. 16, and "The Economic Case against State-Run Gambling," *Business Week*, Aug. 4, 1975, where several so-called experts pronounce on the subject.

9 See Bauer 1984, p. 9, writing in a completely different context about "inducement goods."

10 See Bolen 1976, p. 32, who raises these questions but does not answer them.

11 Tocqueville 1956, p. 18. Richard Heffner, who edited his writings, adds to the Introduction the statement that no wonder revolutions in such societies are rare (p. 18).

12 Ibid.

13 As Heffner, summarizing Tocqueville's views, puts it (ibid., p. 19).

14 Ibid., p. 12.

15 For development of this point in order to explain resistance to innovations in business and science, see Brenner 1987, ch. 5. Also see Schoeck 1969 for extensive discussion about the absence of the notion of envy from the social sciences, and Brenner 1983, 1985, 1987 for discussions about the absence of individuals, entrepreneurship, and chance as well as envy from the social sciences today. And recall that Hegel once said that all philosophical contemplation serves only to eliminate the accidental.

16 Schoeck 1969, p. 238.

17 See discussion on happiness and joy in Brenner 1983, ch. 7, and 1985, ch. 7, as well as the appendix to ch. 1 in Brenner 1985. Whereas in the 1985 book I suggested that one can choose between a policy consistent with recommendations made here and one where the goal is to maintain the somehow achieved status quo, in both the 1987 book and here policies are recommended that favor change. The reason for making this choice today becomes clear in Brenner 1987, ch. 7.

18 Notice that being smart is not on the list. Yet, as Cohen notes, many business tycoons, partly to allay envy and partly to ease their conscience, will say that their success is due to thrift and industriousness. Only a few will admit, as an oil millionaire did, "Whatever else it takes to win in the oil game, the *sine qua non* is luck.... Luck has helped me every day of my life. And I'd rather be lucky than smart, cause a lot of smart people ain't eatin' regular" (1964, p. 146).

19 See Chapter 5, section 1, and Appendix 1 to Chapter 2, section 9, when regressive and progressive taxation are the subject of concern.

20 Unless one talks about addiction – a form of "externality" – which is another issue.

21 These events were recounted by Smith on CBS's "60 Minutes."

22 Ore 1965, pp. 185–6. Today some social scientists refer to "safety valves" when they make such arguments. Sasuly also remarks: "It was scarcely

an accident that a disproportionate number of the new race courses were established in the northern counties of England [historians have made reference to the desperate poverty of the Catholic gentry in the seventeenth and eighteenth centuries]. And it seems highly probable that some of the genuinely great sums staked on Thoroughbred races represented a last hope of paying off debts and preserving a landhold. A direct parallel was seen in backwoods Tennessee early in the nineteenth century. And, at a farther reach in time, place and social class, something rather similar was seen at Detroit Race Course in 1980 when recently unemployed automobile workers went to the races in larger numbers than ever before" (1982, p. 11).

23 Bolen (1976, p. 29), in a somewhat inconsistent essay on gambling, also mentions these points and makes reference to Meriwether's book. Gerald Williams, a poor resident of Harlem, said when buying a lottery ticket and a chance at winning a big prize: "The big difference between Lotto and life is that in this game everyone has the same chance" (quoted in *Newsweek*, Sept. 2, 1985, in an article entitled "The Lottery Craze"). O'Hara remarks that in Australia "for the less wealthy gamblers, gaming and betting provided one of the few opportunities for them to change their station in life. This was particularly relevant in a new society where even a relatively small windfall could place the successful gambler on the path to success" (1987, p. 4).

24 See "Kids Who Sell Crack," *Time*, May 9, 1988, cover story.

25 Yes, apparently there are people who are addicted to fitness, see Charlier 1987. On addiction, see also Duster 1970, ch. 1; Michaels 1986; Chafetz 1987; and sources quoted in Chapter 2, section 5. See also Downes et al. 1976 and Fingarette 1988.

26 Dixon 1980, pp. 115–16, quoting medical opinions of the time. See also Duster 1970, ch. 11.

27 Duster 1970, ch. 1, pp. 22–3, reaching similar conclusions when looking at the campaign against drugs. But see Kerr 1988 and the May 9, 1988, *Time* cover story on a heated discussion in the United States about the legalization of drugs.

28 One cannot discard the possibility of self-interest in claims that governments must find the solution. If one accepts the idea that many of the unfortunate could manage to raise themselves by their own efforts, the role of government and its consultants in redistributing wealth would be significantly reduced.

29 It may be useful, for the last time, to compare our approach in explaining antigambling attitudes with some others. Some have argued that the moral imperatives of Christianity together with pragmatic precepts of industrial capitalism are at the source of the negative attitudes. Others have tried to explain them in terms of the disparity between the publicly avowed principles of the Protestant ethic and the actual practices to which its evolution has given rise; that is, unquestioned affirmation of the primacy of duty, enterprise, frugality, and disciplined work as opposed to self-indulgence, greed, and frivolous consumption. But, as Newman (1972, pp. 85–7) pointed out, these explanations are problematic. As we saw, gambling was condemned in antiquity by Islam, not only in Europe or among Protestants. Thus the explanation must be elsewhere, in a

universal phenomenon independent of specific religions or the existence of middle classes. Such an explanation has been given in this book.

30 See Brenner 1983, 1985, 1987 (first chapter and its appendixes in each book) for reasons justifying this methodology. On the interaction between language and thought in various contexts, see also Bloch 1953; Tuchman 1981, pp. 51–65; Fèbvre 1982; Boorstin 1987, ch. 1. On astrology, see Chapter 1, n. 23. (By the way, this sentence was written well before Donald Regan's revelations about the White House's use of astrology under Ronald Reagan.)

31 This last is added to update the text. Newspapers and magazines published numerous articles about gambling in 1988–9. The *New York Times* had four articles on the subject, starting with one on the front page on May 28, 1989. *Time* put the subject on its cover in a July 1989 issue, and *Business Week* in a May 1989 one. All without exception adopted a condemning, worrying tone. They all mentioned that the poor were playing the lotteries, and that not only was there addiction but much "potential addiction" (whatever that means). Numbers were given in these articles about the total amount wagered, with no mention that 50 percent (in the case of lotteries, and far higher percentages for other games, going up to more than 90 percent for some slot machines) is given back in the form of prizes, significantly diminishing the net outlays on gambling.

However, when some "grayer" articles are written, not those that can be put on the front page, the information confirms the mainly boring, stable image of gamblers. Sturz, for example, writes: "Most weekday bettors [who take the subsidized trips to Atlantic City, where they eat lunch for $2.50, subsidized by the casinos] live on Social Security and pensions. But if they are exploited, encouraged to go in too deep, there's no sign of it. They say they never bet beyond their limit. One after another approvingly recites this refrain: Bet with your head; not over it. Win or lose, these visitors seem to know, and get, what they want: the day's outing to Atlantic City is a welcome way to break up the week. They sit on the boardwalk, dine on restaurant food (and especially prize those places where pickles are free), and most of all, enjoy the thrill of slot machines that swallow endless nickels, quarters and dollar slugs. The casinos also know, and get, what they want. They clear about 18 cents on every dollar wagered. These old people are not nutty about gambling; they are not eager to see casinos come to New York. They enjoy the journey and the long dreamy day. If casinos came closer, the Atlantic City adventure would, like so much else in their lives, be over" (1988).

Of course this is not front-page stuff, and such information does not sell newspapers, magazines, or books. But it is the truth.

Appendix 1 to Chapter 2. Gambling, decision making, and social ranks

1 The deeper philosophical implications of these assumptions are explored in R. Brenner 1983, 1985.

2 Comparison with their views can be found in R. Brenner 1983, 1985, although later in this appendix I shall discuss some facets of these models.

3 Friedman and Savage 1948, for example, argued that the utility function

is sometimes convex, sometimes concave. But if one does not know where exactly, the model will not be falsified. In private correspondence with the author (letter dated June 22, 1987), Friedman said he was wrong when he used the existence of multiple prizes to rationalize the upper concave section of the utility curve.

4 March (1988) attributes risk-taking behavior to a difference between realized wealth and the wealth the individual aspired to. However, he does not present a formal model of risk taking. Yet, interestingly, the sections in the paper are arranged in the same order as in R. Brenner 1983: first a model of risk taking and then an argument about population. But whereas in R. Brenner 1983, 1985 considerable evidence is presented to support the view about the relationship between population and wealth distribution and equilibrium, March does not present any such evidence.

5 The evidence presented in R. Brenner 1983, 1985 suggests that such a distinction should be made.

6 It may be useful to note that whereas people may in effect buy fractional tickets by buying in groups, such pooling is not costless. Somebody who is unemployed may find it difficult to pool resources with others, or people may sometimes forget to pay, in which case, if the group happens to win, considerable friction arises (such cases have reached the courts – in Quebec not long ago, for example). And people may disagree about what to do with the small prizes. One of my colleagues who commented on this paper revealed that he stopped pooling with his father-in-law because he did not want to spend the small winnings on lotteries, whereas his father-in-law did.

7 See R. Brenner 1983, 1985. This problem was brought to my attention by Milton Friedman.

8 It does not take much time to buy tickets; one can even reserve them by phone. However, one may still argue that people buy lottery tickets to daydream. This does not seem to be a reasonable assumption, for a number of reasons. First, people frequently buy tickets at the last minute (queues are the longest the day before the draw). Second, if people daydream about being rich, then the motivation is not daydreaming, but the hope of becoming rich. Third, how can one explain why daydreaming should be condemned and made illegal, as gambling was? Thus, although one sometimes hears the argument about daydreaming, it seems both superficial and lacking in ability to shed the slightest light on facts.

9 If fairness is defined as $(1 - p)h = p(H - h)$, then the same condition is obtained as for lotteries. See R. Brenner 1983, pp. 52–3.

10 The conditions examined next may remind one of the arguments in Rothschild and Stiglitz 1970. But there is a significant difference, since in their model the utility function depends on wealth only, whereas here two variables have to be taken into account.

11 This result contrasts with the result in Rothschild and Stiglitz 1970. The reason is that here an increased variability has both benefits and costs in terms of changing one's *rank*, something that an investment with a smaller spread does not have.

12 R. Brenner 1983, ch. 2; 1985, ch. 2.

13 These issues are discussed in detail in R. Brenner 1983, 1985, 1987. Cancian (1979, ch. 2) makes a somewhat similar distinction too. It may

be interesting to note that Frank Knight's opinion that human conscious-
ness itself would disappear in the absence of uncertainty (discussed in
Arrow 1970, ch. 1) receives a literal interpretation in this model. Also,
Knight's intuition that if all risks were measurable, then risk aversion
would not give rise to any profit, receives a clear interpretation within
this model. Only when innovations take place and demands must be
discovered (a process linked with the notion of uncertainty) will "profits"
exist. Arrow notes that Knight's proposition, "if true, would appear to be
of the greatest importance; yet, surprisingly enough, not a single writer,
as far as I know, with the exception of Hicks . . . has mentioned it, and he
denies its validity" (1970, p. 30). Yet Knight's statement seems accurate
within this model.

14 Or, as pointed out in R. Brenner 1983, p. 56, a person may be called a
terrorist by some and a freedom fighter by others.

15 For a summary of the evidence, see R. Brenner 1983, chs. 1, 2; 1985, ch.
2; 1987, ch. 2.

16 Knight's words, as recalled by Gary S. Becker (1983).

17 R. Brenner 1983, 1985, 1987.

18 See R. Brenner 1983, ch. 1; 1985, ch. 2, where a brief comparison with
Freud's approach to gambling is also made.

19 See the large number of studies in Kahneman, Slovic, and Tversky 1982;
Arkes and Hammond 1986; Hogarth and Reder 1986; Zeckhauser 1986;
Lea, Tarpy, and Webley 1987; March 1988. See also additional references
and discussion in Schoemaker 1982 and Shefrin and Statman 1984; also a
discussion on survey methods in general in Glock 1967 and Moser and
Kalton 1972.

20 See Bloch 1953; Orwell 1957, p. 149; R. Brenner 1983, pp. 25–6, 80–2;
1985, pp. 30–1, 114–15. In the last, additional references can be found
on this point.

21 A point repeated in Viscusi 1987.

22 See Solman and Friedman 1982, pp. 114–15.

23 R. Brenner 1983, 1985, 1987; G. A. Brenner and Brenner 1987. But to
study preference formation, reference should be made to studies based on
direct questions about satisfaction, like Easterlin 1979, and in particular
the numerous ones that Kapteyn has done in collaboration with a number of coauthors (1978, 1982, 1985), Van de Stadt (Van de Stadt, Kapteyn, and van de Geer 1985) in particular. Although their findings strongly support the implication of the model presented here, I give greater
credence to facts than to words (i.e., to the way people answer questions
when their money is not at stake).

24 The model also gives a literal interpretation to the statement made by a
player in the stock market who wrote: "If I hadn't made money some of
the time, I would have acquired market wisdom quicker" (Lefèbvre 1968,
p. 30, quoted by Slovic 1986, p. 188).

Appendix 2 to Chapter 2. A statistical profile of gamblers

1 Other specifications were tried but were not supported by the data. Note
that a more general and complex specification will add an error term to
equation (4).

2 The sample size may even exceed the 10,938 figure, some observations being repeated to respect the weights corresponding to the provinces.

3 35% may be an overestimation, since some people might have reported not buying lottery tickets at all, even though they did buy them. But it is difficult to assess the importance of this problem.

4 The probability of a χ^2_{p-1} exceeding the calculated χ^2 is less than 0.01. Thus we reject the model, subject to the constraint that all regression coefficients (except the constant term) are 0 at a confidence level of 99%.

5 There are actually two sets of solutions corresponding to the adjustment equation, since $\theta_4 = \frac{1}{2} B_2^2 \Rightarrow B_2 = \pm 0.0447$. We use $B_2 = 0.0447$ because with this solution all people in the survey underestimate their lottery expenditures. With $B_2 = -0.0447$, we find that families earning less than $12,000 overestimate their lottery expenditures and that high-income families greatly underestimate their lottery expenditures. But these results contradict the evidence we have from other sources. See R. Brenner 1983, ch. 1; 1985, ch. 2.

6 As shown in Table 6, the underdeclaration reaches slightly over 100% for the very-low-income families, suggesting some difficulties with the truncated series expansion at these levels of income.

7 For further details, see G. A. Brenner, Montmarquette, and Brenner 1987.

8 See R. Brenner 1988.

Bibliographies

Chapter 1

Abt, Vicky, James F. Smith, and Eugene M. Christiansen (1985), *The Business of Risk: Commercial Gambling in Mainstream America*, Lawrence: University of Kansas Press.

Altabella, José (1962), *La Loteria Nacional de España (1763–1963)*, Madrid: Dirección General de Tributos Especiales.

Ashton, John (1969), *A History of English Lotteries* (1893), Detroit: Singing Tree.

(1898) *The History of Gambling in England*, London: Duckworth.

Baker, Leonard (1958), "Should We Have a National Lottery?" *Challenge*, Aug.–Sept., pp. 13–17.

Berlin, Isaiah (1976), *Vico and Herder*, London: Hogarth.

Blakey, Robert G. (1977), *The Development of the Law of Gambling, 1776–1976*, Washington, D.C.: National Institute of Law Enforcement and Criminal Justice.

Blanche, Ernest E. (1950), "Lotteries Yesterday, Today and Tomorrow," in Morris Ploscowe and Edwin J. Lukas (eds.), *Gambling, Annals of the American Academy of Political and Social Science* 269:71–6.

Bloch, Marc (1953), *The Historian's Craft*, New York: Knopf.

Bolen, Darrel W. (1976), "Gambling: Historical Highlights and Trends and Their Implications for Contemporary Society," in William R. Eadington (ed.), *Gambling and Society*, Springfield, Ill.: Thomas, pp. 7–38.

Brenner, Reuven (1985), *Betting on Ideas: Wars, Invention, Inflation*, Chicago: University of Chicago Press.

Caillois, Roger (1958), *Les jeux et les hommes*, Paris: Gallimard.

Clotfelter, Charles T., and Philip J. Cook (1987a), "The Context of Lottery Growth" (manuscript, Duke University).

(1987b) "State Lotteries Today: A Profile" (manuscript, Duke University).

Cohen, John (1964), *Behaviour in Uncertainty*, New York: Basic.

Coste, Pierre (1933), *Les loteries d'état en Europe et la Loterie Nationale*, Paris: Payot.

Desperts, Jean, "Quand Louis XIV jouait à la loterie," *Histoire*, no. 24 (1982): 86–90.

Devereux, Edward C. (1980), *Gambling and Social Structure* (Ph.D. thesis, Harvard University, 1949), New York: Arno.

Dixon, David (1984), "Illegal Gambling and Histories of Policing in Britain," paper presented at the Sixth National Conference on Gambling and Risk-Taking, Atlantic City, December 9–12.

Eade, J. C. (1984), *The Forgotten Sky*, Oxford: Clarendon Press.

Encyclopaedia Judaica (1971), Jerusalem: Keter.

Ezell, John Samuel (1960), *Fortune's Merry Wheel: The Lottery in America*, Cambridge, Mass.: Harvard University Press.

Feinman, Jeffrey P., Robert D. Blashek, and Richard J. McCabe (1986), *Sweepstakes, Prize Promotions, Games and Contests*, Homewood, Ill.: Dow Jones–Irwin.

Fleming, Alice (1978), *Something for Nothing: A History of Gambling*, New York: Delacorte.

Handelsman, Joseph Armand (1933), *La loterie d'état en Pologne et dans les autres pays d'Europe – Les emprunts à lots*, Paris: Marcel Giard.

Henriquet, Paul (1921), "Les loteries et les emprunts à lots," doctoral thesis, Law Faculty, University of Paris.

Huizinga, Johan (1955), *Homo Ludens: A Study of the Play Element in Culture* (1944), Boston: Beacon.

Josephus, Flavius (1959), *The Jewish Wars*, trans. G. A. Williamson, Harmondsworth: Penguin.

Kassuto, M. D. (ed.) (1963), *Torah, Neviim, Ktuvim* (with interpretations), Tel Aviv: Yavneh. (In Hebrew)

Kinsey, Robert K. (1959), "The Role of Lotteries in Public Finance," Ph.D. thesis, Columbia University.

Labrosse, Michel (1985), *Les loteries ... de Jacques Cartier à nos jours*, Montreal: Stanké.

Landau, Michael (1968), *A Manual on Lotteries*, Ramat Gan: Massada.

Lea, E. G., M. R. Tarpy, and P. Webley (1987), *The Individual in the Economy*, Cambridge: Cambridge University Press.

Leonnet, Jean (1963), *Les loteries d'état en France au XVIIIe et XIXe siècles*, Paris: Imprimerie Nationale.

Lorenz, Valerie C. (1985), "The Bible and Gambling," in William R. Eadington (ed.), *The Gambling Studies: Proceedings of the Sixth National Conference on Gambling and Risk-Taking*, vol. 3, Reno: Bureau of Business and Economic Research, University of Nevada, pp. 301–16.

Mackay, Charles (1980), *Extraordinary Popular Delusions and the Madness of Crowds* (1841), New York: Harmony.

Martinez, Tomás H. (1983), *The Gambling Scene: Why People Gamble*, Springfield, Ill.: Thomas.

Mikesell, John L., and C. Kurt Zorn (1985), "Revenue Performance of State Lotteries," paper prepared for the Seventy-eighth Annual Conference of the National Tax Association.

Nussbaum, Martha C. (1986), *The Fragility of Goodness: Luck and Ethics in Greek Tragedy and Philosophy*, Cambridge: Cambridge University Press.

Pryor, Frederic (1977), *The Origins of the Economy*, New York: Academic Press.

The Quran (1972), tr. M. Z. Khan. (2d rev. ed., 1975).

Rosenthal, Franz (1975), *Gambling in Islam*, Leiden: Brill.

Rouse, W. H. D. (1957), *Gods, Heroes and Men of Ancient Greece*, New York: New American Library.

Rubner, Alex (1966), *The Economics of Gambling*, London: Macmillan.

Smith, Stanley S. (1952), "Lotteries," in Herbert L. Marx, Jr. (ed.), *Gambling in America*, New York: Wilson, pp. 61–6. First published in *Journal of Criminal Law and Criminology* 38 (Jan.–March 1948): 547–56, 659–69.

Suetonius, Caius Silentius Tranquillus (1961), *Vie des douze Césars*, Paris: Livre de Poche.

Suits, Daniel B. (1979), "Economic Background for Gambling Policy," *Social Issues* 35(3): 43–61.

Sumner, William Graham, and A. G. Keller (1927), *The Science of Society*, New Haven, Conn.: Yale University Press.

Tacitus, Cornelius (1970), *Germania*, trans. H. Mattingly, rev. S. A. Handford, Harmondsworth: Penguin.

Tester, Jim (1987), *A History of Western Astrology*, Bury St. Edmunds, Suffolk: Boydell.

Thomas, Keith (1971), *Religion and the Decline of Magic*, New York: Scribner.

Vico, Giambattista (1982), *Selected Writings*, ed. and trans. Leon Pompa, Cambridge: Cambridge University Press.

Weinstein, David, and Lillian Deitch (1974), *The Impact of Legalized Gambling: The Socioeconomic Consequences of Lotteries and Off-Track Betting*, New York: Praeger.

Wesley, John (1958–9), *The Works of John Wesley*, Grand Rapids, Mich.: Zondervan.

Woodhall, Robert (1964), "The British State Lotteries," *History Today*, July, pp. 497–504.

Chapter 2 and its appendixes

Alchian, A. A. (1953), "The Meaning of Utility Measurement," *American Economic Review* 42: 26–50.

Allais, M. (1953), "Le comportement de l'homme rationnel devant le risque: Critique des postulats et axiomes de l'Ecole Américaine," *Econometrica* 21(4): 503–46.

Allen, David P. (1952), *The Nature of Gambling*, New York: Coward-McCann.

Alsop, Ronald (1983), "State Lottery Craze Is Spreading, but Some Fear It Hurts the Poor," *Wall Street Journal*, Feb. 24, p. 31.

Arkes, Hal R., and Kenneth R. Hammond (eds.) (1986), *Judgement and Decision Making*, Cambridge: Cambridge University Press.

Arrow, K. J. (1970), *Essays in the Theory of Risk-Bearing*, Amsterdam: North-Holland.

Ashton, John (1898), *The History of Gambling in England*, London: Duckworth.

Becker, G. S. (1983), "The Fire of Truth: A Remembrance of Law and Economics at Chicago, 1932–70" (discussion ed. E. W. Kitch), *Journal of Law and Economics* 24: 163–234.

Bergler, Edmund (1957), *The Psychology of Gambling*, New York: Hill and Wang.

Bloch, M. (1953), *The Historian's Craft*, New York: Knopf.

Blum, W. J., and H. Kalven, Jr. (1966), *The Uneasy Case for Progressive Taxation* (1953), Chicago: University of Chicago Press.

Bolen, Darrell W. (1976), "Gambling: Historical Highlights and Trends and Their Implications for Contemporary Society," in William R. Eadington (ed.), *Gambling and Society*, Springfield, Ill.: Thomas, pp. 7–38.

Borill, J. (1975), "Study of Gamblers and Drug-Takers in H.M. Prison, Pentonville," paper prepared for discussion at a consultation on compulsive gambling, May 22.

Brenner, Gabrielle A. (1985), "Quebeckers and Lotteries," research report, Institut d'Economie Appliquée, Ecole des Hautes Etudes Commerciales, Montreal.

(1986) "Why Do People Gamble: Further Canadian Evidence," *Journal of Gambling Behavior* 2(2) (Fall–Winter): 121–9.

Brenner, Gabrielle A., and Reuven Brenner (1987), "Why Do Lotteries Have Multiple Prizes?" research report, Institut d'Economie Appliquée, Ecoles des Hautes Etudes Commerciales, Montreal.

Brenner, Gabrielle A., Claude Montmarquette, and Reuven Brenner (1987), "Lottery Expenditures: What Do People Say and What Do They Do? An Econometric Analysis," working paper, Department of Economics, Université de Montréal.

Brenner, Gabrielle A., and André Tremblay (1986), "Lotteries: Participation and Business Cycles," Research Report 86–11, Institut d'Economie Appliquée, Ecole des Hautes Etudes Commerciales, Montreal.

Brenner, Reuven (1983), *History: The Human Gamble*, Chicago: University of Chicago Press.

(1985) *Betting on Ideas: Wars, Invention, Inflation*, Chicago: University of Chicago Press.

(1987) *Rivalry: In Business, Science, among Nations*, Cambridge: Cambridge University Press.

(1988) "Numbers, Interpretations, and Macroeconomic Policies," Working Paper no. 8828, Department of Economics, Université de Montréal.

Brinner, Roger E., and Charles T. Clotfelter (1975), "An Economic Appraisal of State Lotteries," *National Tax Journal* 28:395–404.

Brunk, Gregory G. (1981), "A Test of the Friedman–Savage Gambling Model," *Quarterly Journal of Economics* 96:341–8.

Calabresi, G. (1985), *Ideals, Beliefs, Attitudes and the Law*, Syracuse, N.Y.: Syracuse University Press.

Campbell, Angus, and Philip E. Converse (1972), *The Human Meaning of Social Change*, New York: Russell Sage Foundation.

Campbell, Felicia (1976), "Gambling: A Positive View," in William R. Eadington (ed.), *Gambling and Society*, Springfield, Ill.: Thomas.

Cancian, Frank (1979), *The Innovator's Situation*, Stanford, Calif.: Stanford University Press.

Chafetz, Henry (1960), *Play the Devil: A History of Gambling in the United States from 1492 to 1955*, New York: Potter.

Clotfelter, Charles T. (1979), "On the Regressivity of State-Operated 'Number' Games," *National Tax Journal* 32:543–7.

Clotfelter, Charles T., and Philip J. Cook (1987), "Implicit Taxation in Lottery Finance" (manuscript, Duke University).

Coase, Ronald H. (1937), "The Nature of the Firm," *Economica* 4:386–405.

Cohen, John (1964), *Behaviour in Uncertainty*, New York: Basic.

Cohen, John, and Mark Hansel, *Risk and Gambling* (1956), New York: Philosophical Library.

Cornish, D. B. (1978), *Gambling: A Review of the Literature and Its Implications for Policy and Research*, London: H.M.S.O.

Desperts, Jean (1982), "Quand Louis XIV jouait à la loterie," *Histoire*, no. 24:86–90.

Devereux, Edward C. (1980), *Gambling and Social Structure* (Ph.D. thesis, Harvard University, 1949), New York: Arno.

Dixon, David (1980), "The Discovery of the Compulsive Gambler," in Zenon Bankowski and Geoff Mungham (eds.), *Essays in Law and Society*, London: Routledge and Kegan Paul, pp. 157–79.

   (1981) "The State and Gambling: Developments in the Legal Control of Gambling in England, 1867–1923," paper presented at the Fifth National Conference on Gambling and Risk-Taking, Lake Tahoe, Nev., October.

Downes, D. M., B. P. Davies, M. E. David, and P. Stone (1976), *Gambling, Work and Leisure: A Study across Three Areas*, London: Routledge and Kegan Paul.

Eadington, William R. (1987), "Economic Perceptions of Gambling Behavior," *Journal of Gambling Behavior* 3(4) (Winter): 264–73.

Easterlin, Richard A. (1974), "Does Economic Growth Improve the Human Lot? Some Empirical Evidence," in P. David and M. Reder (eds.), *Nations and Households on Economic Growth*, New York: Academic Press, pp. 89–125.

Fisher, Irving (1906), *The Nature of Capital and Income*, New York: Macmillan.

Foster, George M. (1967), "Peasant Society and the Image of Limited Good," in J. M. Potter, M. N. Diaz, and G. M. Foster (eds.), *Peasant Society: A Reader*, Boston: Little, Brown, pp. 300–23.

Freud, Sigmund (1929), letter to Theodor Reik, April 24, in Theodor Reik, *Thirty Years with Freud*, London: Hogarth, 1942, pp. 155–6.

Frey, James H. (1984), "Gambling: A Sociological Review," *Annals: The American Academy of Political and Social Science* 474 (July): 107–21.

Friedman, M., and L. J. Savage (1948), "The Utility Analysis of Choices Involving Risks," *Journal of Political Economy* 56: 279–304.

Gallup Social Surveys (1972), *Gambling in Britain*, London.

Gambling in America (1976), Final Report of the Commission on the Review of the National Policy toward Gambling, Washington, D.C.: Government Printing Office.

Glock, Charles Y. (ed.) (1967), *Survey Research in the Social Sciences*, New York: Russell Sage Foundation.

Grussi, Olivier (1985), *La vie quotidienne des joueurs sous l'ancien régime à Paris et à la cour*, Paris: Hachette.

Guttman, George (1986), "Change the Rules on Death and Taxes," *Wall Street Journal*, October 21.

Heavey, Jerome F. (1978), "The Incidence of State Lottery Taxes," *Public Finance Quarterly* 6 (October): 415–25.

Heckman, James J. (1979), "Sample Selection Bias as a Specification Error," *Econometrica* 47 (January): 153–61.

Herman, Robert D. (1967a), "Gambling as Work: A Sociological Study of the Race Track," in R. D. Herman (ed.), *Gambling*, New York: Harper and Row, pp. 87–104.

   (1967b) *Gamblers and Gambling: Motives, Institutions and Controls*, Lexington, Mass.: Heath Lexington.

Hey, John D. (1979), *Uncertainty in Microeconomics*, New York: New York University Press.

Hogarth, R. M., and M. W. Reder (eds.) (1986), *Rational Choice*, Chicago: University of Chicago Press.

Houthakker, H. S., and Lester D. Taylor (1970), *Consumer Demand in the United States: Analyses and Projections*, 2d ed., Cambridge, Mass.: Harvard University Press.

Kahneman, D., and A. Tversky (1979), "Prospect Theory: An Analysis of Decisions under Risk," *Econometrica* 47 (March): 263–91.

(1986a) "Choices, Values and Frames," in H. R. Arkes and K. R. Hammond (eds.), *Judgement and Decision Making*, Cambridge: Cambridge University Press, pp. 194–210.

(1986b) "Rational Choice and the Framing of Decisions," in R. M. Hogarth and M. W. Reder (eds.), *Rational Choice*, Chicago: University of Chicago Press, pp. 67–95.

Kahneman, Daniel, Paul Slovic, and Amos Tversky (eds.) (1982), *Judgement under Uncertainty: Heuristics and Biases*, Cambridge: Cambridge University Press.

Kallick, Maureen, Daniel Suits, Ted Dielman, and Judith Hybels (1979), *A Survey of American Gambling Attitudes and Behavior*, Ann Arbor: Institute for Social Research, University of Michigan.

Kaplan, H. Roy (1978), *Lottery Winners – How They Won and How Winning Changed Their Lives*, New York: Harper and Row.

(1985a) "Lottery Winners and Work Commitment: A Behavioral Test of the American Work Ethic," working paper, Florida Institute of Technology.

(1985b) "Lottery Winners in the United States," working paper, Florida Institute of Technology.

Kaplan, H. Roy, and Carlos J. Kruytbosch (1975), "A Behavioral Test of Job Recruitment" (mimeograph).

Kaplan, H. Roy, Victor Tremblay, Daniel Koenig, and Marjolaine Martin (1979), "Survey of Lottery Winners: Final Report," submitted to Loto Canada.

Kapteyn, A., B. M. S. van Praag, and F. G. van Herwaarden (1978), "Individual Welfare Functions and Social Reference Spaces," *Economics Letters* 1:173–8.

Kapteyn, A., and T. Wansbeek (1982), "Empirical Evidence on Preference Formation," *Journal of Economic Psychology* 2:137–54.

(1985) "The Individual Welfare Function: A Rejoinder," *Journal of Economic Psychology* 6:375–81.

Keynes, J. M. (1921), *Treatise on Probability*, London: Macmillan.

Kinsey, Robert K. (1963), "The Role of Lotteries in Public Finance," *National Tax Journal* 16(1):11–19.

Knight, F. (1971), *Risk, Uncertainty and Profits* (1921), Chicago: University of Chicago Press.

Koeves, Tibor (1952), "You Can Lose Your Shirt Anywhere in the World," in Herbert L. Marx, Jr. (ed.), *Gambling in America*, New York: Wilson, pp. 55–60. First published in *United Nations World* 2 (March 1948):19–21.

Kuch, Peter, and Walter Haessel (1979), *Une analyse des gains au Canada*, Ottawa: Ministère de l'Industrie et du Commerce.

Kusyszyn, Igor (1984), "The Psychology of Gambling," *Annals of the American Academy of Political and Social Science* 474 (July): 133–45.

Lacroix, Robert, and François Vaillancourt (1981), *Les revenus de la langue au Québec*, Montreal: Conseil de la Langue Française.

Landau, Michael (1968), *A Manual on Lotteries*, Ramat Gan: Massada.

Lazear, Edward P., and Robert T. Michael (1980), "Family Size and the Distribution of Real Per Capita Income," *American Economic Review* 70:90–107.

Lea, S. E. G., R. M. Tarpy, and P. Webley (1987), *The Individual in the Economy*, Cambridge: Cambridge University Press.

Lefèbvre, E. (1968), *Reminiscences of a Stock Operator*, New York: Pocket Books.

Lemelin, Clément (1977), "Les effets redistributifs des loteries québécoises," *L'Actualité Economique* 53:468–75.

Lester, David (ed.) (1979), *Gambling Today*, Springfield, Ill.: Thomas.

Li, Wen Lang, and Martin H. Smith (1976), "The Propensity to Gamble: Some Structural Determinants," in William E. Eadington (ed.), *Gambling and Society*, Springfield, Ill.: Thomas, pp. 189–206.

Lorie, J. H. (1966), "Some Comments on Recent Quantitative and Formal Research on the Stock Market," *Journal of Business* 39:107–10.

McKibbin, Ross (1979), "Working-Class Gambling in Britain 1880–1939," *Past and Present*, no. 82 (February): 147–78.

McLoughlin, Kevin (1979), "The Lotteries Tax," *Canadian Taxation* 1 (January): 16–19.

McNeil, B. J., S. G. Parker, H. C. Sox, Jr., and A. Tversky (1982), "On the Elicitation of Preferences for Alternative Therapies," *New England Journal of Medicine* 306:1259–62.

March, J. G. (1988), "Variable Risk Preferences and Adaptive Aspirations," *Journal of Economic Behavior and Organization* 9:5–24.

Markowitz, M. (1952), "The Utility of Wealth," *Journal of Political Economy* 80:151–8.

(1959) *Portfolio Selection: Efficient Diversification of Investments*, New York: Wiley.

Moser, C. A., and G. Kalton (1972), *Survey Methods in Social Investigation*, 2d ed., New York: Basic.

Nabokov, Vladimir (1981), *Lectures on Russian Literature*, New York: Harcourt Brace Jovanovich.

Newman, Otto (1972), *Gambling: Hazard and Reward*, London: Athlone.

(1975) "The Ideology of Social Problems: A Gambling Case Study," *Canadian Review of Sociology and Anthropology* 12(4):541–50.

Orwell, G. (1957), "Politics and the English Language," *Inside the Whale and Other Essays*, New York: Penguin, pp. 143–59. First published in *Horizon* 76, 1946.

Perkins, Benson E. (1958), *Gambling in English Life (1950)*, London: Epworth.

Robert Sylvestre Marketing Ltd. (1977), "Le marché québécois des loteries" (survey commissioned by Loto-Québec).

Rosen, Sam, and Desmond Norton (1966), "The Lottery as a Source of Public Revenues," *Taxes* 44, 617–25.

Rothschild, M., and J. E. Stiglitz (1970), "Increasing Risk. I: A Definition," *Journal of Economic Theory* 2:225–43.

Rowntree, B. S. (1901), *Poverty: A Study of Town Life*, London: Macmillan.
Royal Commission on Betting, Lotteries and Gaming (1951), *Report*, London: H.M.S.O.
Royal Commission on Bilingualism and Biculturalism (1967), *Report*, Ottawa: Ministry of Supply and Services.
Rubner, Alex (1966), *The Economics of Gambling*, London: Macmillan.
Schoemaker, Paul J. H. (1982), "The Expected Utility Model: Its Variants, Purposes, Evidence and Limitations," *Journal of Economic Literature* 20 (June): 529–63.
Scodel, A. (1964), "Inspirational Group Therapy: A Study of Gamblers' Anonymous," *American Journal of Psychotherapy* 18:115–25.
Sewell, R. (1972), "Survey of Gambling Habits of a Short-Term Recidivist Prison Population," in G. E. Moody (ed.), *The Facts about the "Money Factories,"* London: Churches' Council on Gambling.
Shaw, George Bernard (1965), "Pygmalion," *The Complete Plays of George Bernard Shaw*, London: Hamlyn, pp. 716–57.
Shefrin, H. M., and M. Statman (1984), "Explaining Investor Preference for Cash Dividends," *Journal of Financial Economics* 13:293–302.
Simon, Herbert A. (1959), "Theories of Decision-Making in Economics and Behavioral Science," in E. Mansfield (ed.), *Microeconomics Selected Readings*, New York: Norton, 1971, pp. 85–98.
Skolnick, Jerome H. (1982), "The Social Risks of Casino Gambling," in William R. Eadington (ed.), *Casino Gambling in America*, Reno: Bureau of Business and Economic Research, pp. 22–7. First published in *Psychology Today*, July 1979.
Slovic, Paul (1986), "Psychological Study of Human Judgement: Implications for Investment Decision Making," in Hal R. Arkes and Kenneth R. Hammond (eds.), *Judgement and Decision Making: An Interdisciplinary Reader*, Cambridge: Cambridge University Press, pp. 173–93.
Smith, S., and P. Razzell (1975), *The Pool Winners*, London: Caliban Books.
Solman, P., and T. Friedman (1982), *Life and Death on the Corporate Battlefield*, New York: Simon and Schuster.
Spiro, Michael H. (1974), "On the Tax Incidence of the Pennsylvania Lottery," *National Tax Journal* 27(1):57–61.
Sprowls, Clay R. (1954), "A Historical Analysis of Lottery Terms," *Canadian Journal of Economics and Political Science* 20(3):347–56.
(1970) "On the Terms of the New York State Lottery," *National Tax Journal* 23(1):74–82.
Statistics Canada (1979), *1976 Census of Canada*, Ottawa: Ministry of Supply and Services.
(1982) *Family Expenditures in Canada*, Cat. 62–555, Ottawa.
Stigler, George (1965), *Essays in the History of Economics*, Chicago: University of Chicago Press.
Sullivan, George (1972), *By Chance a Winner – The History of Lotteries*, New York: Dodd, Mead.
Tec, Nechama (1964), *Gambling in Sweden*, Totowa, N.J.: Bedminster.
Thaler, R. H. (1980), "Toward a Positive Theory of Consumer Choice," *Journal of Economic Behavior and Organization* 1:39–60.
(1986a) "Illusions and Mirages in Public Policy," in H. R. Arkes and K. R. Hammond (eds.), *Judgement and Decision Making*, Cambridge: Cambridge University Press, pp. 161–73.

(1986b) "The Psychology and Economics Conference Handbook: Comments on Simon, on Einhorn and Hogarth, and on Tversky and Kahneman," in R. M. Hogarth and M. W. Reder (eds.), *Rational Choice*, Chicago: Chicago University Press, pp. 95–100.

Theil, Henri (1971), *Principles of Econometrics*, New York: Wiley.

Thomas, Lewis (1974), *The Lives of the Cell*, New York: Viking.

Tomes, Nigel (1983), "Religion and the Rate of Return on Human Capital: Evidence from Canada," *Canadian Journal of Economics* 16 (February): 122–38.

Vaillancourt, François (1979), "La situation démographique et socio-économique des francophones du Québec: Une revue," *Analyse de Politique* 4(5):542–52.

Van de Stadt, H., A. Kapteyn, and S. van de Geer (1985), "The Relativity of Utility: Evidence from Panel Data," *Review of Economics and Statistics* 2:179–87.

Viscusi, K. W. (1987), "Prospective Reference Theory: Toward an Explanation of the Paradoxes," (working paper). Forthcoming in *Journal of Risk and Uncertainty*.

Wall Street Journal (1986), "Canada Lotteries Attract U.S. Dollars, As Well As a Lot of American Complaints," April 8.

Weinstein, David, and Lillian Deitch (1974), *The Impact of Legalized Gambling: The Socioeconomic Consequences of Lotteries and Off-Track Betting*, New York: Praeger.

Western Canada Lottery Foundation, "Survey of Purchasers of Lottery Tickets" (mimeographed, Winnipeg).

Zeckhauser, Richard (1986), "Comments: Behavioral versus Rational Economics: What You See Is What You Conquer," in R. M. Hogarth and M. W. Reder (eds.), *Rational Choice*, Chicago: University of Chicago Press, pp. 251–66.

Chapter 3

Ashton, John (1898), *The History of Gambling in England*, London: Duckworth.

Ayres, C. E. (1944), *The Theory of Economic Progress*, Chapel Hill: University of North Carolina Press.

Bailey, Peter (1978), *Leisure and Class in Victorian England*, London: Routledge and Kegan Paul.

Bender, Eric (1938), *Tickets to Fortune*, New York: Modern Age Books.

Bergier, J. F. (1978), "The Industrial Bourgeoisie and the Rise of the Working Class," in Carlo M. Cipolla (ed.), *The Industrial Revolution* (1973), Glasgow: Fontana/Collins, pp. 397–451.

Blakey, Robert G. (1977), *The Development of the Law of Gambling, 1776–1976*, Washington D.C.: National Institute of Law Enforcement and Criminal Justice.

(1979) "State Conducted Lotteries: History, Problems, and Promises," *Journal of Social Issues* 35(3):62–97.

Bloch, Herbert A. (1951), "The Sociology of Gambling," *American Journal of Sociology* 57 (November): 215–21.

Blum, John Morton (ed.) (1973), *The National Experience: A History of the United States*, 3d ed., New York: Harcourt Brace Jovanovich.

Bolen, Darell W. (1976), "Gambling: Historical Highlights and Trends and Their Implications for Contemporary Society," in William R. Eadington (ed.), *Gambling and Society*, Springfield, Ill.: Thomas, pp. 4–38.

Brand, David (1987), "Time Bombs on Legs," *Time*, July 27.

Brenner, Gabrielle A. (1985), "Why Did Inheritance Laws Change?" *International Review of Law and Economics* 5:91–106.

Brenner, Reuven (1983), *History: The Human Gamble*, Chicago: University of Chicago Press.

(1985) *Betting on Ideas: Wars, Invention, Inflation*, Chicago: University of Chicago Press.

(1987) *Rivalry: In Business, Science, among Nations*, Cambridge: Cambridge University Press.

Church, George J. (1988), "Are You Better Off?" *Time*, October 10, pp. 26–8.

Cochrane, Eric, and Julius Kirshner (1986), *The Renaissance*, vol. 5 of *Readings in Western Civilization*, Chicago: University of Chicago Press.

Cohen, John (1964), *Behaviour under Uncertainty*, New York: Basic.

(1966) *Psychological Probability*, London: Allen and Unwin.

Cowing, Cedric B. (1965), *Populists, Plungers and Progressives*, Princeton, N.J.: Princeton University Press.

Cunningham, Hugh (1980), *Leisure and the Industrial Revolution c. 1780–c. 1880*, New York: St. Martin's.

Devereux, Edward C. (1980), *Gambling and Social Structure* (Ph.D. thesis, Harvard University, 1949), New York: Arno.

Dixon, David (1980a), "'Class Law': The Street Betting Act of 1906," *International Journal of the Sociology of Law* 8:101–28.

(1980b) "The Discovery of the Compulsive Gambler," in Zenon Bankowski and Geoff Mungham (eds.), *Essays in Law and Society*, London: Routledge and Kegan Paul, pp. 157–79.

(1981a) "The State and Gambling: Developments in the Legal Control of Gambling in England, 1867–1923," paper presented at the Fifth National Conference on Gambling and Risk-Taking, Lake Tahoe, Nev., October.

(1981b) "Discussion," in Alan Tomlinson (ed.), "Leisure and Social Control," working papers for a workshop of the British Sociological Association/Leisure Studies Association Joint Study Group on Leisure and Recreation, University of Birmingham, January 1980, pp. 21ff.

Duncan, Greg J., with Richard D. Coe et al. (1984), *Years of Poverty, Years of Plenty*, Ann Arbor, Institute for Social Research, University of Michigan.

Duster, Troy (1970), *The Legislation of Morality: Law, Drugs and Moral Judgment*, New York: Free Press.

Elias, Norbert (1986), "An Essay on Sport and Violence," in Norbert Elias and Eric Dunning, *The Quest for Excitement: Sport and Leisure in the Civilizing Process*, Oxford: Blackwell Publisher, pp. 150–74.

Encyclopaedia Judaica (1971), Jerusalem: Keter, vol. 7.

Ezell, John Samuel (1960), *Fortune's Merry Wheel: The Lottery in America*, Cambridge, Mass.: Harvard University Press.

Fabian, Ann Vincent (1982), "Rascals and Gentlemen: The Meaning of American Gambling, 1820–1890," Ph.D. thesis, Yale University.

Feinman, Jeffrey P., Robert D. Blashek, and Richard J. McCabe (1986), *Sweepstakes, Prize Promotions, Games and Contests*, Homewood, Ill.: Dow Jones–Irwin.

Findlay, John M. (1986), *People of Chance: Gambling in the American Society from Jamestown to Las Vegas*, Oxford: Oxford University Press.

Fleming, Alice (1978), *Something for Nothing*, New York: Delacorte.

Geertz, Clifford (1973), *The Interpretation of Cultures*, New York: Basic.

Goldstone, Jack H. (1986), "State Breakdown in the English Revolution: A New Synthesis," *American Journal of Sociology* 92(2) (September): 257–322.

Grussi, Olivier (1985), *La vie quotidienne des joueurs sous l'ancien régime à Paris et à la cour*, Paris: Hachette.

Haller, Mark H. (1970), "Urban Crime and Criminal Justice: The Chicago Case," *Journal of American History* 57(3) (December): 619–35.

Harrison, Brian (1964), "Contributions to Discussion on Work and Leisure in Preindustrial Society, by Keith Thomas," presented at the Seventh Past and Present Conference, *Past and Present*, no. 29 (December): 63–6.

(1971) *Drink and the Victorians*, London: Faber and Faber.

Hood, Christopher C. (1976), *The Limits of Administration*, London: Wiley.

Hughes, Jonathan (1983), *American Economic History*, Glenview, Ill.: Scott, Foresman.

Keynes, John Maynard (1971), *The Economic Consequences of the Peace* (1919), London: Macmillan.

Koeves, Tibor (1952), "You Can Lose Your Shirt Anywhere in the World" (1948), in Herbert L. Marx, Jr. (ed.), *Gambling in America*, New York: Wilson, pp. 55–60.

Koten, John (1987), "Steady Progress Disrupted by Turbulence in Economy," *Wall Street Journal*, March 11.

Lee, Alan J. (1976), *The Origins of the Popular Press in England, 1855–1914*, London: Croom Helm.

Lee, Susan Previant, and Peter Passell (1979), *A New Economic View of American History*, New York: Norton.

Leonard, John D. (1952), "How Britain Gambles on Sports," in Herbert L. Marx, Jr. (ed.), *Gambling in America*, New York: Wilson, pp. 109–12. First published as "The Big 'Flutter,'" *New York Times Magazine*, Oct. 22, 1950.

Levy, Frank (1988), "A Growing Gap between Rich and Poor," *New York Times*, May 1.

McKibbin, Ross (1979), "Working-Class Gambling in Britain, 1880–1939," *Past and Present*, no. 82 (February): 147–78.

McNeill, William H. (1963), *The Rise of the West*, Chicago: University of Chicago Press.

Malcolmson, Robert W. (1973), *Popular Recreations in English Society, 1700–1850*, Cambridge: Cambridge University Press.

(1981) *Life and Labour in England, 1700–1780*, New York: St. Martin's.

Miers, David, and David Dixon (1979), "National Bet: The Re-Emergence of Public Lottery," *Public Law*, pp. 372–403.

Murray, Gilbert (1955), *Five Stages of Greek Religion*, Garden City, N.Y.: Doubleday.

Newman, Otto (1972), *Gambling: Hazard and Reward*, London: Athlone.
Newsweek (1985), "The Lottery Craze," September 2.
   (1987) "What a Deal!" February 9.
North, Douglas C. (1978), "Structure and Performance: The Task of Economic History," *Journal of Economic Literature* 16(3) (September): 963–78.
O'Hara, John T. (1987), "Class and Attitudes to Gambling in Australia: A Historical Perspective," paper presented at the Seventh International Conference on Gambling and Risk-Taking, Reno.
Olmstead, Charlotte (1967), "Analyzing a Pack of Cards," in Robert D. Herman (ed.), *Gambling*, New York: Harper and Row, pp. 136–52.
Ore, Oystein (1965), *Cardano: The Gambling Scholar* (with a translation from Latin by Sydney Henry Gould of Cardano's *Book on Games of Chance*), New York: Dover.
Perkins, Benson E. (1958), *Gambling in English Life* (1950), London: Epworth.
Plumb, J. H. (1967), *The Growth of Political Stability in England*, London: Macmillan.
Razzell, P. E., and R. W. Wainwright (eds.) (1973), *The Victorian Working Class: Selections from Letters to the Morning Chronicle*, London: Cass.
Read, Donald (1979), *England 1868–1914*, London: Longman.
Rosenthal, Franz (1975), *Gambling in Islam*, Leiden: Brill.
Rubner, Alex (1966), *The Economics of Gambling*, London: Macmillan.
Sasuly, Richard (1982), *Bookies and Bettors: Two Hundred Years of Gambling*, New York: Holt, Rinehart and Winston.
Schoeck, Helmuth (1969), *Envy*, New York: Harcourt Brace and World.
Smith, Adam (1976), *The Wealth of Nations* (1776), Chicago: University of Chicago Press.
Smith, Stanley S. (1952), "Age-Old Lotteries," in Herbert L. Marx, Jr. (ed.), *Gambling in America*, New York: Wilson, pp. 61–7.
Spofford, A. (1892), "Lotteries in American History," *American Historical Association Annual Report, 1892*, pp. 174–5 (as quoted in Blakey 1977, p. 75).
Starkey, Lycurgus Monroe, Jr. (1964), *Money, Mania and Morals: The Churches and Gambling*, New York: Abingdon.
Steinmetz, Andrew (1870), *The Gambling Table: Its Votaries and Victims*, London: Tinsley.
Stone, Lawrence (1965), *The Crisis of the Aristocracy 1558–1641*, Oxford: Oxford University Press.
   (1972) *The Causes of the English Revolution 1529–1642*, New York: Harper and Row.
Street, Howard (1937), *Law of Gaming*, London: Sweet and Maxwell.
Thomas, Keith (1971), *Religion and the Decline of Magic*, New York: Scribner.
Thorner, Isidor (1955), "Ascetic Protestantism, Gambling and the One-Price System," *American Journal of Economics and Sociology* 15(1):161–72.
Wagner, Walter (1972), *To Gamble or Not to Gamble*, New York: World.
Wall Street Journal (1987), "Cash for Trash," February 17.
Walvin, James (1978), *Leisure and Society 1830–1950*, London: Longman.
Weber, Max (1946), *From Max Weber: Essays in Sociology*, ed. and trans.

H. H. Gerth and C. Wright Mills, New York: Oxford University Press.

Whang, Paul K. (1933), "The National State Lottery," *China Weekly Review*, August 19, p. 498.

Wiebe, Robert H. (1967), *The Search for Order: 1877–1920*, New York: Hill and Wang.

Chapter 4

Ashton, John (1898), *The History of Gambling in England*, London: Duckworth.

Ayres, C. E. (1944), *The Theory of Economic Progress*, Chapel Hill: University of North Carolina Press.

Bauer, P. T. (1981), *Equality, the Third World and Economic Delusion*, London: Methuen.

Blakey, Robert G. (1977), *The Development of the Law of Gambling, 1776–1976*, Washington, D.C.: National Institute of Law Enforcement and Criminal Justice.

Boyle, James E. (1921), *Speculation and the Chicago Board of Trade*, New York: Macmillan.

Brenner, Reuven (1983), *History: The Human Gamble*, Chicago: University of Chicago Press.

(1985) *Betting on Ideas: Wars, Invention, Inflation*, Chicago: University of Chicago Press.

(1987) *Rivalry: In Business, Science, among Nations*, Cambridge: Cambridge University Press.

Bunce, Harold R. (1952), "The Ethics of Investment," in Herbert L. Marx, Jr. (ed.), *Gambling in America*, New York: Wilson, pp. 134–41.

Carlton, Dennis W. (1983), "The Cost of Eliminating a Futures Market, and the Effect of Inflation on Market Interrelationships" (working paper, University of Chicago).

(1984) "Futures Markets: Their Purpose, Their History, Their Growth, Their Successes and Failures" (working paper, University of Chicago Law School, January).

Coase, Ronald H. (1937), "The Nature of the Firm," *Economica* 4:386–405.

Cohen, John (1964), *Behaviour under Uncertainty*, New York: Basic.

Cowing, Cedric B. (1965), *Populists, Plungers and Progressives*, Princeton, N.J.: Princeton University Press.

Daston, Lorraine J. (1987), "The Domestication of Risk: Mathematical Probability and Insurance 1650–1830," in L. Krüger, L. J. Daston, and M. Heidelberger (eds.), *The Probabilistic Revolution*, vol. 1, Cambridge, Mass.: MIT Press, pp. 237–60.

Dorfman, John R. (1987), "Rating Investment-Advice Givers: The Only Constant Is Inconsistency," *Wall Street Journal*, March 27.

Downes, D. M., B. P. Davies, M. E. David, and P. Stone (1976), *Gambling, Work and Leisure: A Study across Three Areas*, London: Routledge and Kegan Paul.

Eadington, William R. (1973), *The Economics of Gambling Behavior: A Qualitative Study of Nevada's Gambling Industry*, Reno: Bureau of Business and Economic Research, University of Nevada.

Fisher, Irving (1924), "Useful and Harmful Speculation," in Charles O.

Hardy (ed.), *Readings in Risk and Risk-Taking*, Chicago: University of Chicago Press, pp. 346–9.

Flynn, John T. (1934), *Security Speculation*, New York: Harcourt Brace.

Friedman, Milton (1969), "In Defense of Destabilizing Speculation," *The Optimum Quantity of Money and Other Essays*, Chicago: Aldine, pp. 285–91.

Fromson, Brett Duval (1987), "Herd on the Street: 'Garbitrage' Bulls Go Mad," *Wall Street Journal*, June 30, editorial page.

Gardner, Martin (1987), "Giving God a Hand," *New York Review of Books*, August 13, pp. 17–24.

Gilder, George (1989), "The Victim of His Virtues," *Wall Street Journal*, April 18.

Hardy, Charles O. (ed.) (1924), *Readings in Risk and Risk-Bearing*, Chicago: University of Chicago Press.

Hawke, John (1905a), "The Extent of Gambling," in B. S. Rowntree (ed.), *Betting and Gambling: A National Evil*, London: Macmillan, pp. 21–44.

   (1905b) "Existing Legislation," in B. S. Rowntree (ed.), *Betting and Gambling: A National Evil*, London: Macmillan, pp. 135–70.

Hawley, F. B. (1924), "Speculation, Enterprise, and Gambling," in Charles O. Hardy (ed.), *Readings in Risk and Risk-Bearing*, Chicago: University of Chicago Press, pp. 72–9.

Hieronymus, Thomas A. (1971), *Economics of Futures Trading: For Commercial and Personal Profit*, New York: Commodity Research Bureau.

Hughes, Kathleen A. (1986), "Thinking of Buying or Selling a House? Ask Your Astrologer," *Wall Street Journal*, October 10.

Jacoby, Oswald (1952), "The Forms of Gambling," in Herbert L. Marx, Jr. (ed.), *Gambling in America*, New York: Wilson, pp. 19–25. First published in *Annals of the American Academy of Political and Social Science* 269 (May 1950).

Keynes, John M. (1970), *The General Theory of Employment, Interest and Money* (1936), London: Macmillan.

Kolb, Robert W. (1985), *Understanding Futures Markets*, Glenview, Ill.: Scott, Foresman.

Labys, Walter C., and C. W. J. Granger (1970), *Speculation, Hedging and Commodity Price Forecasts*, Lexington, Mass.: Heath Lexington.

Lahey, Edwin A. (1952), "Speculators Have Grown Fat," in Herbert L. Marx, Jr. (ed.), *Gambling in America*, New York: Wilson, pp. 134–41.

Leiren, Hall (1987), "The Feng Shui Men," *Empress*, April, pp. 38–46.

MacDougall, Ernest D. (1936), *Speculation and Gambling*, Boston: Stratford.

Mackay, Charles (1980), *Extraordinary Popular Delusions and the Madness of Crowds* (1841), New York: Harmony.

Malcolmson, Robert W. (1981), *Life and Labour in England, 1700–1780*, New York: St. Martin's.

Marx, Herbert L., Jr. (ed.), *Gambling in America*, New York: Wilson.

Miers, David, and David Dixon (1979), "National Bet: The Re-Emergence of Public Lottery," *Public Law*, pp. 372–403.

Niederhoffer, Victor (1989), "The Speculator as Hero," *Wall Street Journal*, February 10.

Noonan, John T., Jr. (1957), *The Scholastic Analysis of Usury*, Cambridge, Mass.: Harvard University Press.

Owen, Gregory (1982), "Futures Markets: Comments," in J. H. Shideler (ed.), *Agricultural History*, supp. to 56(4) (October): 317–25.

Perkins, Benson E. (1962), *Gambling in English Life* (1950), London: Epworth.

Quebec, Province of (1895), *Rapports judiciaires de Québec*, Cour du Banc de la Reine, vol. 4, Montreal: Gazette Printing Co.

Rowntree, Seebohm B. (ed.) (1905), *Betting and Gambling: A National Evil*, London: Macmillan.

Sasuly, Richard (1982), *Bookies and Bettors: Two Hundred Years of Gambling*, New York: Holt, Rinehart and Winston.

Schama, Simon (1988), *The Embarrassment of Riches*, Berkeley and Los Angeles: University of California Press.

Street, Howard A. (1937), *The Law of Gaming*, London: Sweet and Maxwell.

Telser, Lester G. (1958), "Futures Trading and the Storage of Cotton and Wheat," *Journal of Political Economy* 65 (June): 233–55.

Telser, Lester G., and Harlow N. Higinbotham (1977), "Organized Futures Markets: Costs and Benefits," *Journal of Political Economy* 85(5) (October): 969–1001.

Teweles, R. J., Charles V. Harlow, and H. L. Stone (1969), *The Commodity Futures Trading Guide*, New York: McGraw-Hill.

Thomas, Keith (1971), *Religion and the Decline of Magic*, New York: Scribner.

Train, John (1985), *Famous Financial Fiascoes*, New York: Potter/Crown.

Tuchman, Barbara (1984), *The March of Folly*, New York: Knopf.

United Kingdom (1895), *The Law Reports*, Incorporated Council of Law Reporting, House of Lords, Judicial Committee of the Privy Council, and Peerage Cases, London: Clowes.

Whitaker, Mark, Tony Clifton, and Donna Foote (1987), "Thatcher's Two Britains," *Newsweek*, June 22.

Williams, Jeffrey C. (1982), "The Origins of Futures Markets," in J. H. Shideler (ed.), *Agricultural History*, supp. to 56(4) (October): 317–25.

Wilson, A. J. (1905) "Stock Exchange Gambling," in B. S. Rowntree (ed.), *Betting and Gambling: A National Evil*, London: Macmillan, pp. 45–69.

Chapter 5 and its appendix

Ashton, John (1969), *A History of English Lotteries* (1893), Detroit: Singing Tree.

Blair, William G. (1986), "16 States Consider Joint Lottery Game," *New York Times*, July 13.

Blakey, Robert G. (1977), *The Development of the Law of Gambling, 1776–1976*, Washington, D.C.: National Institute of Law Enforcement and Criminal Justice.

(1979) "State Conducted Lotteries: History, Problems and Promise," *Journal of Social Issues* 35(3):62–87.

Blum, W. J., and H. Kalven, Jr. (1966), *The Uneasy Case for Progressive Taxation* (1953), Chicago: University of Chicago Press.

Brenner, Reuven (1983), *History: The Human Gamble*, Chicago: University of Chicago Press.

(1985) *Betting on Ideas: Wars, Invention, Inflation*, Chicago: University of Chicago Press.

(1987a) *Rivalry: In Business, Science, among Nations*, Cambridge: Cambridge University Press.

(1987b) "Bureaucracy – A Useless Abstraction," Research Report no. 1787, Centre de Recherche et Développement en Economique, Université de Montréal.

Chafetz, Henri (1960), *Play the Devil: A History of Gambling in the United States from 1492 to 1955*, New York: Potter.

Clotfelter, Charles, and Philip J. Cook (1987), "The Context of Lottery Growth" (manuscript, Duke University).

Devereux, Edward C. (1980), *Gambling and Social Structure* (Ph.D. thesis, Harvard University, 1949), New York: Arno.

Dixon, David (1984), "Illegal Gambling and Histories of Policing in Britain," paper presented at the Sixth National Conference on Gambling and Risk-Taking, Atlantic City, December (Faculty of Law, University of Hull).

(1987) "Responses to Illegal Betting in Britain and Australia," paper presented at the Seventh International Conference on Gambling and Risk-Taking, Reno.

Dunnan, Nancy (1987), "Yuan to Invest," *New York Times*, supp. "The Business World," November 29.

Eichenwald, Kurt (1987), "Are Lotteries Really the Ticket?" *New York Times* supplement, January 4.

Fabian, Ann Vincent (1982), "Rascals and Gentlemen: The Meaning of American Gambling, 1820–1890," Ph.D. thesis, Yale University.

Gruson, Lindsay (1987), "Delaware Joins 3 States in Big Lottery," *New York Times*, April 19.

Harrison, Brian (1971), *Drink and the Victorians*, London: Faber and Faber.

Herman, Robert D. (ed.) (1967), *Gambling*, New York: Harper and Row.

Hood, Christopher C. (1976), *The Limits of Administration*, London: Wiley.

Joyce, Kathleen M. (1979), "Public Opinion and the Politics of Gambling," *Journal of Social Issues* 35(3):144–65.

Kaplan, H. Roy (1984), "The Social and Economic Impact of State Lotteries," *Annals of the American Academy of Political and Social Science* 474 (July): 91–106.

Leonnet, Jean (1963), *Les loteries d'état en France du XVIIIe au XIXe siècles*, Paris: Bibliothèque Nationale.

Livernois, John R. (1985), "The Redistribution Effects of Lotteries in Western Canada," Research Paper no. 85–23, University of Alberta.

McKibbin, Ross (1979), "Working-Class Gambling in Britain 1880–1939," *Past and Present*, no. 82 (February): 147–78.

Miers, David, and David Dixon (1979), "National Bet: The Re-Emergence of Public Lottery," *Public Law*, pp. 372–403.

Mikesell, John L., and C. Kurt Zorn (1985), "Revenue Performance of State Lotteries," paper prepared for the Seventy-eighth Annual Conference of the National Tax Association, Tax Institute of America, Denver, October 16.

Mishan, E. J. (1960), "A Survey of Welfare Economics, 1939–51," *Economic Journal* 70 (June): 197–265.

Mitchell, B. R., and Phyllis Deane (1962), *Abstract of British Historical Statistics*, Cambridge: Cambridge University Press.

O'Hara, John (1987), "Class and Attitudes to Gambling in Australia," paper presented at the Seventh International Conference on Gambling and Risk-Taking, Reno.

Read, Donald (1979), *England 1868–1914*, London: Longman.

Reuter, Peter (1985), *Disorganized Crime*, Cambridge, Mass.: MIT Press.

Rosten, Leo (1941), *Hollywood: The Movie Colony – the Movie Makers*, New York: Harcourt Brace.

Rubner, Alex (1966), *The Economics of Gambling*, London: Macmillan.

Shaw, George Bernard (1926), *The Intelligent Woman's Guide to Socialism and Capitalism*, London: Constable.

Suits, Daniel B. (1979), "Economic Background for Gambling Policy," *Social Issues* 35(3):43–61.

Wall Street Journal (1986), "Odds Improve for Legalized Gambling in Several States," March 6, p. 1.

Walvin, James (1978), *Leisure and Society 1830–1950*, London: Longman.

Weinstein, David, and Lillian Deitch (1974), *The Impact of Legalized Gambling: The Socioeconomic Consequences of Lotteries and Off-Track Betting*, New York: Praeger.

Whang, Paul K. (1933), "The National State Lottery," *China Weekly Review*, August 19, p. 498.

Williams, Penry (1956), "Lotteries and Government Finance in England," *History Today* 6:557–61.

Chapter 6

Baker, Leonard (1958), "Should We Have a National Lottery?" *Challenge*, August–September, pp. 13–17.

Bauer, Peter (1984), *Reality and Rhetoric*, Cambridge, Mass.: Harvard University Press.

Blair, William G. (1986), "16 States Consider Joint Lottery Game," *New York Times*, July 13.

Bloch, Marc (1953), *The Historian's Craft*, New York: Knopf.

Bolen, Darrell W. (1976), "Gambling: Historical Highlights and Trends and Their Implication for Contemporary Society," in William R. Eadington (ed.), *Gambling and Society*, Springfield, Ill.: Thomas, pp. 7–38.

Boorstin, Daniel J. (1987), *Hidden History*, New York: Harper and Row.

Brenner, Reuven (1983), *History: The Human Gamble*, Chicago: University of Chicago Press.

   (1985) *Betting on Ideas: Wars, Invention, Inflation*, Chicago: University of Chicago Press.

   (1987) *Rivalry: In Business, Science, among Nations*, Cambridge: Cambridge University Press.

Chafetz, Morris E. (1987), "The Third Wave of Prohibition Is upon Us," *Wall Street Journal*, July 21.

Charlier, Marj (1987), "Overdoing It: In Name of Fitness, Many Americans Grow Addicted to Exercise," *Wall Street Journal*, October 1.

Cohen, John (1964), *Behaviour in Uncertainty*, New York: Basic.

Dixon, David (1980), "'Class Law': The Street Betting Act of 1906," *Interna-*

tional Journal of the Sociology of Law 8:101–28.

(1981) "The State and Gambling: Developments in the Legal Control of Gambling in England, 1867–1923," paper presented at the Fifth National Conference on Gambling and Risk-Taking, Lake Tahoe, Nev., October.

Downes, D. M., B. P. Davies, M. E. David, and P. Stone (1976), *Gambling, Work and Leisure: A Study across Three Areas*, London: Routledge and Kegan Paul.

Duster, Troy (1970), *The Legislation of Morality: Law, Drugs and Moral Judgement*, New York: Free Press.

Fèbvre, Lucien (1982), *The Problem of Unbelief in the Sixteenth Century: The Religion of Rabelais*, Cambridge, Mass.: Harvard University Press.

Fingarette, Herbert (1988), *Heavy Drinking*, Berkeley and Los Angeles: University of California Press.

Haller, Mark (1970), "Urban Crime and Criminal Justice: The Chicago Case," *Journal of American History* 57(3) (December): 619–35.

Hornby, A. S., E. V. Gatenby, and H. Wakefield (1963), *The Advanced Learner's Dictionary of Current English*, Oxford: Oxford University Press.

Kallick-Kaufman, Maureen (1979), "The Micro and Macro Dimensions of Gambling in the United States," *Journal of Social Issues* 35(3):7–27.

Kaplan, H. Roy (1985a) "Lottery Winners and Work Commitment: A Behavioral Test of the American Work Ethic" (working paper, Florida Institute of Technology).

(1985b) "A Study of Lottery Winners in the United States" (working paper, Florida Institute of Technology).

Kerr, Peter (1988), "The Unspeakable Is Debated: Should Drugs Be Legalized?" *New York Times*, May 15.

Koeves, Tibor (1952), "You Can Lose Your Shirt Anywhere in the World" (1948), in Herbert L. Marx, Jr. (ed.), *Gambling in America*, New York: Wilson, pp. 55–60.

McKibbin, Ross (1979), "Working-Class Gambling in Britain 1880–1939," *Past and Present*, no. 82 (February): 147–78.

Meriwether, Louise (1970), *Daddy Was a Number Runner*, Englewood Cliffs, N.J.: Prentice-Hall.

Michaels, Robert J. (1986), "The Market for Heroin before and after Legalization," draft of a chapter in Ronald Hamowy (ed.), *Dealing with Drugs: Consequences of Government Control*, Lexington, Mass.: Heath Lexington, 1987.

Newman, Otto (1972), *Gambling: Hazard and Reward*, London: Athlone.

Newsweek (1985), "The Lottery Craze," September 2.

O'Hara, John T. (1987), "Class and Attitudes to Gambling in Australia: A Historical Perspective," paper presented at the Seventh International Conference on Gambling and Risk-Taking, Reno.

Ore, Oystein (1965), *Cardano: The Gambling Scholar* (with a translation from Latin by Sydney Henry Gould of Cardano's *Book on Games of Chance*), New York: Dover.

Passell, Peter (1989), "Lotto Is Financed by the Poor and Won by the States," *New York Times*, May 21.

Rubner, Alex (1966), *The Economics of Gambling*, London: Macmillan.

Sasuly, Richard (1982), *Bookies and Bettors: Two Hundred Years of Gambling*, New York: Holt, Rinehart and Winston.

Schoeck, Helmut (1969), *Envy*, New York: Harcourt Brace and World.

Sturz, Herbert (1988), "A Sure Thing in the Casino: What Older People Spend Best Is Time," *New York Times*, April 3, editorial page.

Time (1988), "Kids Who Sell Crack," May 8, cover story.

Tocqueville, Alexis de (1956), *Democracy in America* (1835), ed. and abridged Richard D. Heffner, New York: New American Library.

Trattner, Ernest R. (1966), *Architects of Ideas* (1938), Westport, Conn.: Greenwood.

Tuchman, Barbara W. (1981), *Practicing History*, New York: Ballantine.

Wayne, Janie (1984), "Lottomania: Fever Hits Epidemic Proportions," *Financial Post*, December 29.

Index of names

Subject index

addiction, 141. *See also* compulsion; gambler, compulsive; gambling, compulsive, excessive
ages of gamblers, 22–3, 27–32, 37. *See also* gamblers, statistical profile of
alcohol, 37, 197, 248 n. 55, 249 n. 6; taxation of, 1, 68. *See also* drink; leisure
ambition, theory of, 144–80
astrology, 6–7, 100, 102, 239 n. 19; in England, 7; in the White House, 211 n. 25

"bank nights," 85–6
banks, banking, 13, 14, 15, 78, 80, 81, 243 n. 1. *See also* financial institutions
bingo, 18, 24–5, 83. *See also* entertainment; gambling; leisure; pastimes
bookmaking, 122–4. *See also* gambling; horse racing
bootlegging, 140
bucket shops, 92, 107, 236 n. 3
bureaucracy, 15, 38, 111–12, 130–2

cases, law, *see* law cases
casinos, 18, 19, 21, 27, 80. *See also* entertainment; gambling; leisure; pastimes
chance: of becoming rich, 7, 49; and providence, 5, 51–5; and religion, 1–7, 57–8, 87–8, 137; and wealth, 55, 57, 217 n. 28. *See also* happiness; hope; luck; optimism
children, 62; of gamblers, 22–3, 27–31, 85, 182–4. *See also* gamblers, statistical profile of; winners
class, social, 15–16, 22, 26–9, 40–1, 57, 60–1, 63, 67–72, 74–7, 81–2, 88–9, 102–6, 127–8, 136, 139–40, 227 n. 64; and decision making, 143–80. *See also* laws; poverty; rank; rich, the; wealth

clergy, 57, 59, 82, 237 n. 113. *See also* religion
cockfighting, 61. *See also* gambling
competition, competitors, 59, 64, 80, 128, 134. *See also* innovation; monopoly; rivalry
compulsion, compulsive behavior, 46–8, 50. *See also* addiction; gambling, excessive
contests, 84–5. *See also* sweepstakes
crime, 21, 64, 78, 100; and gambling, 37–42, 126, 219 n. 66; and prohibitions, 10, 125–7, 132; and redistribution of wealth, 164–8. *See also* class; decision making; fraud; poverty

decision making, 5–7; in the Bible, 1–3, 51; in Islam, 3–4, 53–4; theory of, 143–80. *See also* astrology; dice; lot casting; social sciences
deficits, 113, 198–207. *See also* taxation
depressions: and gambling in the USA, 18, 83–8, 113–14; in England, 74
destiny, 1, 5. *See also* fate; lot casting
dice: throw of, 2, 5–7, 78, 210 n. 8, 211 n. 26. *See also* games of chance; lot casting; religion
divination, 57. *See also* astrology; decision making
dog fighting, 87, 89
dressing up, 71, 140
drink, drinking, 46, 57, 68, 73, 82, 127, 228 n. 72, 230 n. 94, 231 n. 107; taxation of, 1, 126. *See also* alcohol; tea; temperance movement

economic theory, economists: and gambling, 20, 142; and theories of attitudes toward risks, 111–12, 143–80, 253 n. 13. *See also* social sciences